"Gary Moon has given every parent another marvelous tool in helping their children know more about the Scriptures by writing *The Bible Ride, Book Two.* This book is a must for parents who want their families to become more knowledgeable, have fun, and grow closer to each other at the same time. My suggestion is that families everywhere take advantage of this creative system of Bible study that will be a blessing indeed!"

DWIGHT "IKE" REIGHARD
author, motivational speaker, and
Senior Pastor of NorthStar Church
Kennesaw, Georgia

THE BIBLE RIDE
BOOK 2

More Adventures that
Bring the Gospel to Life

GARY W. MOON

VINE
BOOKS

Servant Publications
Ann Arbor, Michigan

Vine Books is an imprint of Servant Publications especially
designed to serve evangelical Christians.

Unless otherwise indicated, Scripture quotations are from *THE
MESSAGE.* © by Eugene H. Peterson 1993, 1994, 1995. Used by permission of NavPress
Publishing Group.

Published by Servant Publications
P.O. Box 8617
Ann Arbor, Michigan 48107

Cover design and illustrations: Hile Illustration and Design, Ann Arbor, Michigan

97 98 99 00 10 9 8 7 6 5 4 3 2 1

Printed in the United States of America
ISBN 0-89283-981-3

LIBRARY OF CONGRESS CATALOGING-IN-PUBLICATION DATA

Moon, Gary W.
    More adventures that bring the Gospel to life / Gary W. Moon.
        p. cm.   (The Bible ride : bk. 2)
    Includes bibliographical references.
    1. Jesus Christ—Prayer-books and devotions—English. 2. Family—Prayer-books and
devotions—English. I. Title. II. Series.
BT306.5.M67 1997
249—dc21   97-7782
                                                                                  CIP

ACKNOWLEDGMENTS

I wish to say a brief "thank you" to some folks who have made it possible for this book—in fact this whole *Bible Ride* series—to pass from ideas to paragraphs.

Les Parrott. Thanks for being a good friend and for passing the manuscript on to Bert Ghezzi. You're the best agent I never paid.

Bert Ghezzi. Thanks for taking such a gamble, all the encouragement, and for the "Family Discussion" idea.

Gwen Ellis. Thanks for leaving the music in—and for all the notes and measures you added.

Phil Genetti. Thanks for mentioning that a dog might just make a fine narrator and for all the help in sewing the infinitives back together and undangling all those pesky participles.

PREFACE

I hope the fact you are reading this sentence means that you have already read volume 1 of the *Bible Ride* series. I already know it means you are a serious reader. Who else would bother with a preface!

Since you are such an ardent consumer, I had better be honest with you about something. You'd find me out anyway. Putting the greatest stories ever told in chronological order is no small task—as I now know.

I'm afraid that if I had known just how immense an undertaking it would be, I probably would have shied away from the project. But once the Pilgrim family had begun driving over the pages of the four Gospels it was too late to turn back. I couldn't just leave them there. And I couldn't cheat—bring them back in a manner that was unfair to the chronology of the accounts of Christ.

So, I continued to rely on the scholarship of Kurt Aland, editor of the frightfully academic text, *Synopsis of the Four Gospels*. But even Aland himself was not convinced about how to best handle a difficulty that arises in the early autumn of Jesus' third year of public ministry. (Actually, it's only a difficulty for someone who is trying to line up the scenes of the Gospels in chronological order. It's not even a speed bump for the devotional reader.)

It is known—in John's Gospel—that Jesus traveled south, from his headquarters in Capernaum, to attend the Feast of

Tabernacles. This celebration was held in Jerusalem, October 15-21. Jesus would have been thirty-two years old, rapidly approaching his thirty-third birthday.

It is also reported by John that Jesus was in Jerusalem on December 25 for the first of the eight days of the Feast of Lights (Fears of Dedication)—which is now called Hanukkah. And, of course, he was back in Jerusalem at least a week before April 14—the date of his Passover meal with his twelve disciples (well, actually it was just eleven "disciples"—since we've started getting academic).

What is not clearly known, however, is whether or not he made a return trip to the north during those six months— between mid-October and early April. It is possible, given the length of the trip, that he did not return to Galilee during this period of time. We do know that during those months he went out into the Judean wilderness and that he passed through Jericho and saw a very small man up a rather large tree.

An additional problem—to the chronologist—is that there is a section of Luke's Gospel (from 9:51 to 18:14) which stands alone from the other accounts. Luke is the only one of the four accounts to offer this wonderful collection of Jesus' parables. And Luke does this without giving us a notion of time and place.

Fortunately, the time period encompassed is relatively short. And, as the respected scholar Alfred Edersheim observes, these narratives from Luke fit remarkably well into John's October 15 to early April descriptions.

All of this is to confess that I resolved the chronology dilemma—for the purpose of this project—by following Edersheim's hunch. I complied with the chronology presented in Luke's stand-alone passage and placed it within John's overall framework. With this solution, Jesus does not return to Galilee after his early October trip south.

While I am very comfortable with this resolution (it follows Edersheim's best hypothesis and does not violate the sequencing of Aland), I am confessing that, truly, it is unknown whether or not Jesus returned to Galilee after October 15 of his thirty-second year.

Finally, before I rapidly back out of academia and get back to an arena in which I am more comfortable—storytelling, I would like to borrow again from Edersheim.[1] While you will pass through a period in this volume where precise ordering is unknown, I hope his "three vital conditions for following Christ" will be clearly apparent on every page. These are:

1. Immediate and entire self-surrender to Christ and his work.
2. A heart undivided and set on Christ.
3. Absolute self-denial and an awareness that the world is not our true home.

And for each of us who is willing to dare a level of self-surrender that would leave us homeless pilgrims, the rest is Divine history.

EVEN MORE GOOD NEWS

We were racing toward the strangest sight my dog eyes had ever seen— at certain-death speed!

Jesna was still feverishly pushing buttons and pulling levers. Her five-year-old shoulders were tense with the weight of the world. Pete was screaming with glee. To him this was simply the world's greatest roller coaster.

Between the two contrasting sets of shoulders I peered out. What I saw would have caused astonishment—if my fear had left room for another emotion.

A broad band of blue water was rapidly getting bigger and bigger. So was a straight stripe of brown mud. The brown— right across the middle of the blue—seemed bizarrely out of place, like the misplaced crayon mark of a child. But as the unnatural picture grew bigger, its bizarreness doubled in weirdness.

Even from our bouncing vantage point I could see that the brown streak was a road that had been carved through the middle of a huge sea. The road, however, was on the surface of the sea-bottom. Whatever was holding the walls of water back was clearly invisible to my bobbing eyes.

"Wow!" Pete exclaimed. "That looks just like the Sunday School pictures of Abraham crossing the deep blue Sea."

"That's 'Moses' and the 'Red Sea,' you little family-crasher!" Priscilla managed to scold, through clenched teeth.

"Oh, yeah," Pete shot back. "Hey, do you suppose that really is Moses down there?"

"Why don't you ask him? Right after you smash into his face!" Priscilla said, her lips still pursed. Her hands were firmly gripping the side of our speeding car.

At this point we were approaching the road through the Red Sea at break-neck speed—literally. Jesna was still working with the control panel with all the seriousness of a brain surgeon working on her own child. At the far end of the sea-ditch a multitude of people were spread out on the shore like tens of thousands of wildflowers—petals raised skyward. Either they were bouncing up and down, or I had doggie motion sickness.

At the opposite end of God's fingerswipe through the water was a charging army of horses, chariots, and spear-chuckers. Their swords, spears, and metal skirts were sparkling in the sun-light like a tangled string of blinking Christmas lights.

"1,000 feet!" Jesna shouted.

"Why are you so serious, Jesna? We've crashed through stuff before. We can't get hurt."

"Oh yes, we can! The ride is set for 'total reality'!" Jesna answered Pete, her face now tightly drawn. "Five hundred feet! Put your heads between your knees. *Now!*"

Pete turned around and looked at his parents. He was white as a sheet.

"One hundred feet," Jesna said as she turned the smallest dial. I think my *fur* was white as a sheet.

With Jesna's last effort my throat took a quick trip through my stomach and out my feet as our car drew a ninety-degree angle—in mid-air. We shot over the Egyptian army, just above spear height, and down the middle of an alleyway of four-story aqua-blue walls. You should have seen the startled looks on the faces of a few thousand fish that were staring right at us.

With Jesna now in control of our craft we began to race along the corridor. It was some mighty thin inches that separated us from the muddy floor of the Red Sea.

"Yee-haw!" Pete crowed, his face now back to its normal pink color. "We're leaving them Egyptians behind like they were standing still."

And he was right, except that they weren't standing still. They were still racing toward the nation of unarmed Israelites.

"Hey, Jesna," Pete continued, "this reminds me of the first *Star Wars* movie. See if you can squeeze off a shot into the enemy's main reactor. The force will be with you."

"There aren't any enemies in front of us, Pete," Jesna said, "only Moses and a few hundred thousand of his closest friends. Obviously God's force is with *them.*"

"Yeah," Pete said. "They better hope it's with them!"

We all looked ahead to get a better view of what, and who, Jesna and Pete were describing. But just then an unearthly crashing sound began to explode behind us. I spun my head around so fast I could see my tail. I also saw that God was quickly causing the monstrous gash we were driving through to heal shut. Two giant, fast-moving waterfalls were racing toward us and tossing the entire Egyptian army around like a child's pool toys near an open fire hydrant.

"You better step on it, Jesna!" Pete said. "There's a tidal wave in the passing lane!"

As the first spray from the crashing water came down on us we zipped up the bank and over the heads and clapping hands of the cheering crowd of Israelites.

"Ride 'em cowboy!" Pete shouted. Then he said, "Hey, did

you notice that Moses doesn't look a thing like Charlton Heston? Talk about bad casting."

But before anyone could laugh, Jesna caused the sky to become a swirling kaleidoscope of time-travel colors. By the time it had turned back into a canopy of black with pinpricks of light, we had landed on the crackling sand of first-century Bible Land. Right on top of the very same dirt indentations and rocks we had blasted off from—twenty seconds and a million heartbeats ago.

We all sat motionless in the prodigal car, allowing our breathing and heart-beating to slow to a more normal pace.

SCENE 91
BACK TO THE PAST—
TWO MORE PARABLES[2]

Cooking smells began to waft out from the house and across the courtyard. Pete was the first to pop out of his seat and follow the aroma to its source. We all tagged behind, like a pack of steely-eyed zombies. I wasn't sure if Pete was being led by his nose or his desire to keep some distance between his bottom and his father's hand. In either event, he plopped down at the feet of Jesus, safe at last.

Jesus was continuing his private lessons with the disciples. A quick wink at Pete was all that let us know he was aware of our near-baptism experience in the Red Sea.

"God's kingdom is like a treasure hidden in a field for years and then accidentally found by a trespasser. The finder is ecstatic—what a find!—and proceeds to sell everything he owns to raise money and buy that field.

"Or, God's kingdom is like a jewel merchant on the hunt for excellent pearls. Finding one that is flawless, he immediately sells everything and buys it."[3]

"The first thing he said reminds me of a movie I saw on TV one time," Pete turned to us and said excitedly.

"We just *lived* a movie you saw on TV one time, Pete," Priscilla said, still breathing deeply from Pete's joy ride.

"It was about a family that

took an exciting trip. They sold everything they had and bought a wagon with a round tent on the top of it. They hitched it to some horses and took their new house all the way to California. When they got there, they sold their mobile home, bought some land, and started digging for gold."

"Did they find any?" Priscilla asked, seeming slightly upset with herself that Pete had pulled her into a conversation.

"Nope, not at first. They just dug in the ground, built a real ugly house out of logs, and lived like they were a family of bears.

"When winter came one of the kids got real sick. They didn't have anything to eat but stuff their dad could shoot. And I don't think he was a very good shot, because they all were looking pretty skinny before springtime. When spring came they were back at it, digging like four dogs looking for the last bone on earth." (I yipped once just thinking about it. *Umm, bones!*)

"Then, after their horses died and a bear scared them up a tree and Old Yeller had puppies, they found some gold. You should have seen them whooping and hollering and dancing around—like they had found a calendar where every day was Christmas and every night New Year's Eve."

"So, what happened to them?"

"Well, Sis, I don't know."

"You don't know?"

"No! I fell asleep right after they found the gold. But I bet they moved to the city, took baths, and bought a toy store. Anyway, Jesus' story reminds me of that movie."

"And with good reason, Pete," Jesna said. "He's talking about a treasure to be found that is worth far more than gold."

Pete's eyes became as wide as saucers.

"You are the field. Like the land in California," Jesna went on.

"Huh?"

"And buried down deep inside you is a hidden treasure—a soul that can live and dance in God's kingdom. If you find that treasure and let your soul start to enjoy the 'kingdom,' then you just might start whooping and hollering yourself. Because every day can be a Christmas," she told him.

"It sounds like that's worth selling out for, Jesna," Mr. Pilgrim echoed. "But first, Pete has a different type of whooping and hollering to get out of the way."

"Couldn't you just give me a time out, Dad?"

"People don't usually live that long, son."

FAMILY DISCUSSION

1. What are some ways you can let God's kingdom shine out for others to see?
2. Have you ever thought about the fact that your soul with its ability to enjoy life in God's kingdom is the most valuable possession you own?

SCENE 92
THE PARABLE OF THE NET[4]

After a while, Pete and his father went off to take care of Pete's discipline problem, and Jesus continued to instruct his disciples about the "kingdom."

" ... God's kingdom is like a fishnet cast into the sea, catching all kinds of fish. When it is full, it is hauled onto the beach. The good fish are picked out and put in a tub; those unfit to eat are thrown away. That's how it will be when the curtain comes down on history. The angels will come and cull the bad fish and throw them in the garbage. There will be a lot of desperate complaining, but it won't do any good."[5]

"I bet those fish cooking in there … " Pete pointed toward the house, "are good ones. I know they sure smell good to me."

No one responded. Mrs. Pilgrim and Priscilla had their attention glued on Jesus.

Pete continued in a louder voice. "Y'know, I remember seeing Peter and some of his friends throw out a big ol' rope net and haul in a bunch of fish. They poured them into the bottom of their boat and they—the fish, not the disciples—were really doing some flipping, flapping, and flopping."

He still didn't have anyone's attention but mine. I wagged my tail encouragingly.

"Ahhummmphum!" Pete cleared his throat. "And it was just like Jesus was saying. When we got back to the shore Peter started grabbing some of those fish—some of the biggest ones—and he threw them away. If I had tried to pick up one of those slimy things it would've been like trying to pick up soap out of a bathtub full of water or a watermelon seed off a waxed floor. But he could do it.

"Remember, Dad, you told me they were probably carp that he was throwing back. Remember you said, 'The only way a guy can eat a carp is if he leaves it on a board out in the hot sun for a week, and then scrapes off the carp and eats the board?'"

"Pete!" Priscilla said. "Are you still talking?"

"Yeah! Weren't you listening? I was saying the same thing Jesus was—about how you shouldn't be a carp or the angels will throw you away. But how can a person, like me," Pete said with his head turned sideways, "keep from being a bad-tasting fish?"

That got Jesna's attention. "Bad-tasting fish, Pete, generally get that way because of the way they live—because of what they eat. You know, the habits they have."

"You mean the low-down, bottom-dwelling, scum-suckers usually are the worst-tasting?" Pete asked.

"Well," Jesna said, "if not the worst-tasting, they might be the worst *for* you. Because it's the habits of a fish, or a person, that can...."

"Cause the angels to keep 'em or cull 'em?"

"You got it, Pete," Jesna said. "It's how we respond to God, what we *do* with our lives, that determines if we are wheat or tares, sheep or goats, fish or, uh … "

"Foul fish," Pete said. "And that's probably why Dad has to give me a habit adjustment every now and then. Huh, Dad?"

FAMILY DISCUSSION:
1. What are the best "habits" of your life?
2. What are some of the worst?
3. What do you intend to do to change your habits?
4. Have you ever asked the Lord Jesus to help you?

SCENE 93
NEW AND OLD TREASURES[6]

"Time to come in and eat," said a pleasant-sounding voice from inside the house. (Jesus and his disciples were still staying with a family that had been coming out to hear him preach.)

"She sounds as pleasant as Mrs. Santa," Pete observed.

Jesus stood to his feet. As he was entering the doorway he stopped and faced his disciples, who were close on his heels, and asked,

"Are you starting to get a handle on all this?"

Most of them began nodding.

"Then you see," he said, "every student who is well trained in God's kingdom is like the owner of a general store who can put his hands on anything you need, old or new, exactly when you need it."[7]

Jesus studied their faces, then stood in the doorway and motioned for his disciples to enter ahead of him. From the smell of things inside, God's kitchen-keepers too had put their hands on exactly what Jesus and the disciples needed, and they had cooked it to mouth-watering perfection.

After a long, leisurely meal of a roasted goat, fruits, vegetables, and mounds of golden bread, Jesus and his disciples began talking with their hosts. When minds were as full as bodies, pallets were prepared for everyone to sleep on the floor. That night was the first time that Jesus had not slept outside in many moons.

The next morning Jesus awoke when the first rays of dawn splashed color on his face. He shook his friends awake and whispered to each one that they would be traveling back to Nazareth that day. From the looks on some of their faces, it appeared they thought his words were part of a bad dream.

Having heard the disciples' stirrings, their hosts came into the room. Mrs. Host insisted that Jesus and his friends fill their packs with leftovers from the feast before leaving. Mr. Host was equally insistent that Jesus accept a small leather bag filled with jingling coins.

Jesus' eyes welled with tears—he almost always seemed a little surprised whenever someone truly came to understand his message of selfless love. He hugged him and then handed the money to Judas. Judas was the group's treasurer, since he loved money more than any of the rest.

Judas looked as surprised at the gift as Jesus had the giver. Judas' astonishment was so great that Mr. Host offered an explanation. "Jesus has thrown open the gates to his Father's kingdom and invited us to live there. The least we can do is to help ease the discomfort of his and your travels. The money is just street-dust compared to the gift I have been given."

Judas still looked puzzled. Apparently he hadn't listened very carefully when Jesus had talked about God's kingdom.

"Do you ever wonder if Jesus thinks he picked the wrong disciple when he nabbed Judas?"

"Hush, Pete!" said Mr. Pilgrim, cupping a large hand around his son's never-resting mouth.

That day we all made the trip to Nazareth. Jesna's driving skills seemed to be improving. My upper and lower canine teeth smacked into each other only two or three times when we hit the natural speed bumps that seemed so common along the way.

That first evening in Nazareth, Jesus was speaking in a meeting house—the house where he grew up. This was his first trip back home since the good folks of Nazareth had tried to push him over a cliff just outside town.

Mary and the rest of Jesus' family were sitting right in the front row.

When he had finished speaking and the crowd was milling around him, I couldn't resist weaving in and out of the forest of legs to hear what everyone was saying. The reviews were not all positive. There were as many thumbs pointing down as up.

"We had no idea he was this good!"

"How did he get to be so wise? Where'd he get such speaking ability?"

"We've known him since he was a kid; he's the carpenter's son. Who does he think he is, talking that way!"

Jesus was aware of the cutting words. When the crowd was gone, and he was alone with his disciples, he said,

> "A prophet is taken for granted in his hometown and his family."[8]

He did very few miracles in Nazareth before leaving town.

FAMILY DISCUSSION
1. What do you think Jesus meant by saying, "A prophet is taken for granted in his hometown"?
2. How can you keep from taking Jesus for granted in yours?

SCENE 94
THE HEALING AT THE POOL[9]

Soon Jesus left his hometown for the third time in less than three years. While it wasn't his first time to leave home—and no one had tried to kill him this time—there was still pain on his face.

"Where are we going?" Pete asked Jesna as Nazareth was becoming a smaller and smaller bouncing blur in the rearview mirror.

"Jesus is heading down south, to Jerusalem," Jesna said. "There is going to be a religious feast in the Temple that he wants to attend."

Five minutes of Bible time passed as the car rolled onward. Then Pete asked, "Are we there yet?" Even from the back seat I could see both of his parents rolling their eyes with their whole heads.

"No, Pete, we're not there yet," Jesna responded. "Do you remember when we made the trip with Mary and Joseph to Bethlehem?"

"Sure I do. I'm real glad you didn't say we're going to Bethlehem. It took more than a week to get there."

"Well, there's good news and bad news, Pete. Bethlehem is only about five miles south of Jerusalem."

"What's the good news?" Pete moaned.

"We're not traveling with an expectant mother this time. So we'll be able to make the trip in four or five days."

"Y'know," Priscilla sighed, "with a monorail like they have back at Daffy World, Jesus could have done ten times the work."

"I don't know, Priscilla. Take a look at him now," Jesna said while motioning to Jesus with her head.

Jesus seemed to have put the pain of Nazareth behind him. He was laughing and talking with the disciples with an arm draped around the shoulder of one of them.

"I think he does his most important work between destinations."

The journey passed quickly. On the day before Sabbath, we camped outside Jerusalem at sunset. The next morning we entered Jerusalem through one of its magnificent city gates.

"I always feel like we are driving into a big castle when we go in this gate," Pete observed. "I wonder if there's a drawbridge for this thing."

Once inside the holy city we quickly became engulfed by the crowds of people. It was only because we could pass through them that we were able to keep up with Jesus.

After about an hour of navigating through the crowded streets, we found ourselves in a large, stone building. It smelled of fresh spring water.

"Everybody out," Jesna said.

We piled out of the car and everyone stretched. We ran to catch up with Jesus. He was descending a steep and winding flight of stone steps. Footsteps echoed off the pool of water below.

The last step ended in the middle of a large room-sized opening that was carved from stone. There in the center of the room was a long, narrow pool of crystal-clear water. Five alcoves, each with a stone porch, surrounded the pool.

"Cool!" Pete shouted. "An indoor pool."

"Not quite indoors, little brother," Priscilla said, directing his gaze up at the blue sky.

The crowd of people gathered by the pool were further evidence that this was no typical swimming pool. Most had twisted limbs or eyes that were matted shut. Some were lying on their backs on straw mats, reaching up to no one in particular with helpless hands.

"What *is* this place?" Pete squeaked. "Is this hell? But I didn't think there would be any water there. All these broken people are giving me the creeps."

"No, Pete," Jesna reassured. "We didn't go *that far* down the steps. This is the pool of Bethesda, a place where sick people come in hopes of getting well."

"Why does Jesus seemed to be attracted to sick people?" Pete asked. "It seems like they are Jesus-magnets."

"Love is always attracted to pain, if it's true love," Jesna answered.

Then she continued. "Bethesda means 'house of grace.' The water is from a spring-fed pool, and these people believe that sometimes angels visit and splash in the water. They also believe that if they are the first to get in after an angel touches the water, they'll be healed."

"Wow!" said Pete with his eyes flashing excitement. "You mean we might get to see a real, live angel?"

"I don't know," Jesna answered, "but the Angel-maker is here now. He's standing right by your side. Take a look and you'll see what's splashing around in his mind."

Jesus was kneeling on one knee over the motionless body of a man. The man was lying on a dirty mat of straw and whispering to Jesus with a raspy voice.

"I've been a cripple for thirty-eight years. My son brings me to this pool every day. But when the water is stirred, I don't have anybody to put me into the pool—my son is away working. By the time I am able to roll myself in, somebody else is already splashing around in my healing."

"I see," Jesus said.

"You do?" the man said excitedly. "Will you help me get in?"

"Oh, I'll do more than that," Jesus answered—

"Get up, take your bedroll, and start walking."[10]

Jesus' words caused shockwaves to cross the caverns of the man's hollow face. But it was nothing compared to the Richter-scale readings his face registered when his legs and arms began to shake with Divine energy.

The man rolled to his knees and then stood to his feet, astonished.

He ran from the pool area, up the steps, grasping every bystander's hand as he passed, babbling with joy all the way. Jesus was looking up into the blue sky, smiling at his Father. Pete and Priscilla did high fives and I halfway expected to see angels doing them too.

FAMILY DISCUSSION
1. Why do you think Jesus visited the pool of Bethesda before going to the Temple?
2. Why do you think that Jesus' "true love" caused him to be attracted to those in pain?
3. If you were in terrible pain or paralyzed, what could you do about it?

SCENE 95
CONFRONTATION IN THE TEMPLE[11]

In the same way that a mother bird watches its chick's first flaps of flight, Jesus watched the gleeful man as he ascended the winding steps. After he was out of sight, he turned and began ministering to others by the pool. No one seemed disappointed that an angel hadn't shown up that morning. No one even thought about jumping into the pool.

"Come on," Jesna said. "We've got to catch up with the man Jesus just healed."

"Which one?" Priscilla asked with a smile.

"The first one," Jesna winked back, "the one who couldn't walk."

"Which one?" Priscilla teased again, as another former cripple danced by the pool.

"Can't we stay here with Jesus?" Pete asked.

"Jesus will come along soon. But you need to see what happens next."

Jesna let me sniff out the lame man's trail. It wasn't easy. His feet, which had been dragging uselessly for over thirty-eight years, were barely touching the ground now. When we caught up with him he was in the courtyard of the Temple—encircled by an unfriendly gang of men.

"Hey! What are you doing carrying your bedroll around on the Sabbath?" an angry-faced man shouted.

"Yeah," said another, in a grumpy voice. "You know it's against the rules! Are you trying to provoke God's anger?"

The smile faded from the newly-healed man's face. He looked as confused as a dog being beaten by its master. He began to stammer, "Th-the man who made me well told me to carry it. He said, 'Take your bedroll and start walking.'"

"Who told you to break the Sabbath rule?" another angry face asked, apparently missing the fact that a certifiable miracle had been performed.

The healed man couldn't answer the question. He had never seen Jesus before. And he'd left Jesus back by the pool when he had scampered off.

"This is a matter for the Temple council," someone declared. Then the group spun around as if on one heel, and followed their anger through the door of a stone building next to the Temple.

People from the crowd approached the healed man. Some reached out and touched him tentatively, as if to make sure he was still the same pitiful fellow they had stepped over yesterday when he was crippled.

"I didn't know you *had* feet," a little girl exclaimed.

Then Jesus came into the courtyard with his band of disciples.

"Why isn't there a crowd of people around him here, like up north?" Priscilla asked.

"Most all of Jesus' ministry has been around the Sea of Galilee—almost a hundred miles to the north. There are no telephones or TVs, so people down here don't know much about him. He is only known in Jerusalem by the few who have traveled to hear him. He's probably best known in Jerusalem by the Sanhedrin, the religious rulers. They've kept up with him through their spies. Now, they're about to find out he's right under their noses."

"Sounds like there might be a shoot-out at the OK Corr ... Courtyard," Pete mused out loud.

"Sooner than you think," Jesna said.

"That's him! That's the man!" the healed man was crying at the top of his lungs, and he ran to grab Jesus by the knees.

"Shhh!" Pete sprayed. "It's a trap!" But it was too late.

"You look great!" Jesus said. "Now go and stay far from sin."

The man went bouncing off in the direction his gang of accusers had taken. Before you could say "lynch mob" the gang had returned—quadruple in size and peppered with black-robed Pharisees.

"Are you the one who breaks the Sabbath rules?" one shouted as they approached Jesus.

"My Father—God—doesn't take the Sabbath off. Why should his Son?"

"Uh-oh," Pete sighed. "Them's fightin' words."

The mob of angry men stopped dead in their tracks a few feet from Jesus, as if they had run into an invisible wall. Their noses almost seemed flattened by the impact of Jesus' statement. Disciples tried to hide from the mob behind Jesus' back. Pete stepped in front of Jesus and balled up his fists. He was staring at a black-robed man in the kingpin position of the mob.

"Did you hear that?" the first to find his voice shouted. "He said he was … I can't say it. He's not only broken the Sabbath, but he's a blasphemer. *He must be put to death!* Go tell the Sanhedrin."

"You can tell your mamma if you want to," Pete shouted back. "Me and Jesus ain't backing down. And tell her I said this Temple ain't big enough for the both of us. I mean the three of us."

Pete was right.

Jesus, far from backing down, spoke with a clear and confident voice.

"You have your heads in your Bibles constantly because you think you'll find eternal life there. But you miss the forest for the trees. These Scriptures are all about *me!* And here I am, standing right before you, and you aren't willing to receive from me the life you say you want.

"I'm not interested in crowd approval. And do you know why? Because I know you and your crowds. I know that love, especially God's love, is not on your working agenda.

" … How do you expect to get anywhere with God when you spend all your time jockeying for position with each other, ranking your rivals, and ignoring God?

" … If you won't take seriously what (Moses) wrote, how can I expect you to take seriously what I speak?"[12]

Jesus turned—leaving his accusers too shocked for words behind their wall of disbelief—and walked away.

"Now I bet I know why Jesus went to Bethesda first this morning, before coming here," Priscilla said as she stared at her wrist-computer.

"Why?" Jesna asked.

"It's the Sabbath, right?" Priscilla chirped proudly. "Where else would he go first—Bethesda, 'house of grace,' or, uh, … "

"The 'Temple of doom'?" Pete assisted.

FAMILY DISCUSSION

1. How could someone have his head in the Bible all the time and still miss the most important stuff?
2. If you had been there with Jesus, what would you have said to his accusers? To Jesus?

SCENE 96
COMMISSIONING THE TWELVE[13]

We didn't stay in Jerusalem very long. We were only there enough time for Jesus and his friends to attend the feasts and for him to tell a few small groups about his favorite subject— "the kingdom."

He also kept doing what he said he would do when he was back in the synagogue in Nazareth. When he left Jerusalem there were fewer blind or crippled people there. There were fewer captives of sin, fewer oppressed by fear. And, for many with soft hearts, the "good news" of the gospel had been written inside them—in the "holy of holies" of their living temples.

During the return trip to Galilee, Jesus gathered his disciples together one night. By the light of their campfire he said to them all: "Do you remember when I told you that the 'fields are overflowing—ready for harvest—but the harvesters are few'?"

They all nodded. So did Pete. He probably was remembering getting a special hug from

Jesus that day—after he had declared his intent to be a soul farmer.

"You've seen that what I say is true. You have all been wonderful helpers, wonderful harvesters. Now it's time for you to go off on your own for a while."

Everyone froze in place. It became so quiet you could have heard a bird feather drop on a disciple's beard. At last, Peter broke the silence. He sounded like a five-year-old who had been asked to get a job away from home. "What's wrong, Master? Did we do something wrong?"

Jesus laughed from his belly. "No! Just the opposite. You've been doing everything right. That's why it's time for you to do more—to put all that you have been learning into practice, on your own."

Then he told them:

"Don't think you need a lot of extra equipment for this. *You* are the equipment. No special appeals for funds. Keep it simple."

"I thought he was going to say, 'stupid,'" Pete said.

"If you're not welcomed, not listened to, quietly withdraw. Don't make a scene. Shrug your shoulders and be on your way."[14]

The next morning, twelve disciple-birds were sent out of the nest in pairs. They flew away with joy and a sense of urgency. We didn't get to follow any of them—Jesna said those scenes weren't recorded in Scripture. "But," she said with a confident smile, "don't worry about them. They've had a great Teacher. Before they're through they'll tell the world that life can be radically different for those who are willing to take the risks, spread their wings, and fly."

FAMILY DISCUSSION

1. What do you think are the most difficult things about taking the risks to live a radically different life—a life of a true disciple?

2. If Jesus were to send you out tomorrow to tell people about his kingdom, could you do it? How would you feel?

SCENE 97
THE DEATH OF JOHN THE BAPTIST[15]

Jesus and the disciples were separated for a while. It's hard to know exactly how long when all you are seeing of time is the pushing of buttons and the whirling colors. When the Bible-world stopped spinning around we were back in the palace of King Herod. Jesna told us where we were, but I would have recognized the smells of overfed royalty anywhere.

We were in the middle of a huge banquet room. On one side were long tables piled high to overflowing with rich, spicy-smelling foods. Across the front were other, longer tables, surrounded by eaters in bright, flowing clothes. Besides the wonderful smells of bread and roasted meat, the room was also filled with music, barely-dressed dancers, and the sounds of a hundred mouths smacking. I was the only dog in the place.

"That's King Herod, there, isn't it?" Pete asked, then answered his own question. "I recognized him from our last trip here."

"I guess that big crown on his head was another good clue, huh?" Priscilla said facetiously.

"Yeah, that was a good one. But it was the lamb leg in each hand that really gave him away. Hey," Pete continued, "do you know what a glutton is? My friend, Joey, told me this one. A glutton is someone who has food in each hand and then asks for third helpings. If Herod asks for more mutton, we'll know he's a glutton."

Everyone moaned but Jesna. She seemed very sad and serious. Mrs. Pilgrim noticed it first. She said, "Jesna, why are you so glum?"

"Yeah," Pete chimed in, "there's a party going on."

"It's more like a wake," Jesna said. Then, in soft tones, she began to explain. "John, you know, is in prison here."

"Oh," Pete said quietly, then tucked his head. "I forgot."

"So he's still here?" Mr. Pilgrim said.

"Yes. At least for a little while longer."

"What does *that* mean?" Priscilla asked. " … 'for a little while longer'?"

"Is he about to get out of jail?" Pete interrupted. "Is he going back home?"

"In a manner of speaking, Pete. In a manner of speaking, yes, he's homeward bound."

Jesna was staring at the stone floor of Herod's palace as she was answering Pete. Tears were spilling down her cheeks.

"John is a great prophet, you know. Jesus said he was the greatest ever. But prophets have a real hard time keeping quiet about truth—especially if someone is breaking God's rules."

"I remember," Priscilla said. "That's why Herod sent his soldiers to arrest him. He was preaching that it was wrong for Herod to be married to … uh … "

"Herodetta," Pete proudly interrupted.

"Herodias," Jesna softly corrected. "Herodias is also Herod's brother's wife. John hasn't stopped being a prophet, hasn't stopped preaching, even in Herod's dungeon. He's been booming away from his small cell, every day—just like when he was out in the wilderness. And he hasn't stopped preaching against Herod's marriage to Herodias."

"Herodias has wanted John dead for a long time. But Herod knows John is a holy man. Some days, he even goes down to the dungeon and listens. His guilt has almost driven him to repentance. And Herodias knows that if he repents …."

"She's out with the trash?" Pete inserted.

"Yes, you could say that. It frightens her very much."

"Oh my goodness!" Mrs. Pilgrim said. "Somebody cover Pete's eyes. Quick!"

This caused everyone, especially Pete, to pay extra attention to what was going on.

The music had changed. It had become louder and faster. In the center of the room a young woman was jumping, gyrating, and swirling to the music; and throwing away what few clothes she was wearing as she went.

"That's Herodias' daughter," Jesna said calmly.

By this time Mr. Pilgrim had his hand over Pete's eyes and Mrs. Pilgrim had her hands over Mr. Pilgrim's. Herodias' daughter's hands were a blur. She was putting on a show that was enough to make a monkey blush.

When the music stopped, so did she. She was breathless, and so was King Herod. But he somehow managed to bellow out, "Ask me anything. I'll give you whatever you want. I'll give you up to half my kingdom. Name your price for the dance."

Before she answered, the girl looked to the eyes of her mother, who sat beside the king like a snooty afghan hound. Her mother gave one long, satisfied nod.

"I'll take the head of John the Baptist—on a platter—and I want it now!" the girl said.

The king's countenance fell. It was obvious that half his kingdom would have been easier to give. But even as he stared at the floor, he raised his hand over his head and snapped his fingers.

Two men wearing metal Xs across their muscular chests left the room.

Jesna was anxiously punching buttons that were wet with the tears of her grief. "Some scenes are better left unseen," she said.

FAMILY DISCUSSION

1. What do you think Jesus would have said to John if he had been there?
2. Why was John being killed? Is there anything you are willing to die for?
3. How do you think John maintained the courage to keep preaching in prison?

SCENE 98
THE RETURN OF THE APOSTLES[16]

More buttons were pushed, more tears splashed, more colors set a-swirl. We came to rest in the middle of a wonderful, peaceful, and familiar sight—the rocky shore of the Sea of Galilee. Less than a good cheetah-leap away, Jesus was sitting on a large rock. His back was to the sea as he gazed out across the brown-green landscape.

"Do you think he knows about John?" Pete asked.

"I'm sure he does," Jesna said. "Even if his Father hasn't told him during one of their daily conversations, it's become common knowledge by this time."

"Well, I just wondered if that's why he looks a little sad right now."

"He's not sad now, Pete. He's just praying. This is the day his disciples are supposed to come back and report on all that happened during their 'solo' flights. His mind is on them."

"I'm sure, though," Jesna continued, "that the cruel death of his cousin John has been on his mind today. It's a horrible reminder of how high the stakes are for those who are brave enough to challenge this dark world with kingdom-light."

Time passed. Jesus skipped rocks, smelled the flowers, and watched butterflies.

As the sun was reaching its highest point in the sky, we saw two figures separating themselves from the horizon. When they were about five hundred yards away they apparently recognized the man by the lake as Jesus and they broke into a gallop. He met them halfway.

The three walked back to the meeting spot together. Before

they could take a seat, two more disciples were spotted. By the time it was necessary to start preparing supper, all were present and accounted for.

The peaceful evening hours were spent eating fish and telling stories about all that had been done, seen, and taught. Jesus listened intently like the proud parent he was. He listened until an impatient rooster crowed—just before dawn.

Before they finally pulled what was left of the warm night sky over their heads to go to sleep, Jesus said, "Tomorrow we'll go off by ourselves. It's time to take a break and get some rest. And I'd like to hear all of your stories again."

No one argued. They were all big boys now.

FAMILY DISCUSSION

1. Why do you think the disciples were sent out by twos, instead of ones, or threes?
2. How does it feel to know, that because of the Holy Spirit, you can never be alone?
3. Do you tell Jesus about your day before you go to sleep? Did you know he is interested enough to want to hear everything you have to say?

SCENE 99
FIVE THOUSAND FED[17]

Jesus and his partners didn't ask for a wake-up call the next morning. They all slept in for as long as their eyelids could keep out the rays of early morning sun. Eventually the sun won.

I don't know if the disciples had spent more energy completing their first internship or in telling each other about it. But the combination had left them exhausted.

Pete and Priscilla weren't quite so tired. They had amused themselves by exploring the seashore, bouncing in a boat that Jesus had left tied to a conveniently shaped rock, and trying to keep the roosters quiet. Mr. and Mrs. Pilgrim had enjoyed a long walk by the lake and an even longer chat on a rocky love seat. They were holding hands a lot lately, which was quite a change from how things had been for them before this ride began.

I spent the morning swimming in the shallow water near the shore, while Jesna waited as patiently as a cat-napping cat.

Eventually, the disciples and Jesus were all out of their bedrolls and eating a light brunch of bread and dates. "That seems to be about all the food we have in camp," one said. "I guess so," said another. But no one seemed concerned about the prospects for the next meal.

True to his suggestion the night before, Jesus told the disciples to get into a boat that he had borrowed. "I want us to go across the lake to a quiet place where we won't be disturbed. We all can use the rest and the time together."

"You know," Pete said, "even the tax taker, Matthew, has learned his way around the campsites and boats. Look at him go."

It wasn't long until they had pushed off from the shore, heading, it appeared, to the northeast corner of the lake. We Pilgrims were right by their side, the shiny metal fender of our car jostling the weathered wooden bow of their boat.

"Is Jesus still the only one of them that can see us?" Pete asked.

"Yes, Pete," Jesna said.

"Shoot! I thought one of them was making a funny face at me."

"No, that was Bartholomew. I think he's a little seasick."

"Oh. Do you think we'll get to see him hurl?"

"Pete!"

Personally, as a dog, it was hard for me to feel very sorry for anyone who's last name ends with "mew." But there were plenty of things to be interested in. For instance, I began noticing light flashes and patches of color along the shoreline. I began to suspect that a pack of humans was following the course of our boats. I wondered if Jesus and the disciples would get the rest break they needed.

A couple of hours passed before the spot that Jesus had picked for us was in view. It was beautiful. The boundaries of the shore opened up to form a large inlet of still, blue water. Gentle slopes of golden grass kept the water in its place and the winds out of the cove. The hillsides were patched with green olive trees and large gray rocks.

And oh yes, the hills were also alive with the sounds of people. Apparently, a huge crowd had anticipated Jesus' destination and was now awaiting his next message and miracles.

"Can you believe it? Let's turn back," one of the disciples said. "Yeah," said another, "I haven't had enough sleep for this."

But Jesus was wearing a broken heart on his sleeve. "No," he said. "Look at them—like sheep without a shepherd. Our rest today will be in doing my Father's work."

And that's just what they did. Minutes after securing the boat, Jesus was alternately preaching at the top of his voice and talking to his Father about those who needed miracles. The disciples left the preaching to him, but freely joined in praying for the sick and helpless.

Much of the afternoon passed, and stomachs and disciples began to grumble.

"The day is gone and no one has eaten," one disciple said.

"Yeah, we're a long way from any town, even if the market were still open."

"Jesus," another said, "don't you think it's time to send these folks home for supper? It'll be dark soon."

"Boy!" Priscilla said. "It doesn't take these disciples much time to forget, does it? The time between shouting the victory to grumbling the defeat is about as quick as the interval between a traffic light turning green and hearing the first horn blow."

"Yeah. Dad says that's the shortest interval of time known to mankind, huh, Dad?"

Mr. Pilgrim said nothing.

"But why all the complaints?" Pete said. "Why don't they just order out? Pizza places never close."

"Only a few minor glitches, little brother. Remember, no one has a cellular phone; it's a few millennia until the first pizza place will open in the Holy Land, and it's a long way to Italy!"

"Well, Jesus could invent pizza if he wanted to," Pete replied. "He's already invented all the ingredients."

But Jesus had another idea. "You fix supper for them," he said to his disciples.

"You can't be serious!" Judas said, as he jingled a leather pouch of coins in front of Jesus' face. "It would cost a fortune to feed this multitude!"

"Plus," said Matthew, "there's no place to buy food."

"How much food do you have?" Jesus asked.

"None," said Simon Peter. "I finished it off this morning. But I was just talking to a little boy who has five loaves and a couple of fish. He wanted to give it to me after I prayed for his mother's eyes to be healed."

"Go and ask him if I can borrow his supper."

"Borrow?" Peter questioned, with wide eyes and a wrinkled brow. But he did as he was told.

In a moment Peter was back with a little guy, waist-high, by his side. With two straight arms, he was holding out to Jesus a rough, cloth sack. He seemed prouder than a peacock. His mother was a few steps behind, looking at everything in wide-eyed wonder.

"Do you want some of my lunch?" the boy said to Jesus in an excited little voice. "You can have all of it if you want. I'm too happy to be hungry."

"What do you have there?" Jesus asked, as he opened the brown cloth bag.

From where I sat I could see it all—five round, golden, oversized biscuits and two dried fish—just the way I like them (heads still attached). Jesus let the food slide back to the bottom of the sack.

"Get the people to sit down in groups of fifty or a hundred," Jesus said to his bewildered disciples. Then turning back to the boy, he said, "Will you help me serve lunch?"

The boy eagerly nodded his head and then he and Jesus began to take turns reaching into the bag, pulling out fish and bread.

"One loaf, two," Peter began to count. "One fish, two …." By the time Peter was saying "eight loaves, nine,…" Priscilla was staring with her mouth agape. This didn't compute.

By the time they had filled two large straw baskets with bread and fish the disciples were returning for more, Pete was saying to his gaped-mouth sister, "Hey, Priscilla, did you know you have two fillings?"

Before sunset, more than 5,000 people had been fed

(Priscilla counted them—twice), twelve interns realized they still had a lot to learn, and Jesus had returned the five loaves and two fish he had borrowed from a big-hearted little boy—along with twelve baskets filled and overflowing with "interest."

"Thank you," Jesus said to his little friend with the big heart.

"Anytime, Jesus," his chef-mate said.

"Apparently," Mr. Pilgrim said, "it's hard to outgive Jesus."

FAMILY DISCUSSION

1. Do you think, from the discussion Jesus and the disciples had, they were still having trouble believing in him? Why?
2. What do you have that you are willing to give Jesus to use in helping others?
3. What are you willing to give Jesus for him to use any way he wishes?

SCENE 100
WALKING ON WATER[18]

As soon as the clean-up crew had finished, Jesus told the disciples to get back into the boat and go on to the other side of the lake. "I'll catch up with you," he said. They obeyed him mechanically, not even wondering how he could catch up if they took the only boat.

He was dismissing the crowd as they were pushing off from the shore. Then Jesus climbed higher up the hillside. We watched from the shoreline.

"He must still need time in a lonely place, like he was talking about in the first place," Mr. Pilgrim said.

"You're right. He'll be up there praying half the night,"

Jesna said, then continued on. "Some people say that's the secret to his ministry."

"What's a secret?" Pete asked, his attention suddenly refocused.

"His taking so much time to be alone with his Father, asking questions, listening for answers. Some say that's how he's able to do what he does—what he's about to do—taking the time to be with his Father."

"Fascinating!" Mr. Pilgrim said. "It's almost like God is his energy supply and he's a reusable battery."

"I'm not sure about the theology of that one, Mr. Pilgrim. But I think you've got the big picture."

As she was converting our car into a boat and inching it into the water, Jesna told us we should soon be catching up to the disciples. She said she thought that Jesus would join us before morning.

"So we'll be across the lake by morning?" Pete asked.

"I didn't say that, Pete."

Pete looked puzzled, but he kept quiet for a long while and amused himself by dabbling in the boat wake as we drifted along behind the boatload of disciples.

When Pete could stand it no longer he blurted out, "But how can it be that ... "

A distant crack of thunder broke Pete's sentence in two and caused the second half to be lost. My doghair stood up straight along my spine. A thunderstorm—and all of us out on a lake with no place to hide! Dark, angry clouds began to fill the sky. As the thunderstorm came nearer, the time between lightning flash and thunder crash shrank and shrank until they happened right together and directly overhead.

What had at first been a gentle rain turned into an open fire hydrant in the sky. Winds blew hard and the Sea of Galilee became a frightening roller coaster ride. Only fearless Pete was saying, "Wheeeee!" Everyone else was holding on for dear life; Priscilla had a stranglehold on me.

If the disciples' boat had not been passing right through ours, it would've sunk us a hundred times. This was the second time we had been out on the lake in a storm so bad that it was enough to make suntanned sailors turn ghostly white. But this time, Jesus was not around to tell the storm to shut up.

"What's *that?*" a disciple shouted, his face, somehow, even whiter.

"Where?" another called.

"There!—" the first disciple pointed.

I looked out and saw a strange sight. A man seemed to be *walking* over the rolling waves as if they were a hilly pasture.... My hackles stood on end in spite of the lashing rain.

"It's a ghost!" a frightened disciple cried out. "It's a sign. We're all going to die!"

"Be calm. It's just me. Don't be afraid," the figure on the water said in a familiar voice.

"That sounds like *Jesus,*" Pete said. "What in the world is he doing?"

"Nothing of this world, little brother. That's for sure."

"Master!"

It was the voice of Simon Peter. "If it's really you, call me to come to you—on the water."

"Me, too! Me, too!" Pete shouted.

Jesus said, "Come ahead."

Mr. and Mrs. Pilgrim assured

Pete that Jesus was talking to the other Peter, and they both held him too tightly to wriggle.

The disciple Peter sprang from the boat and began to walk to Jesus. On *top* of the water! Everyone was mesmerized by the sight—Peter and Jesus ambling over the rough Galilean water as if it were a dark-blue jumble of AstroTurf.

"That must be some kind of hard water!" Pete said. "Can fish still swim in it?"

"It's not the hardness of the water, Pete, it's the faith of the walkers," Jesna told him.

Suddenly, Peter cried out, "Help me! Help me, Jesus!"

Peter was sinking, as if he were in quicksand. He had looked down, seen the waves rolling beneath his feet, and lost both his nerve and his faith.

Jesus didn't hesitate. He reached down and grabbed Peter by his hand. Then he said, "Oh man of little faith, why did you doubt?"

He helped Peter into the boat. The wind died down, and the waves unrolled. The disciples were shaking their heads and saying,

"This is it! You are God's son for sure!"[19]

"Now I've seen everything," Mr. Pilgrim said.
"Oh, no," said Jesna. "It's just beginning."

FAMILY DISCUSSION

1. What are some problems you have that you wish you could walk on top of like Jesus did on the water?
2. If you had been in the boat with the disciples do you think you would have jumped out of the boat like Peter did, or would you have stayed in the safety of the boat?
3. Can you believe the disciples said, "You are God's Son for sure"?

SCENE 101
HEALINGS AT GENNESARET[20]

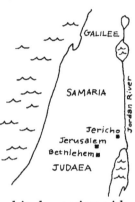

Not too long after the sun had awakened and stretched out its morning
rays, we completed our long voyage
across the lake. Well, actually, we made
a voyage and Jesus strolled a good part
of the way. In the cool of early morning, the designated disciples piled out
into ankle-deep water and began to tie
up the boat. Jesna just drove our frog-
mobile right onto the beach and stopped its humming with
the slide of a lever.

"Hey, we've been here before," Pete said.

"Yeah, I know this place, too. Look how lush and green it
is." Priscilla's eyes swept back and forth over a sea of green.

"You both have good memories," Jesna affirmed. "This rich
green plain stretches out in front of us for a few miles; it's
called the land of Gennesaret. We're on the northwest shore
of the Sea of Galilee."

"Yeah, I remember it, because it ain't got so many rocks."

"'Doesn't,' Pete. Doesn't have so many rocks,'" Mrs. Pilgrim
corrected.

"You're right, Mom. I doesn't see even one rock."

Mrs. Pilgrim sighed as Jesna continued. "Of all the land
that borders the Sea of Galilee, this is the most fertile and the
only area that is easy for farmers to till with their oxen-drawn
plows."

The land of Gennesaret was not only alive with plants, but
also with people. The sight of Jesus had caused farmers to
drop their hoes and fishermen to pull up their nets to run.

Some ran away, toward the local village. Some ran toward us.

Even though we had left a huge crowd behind on the other side of the lake, it didn't take ten minutes for another congregation to be created. A bumper crop of needy people quickly sprang up like weeds from the rich land of Gennesaret. There they were, the weak, the strong, the helpless on pallets, and the helpers standing tall and erect. There they were, present cynics and future disciples.

For a crowd to gather so quickly was not unusual, as it turned out. For the next several weeks, wherever Jesus traveled, in villages, cities, or in the country, crowds formed and laid their sick before him. And all who so much as touched the fringe of his robe were made well.

It was an incredibly exciting time to be on the road with Jesus. Every day that passed produced bushels of miracles and fields full of beaming smiles from the recipients of these signs and wonders. And not a day went by that a chant of "Jesus for our King" didn't erupt within the midst of his followers.

I think only a few realized that he already was a King or that they were being invited to leave their present realm and become subjects in his invisible, upside-down kingdom. Certainly the zealots, who were the loudest in proclaiming the need for Jesus to be an earthly king, had no idea that their suggestion of a golden crown and a purple robe was an unfathomable demotion for Jesus, the King and Creator of the universe.

FAMILY DISCUSSION

1. Why would it be a "demotion" for Jesus to become an earthly king?
2. Couldn't he do a lot of good as a king?
3. What good thing would you like Jesus to do in your life, this very minute?

SCENE 102
THE BREAD OF LIFE[21]

I almost forgot! One of the most interesting things that happened during this special time of Jesus' ministry occurred a few days after we came ashore at Gennesaret. We had walked over to Capernaum. Jesus was teaching there in the synagogue. A stream of people began to file through the front door—a long stream. I recognized some of them from the other side of the lake. They had been among the five thousand people Jesus had fed with a few loaves and fewer fish.

"Teacher!" someone from the stream called out. "When did you get here?"

"And how?" another asked.

Jesus answered,

"You've come looking for me not because you saw God in my actions, but because I fed you, filled your stomachs—and for free."

"Boy, Jesus doesn't mince words," Pete burst out.

"Don't waste your energy striving for perishable food like that. Work for the food that sticks with you, food that nourishes your lasting life, food the Son of Man provides. He and what he does are guaranteed by God the Father to last."

"How do we get in on this?" someone who had been on the other side of the lake asked. "What kind of work are we supposed to do?" asked another.

Jesus answered,

"Throw your lot in with the One that God has sent. That kind of a commitment gets you in on God's works."[22]

The crowd did not respond appropriately. They had just been offered a treasure-trove, a better prize than winning the lottery, and their only response was to mumble among themselves. Finally, someone summed up the grumbles with a question. "Why don't you show us a sign? Show us what you can do. Moses did. It says so in Scripture: 'He gave them bread from heaven to eat.'"

"They really haven't been paying attention, have they, Jesna?" Pete asked. "If they'd listened, they would know that Jesus is the Bread from Heaven."

Jesna's mouth slid open in amazement at Pete's insight. But not nearly as wide as those of Pete's parents'. All three sets of lips slowly came back together as Jesus continued:

"The real significance of that Scripture is not that Moses gave you bread from heaven, but that my Father is right now offering you bread from heaven, the *real* bread. The Bread of God came down out of heaven and is giving life to the world."

At this the crowd finally showed unbridled excitement. The spokesperson said: "Teacher, give us this bread, now and forever!"

Jesus answered,

"I am the Bread of Life. The person who aligns with me hungers no more and thirsts no more, ever ... This is what the Father wants: that anyone who sees the Son and trusts who he is and what he does and then aligns with him will enter *real* life, *eternal* life. My part is to put them on their feet alive and whole at the completion of time."[23]

Some in the crowd seemed transfixed by Jesus' words. Perhaps "kingdom seeds" were taking root in their hearts.

Others went back to murmuring. "Isn't this Joseph's boy?" "We know his father and mother." "How can he say, 'I came down out of heaven' with a straight face?"

"Jesna," Priscilla said thoughtfully.

"Yes, Priscilla."

"I've been thinking. What Jesus is saying about being the 'Bread of Life' refers not only to Moses and the manna and to when he fed all those people, but also to the future."

"What do you mean?" Jesna asked, with a knowing smile on her lips.

"To the celebration of communion," Priscilla said while squinting and looking at the sky, "or of the Eucharist. You know, when Christians gather together to take 'the Bread of Life' into themselves."

"Do you think Priscilla is right about what Jesus is referring to?" Mr. Pilgrim asked.

"I believe I'll let Jesus answer that one," Jesna said.

"I'm telling you the most solemn and sober truth now: whoever believes in me has real life, eternal life. I am the Bread of Life. Your ancestors ate the manna bread in the desert and died. But now here is Bread that truly comes down out of heaven. Anyone eating this Bread will not die, ever. I am the Bread—living Bread!—who came down out of heaven."

"Just like the manna did, huh? Looks like Prissy finally got one."

"Shhh."

"Anyone who eats this Bread will live—and forever! The Bread that I present to the world so that it can eat and live is myself, the flesh-and-blood-self ... By eating my flesh and drinking my blood you enter into me and I into you."[24]

FAMILY DISCUSSION

1. What do you think Jesus meant by saying "Work for the food that sticks with you?"
2. How does it feel to know that every time you participate in communion (the Eucharist)—every time you ask Jesus to live in your heart—you are being reminded of the fact that you have won a prize far greater than winning a million dollars?

SCENE 103
DEFILEMENT— TRADITIONAL AND REAL[25]

Not long after Jesus talked about being "the Bread of Life" in the synagogue in Capernaum, he and his disciples were invited to have supper at the home of one of his best listeners (judging from the amount of nodding and smiling she was doing). Jesus accepted the kind offer.

Later that evening, they were gathered next to her home, which bordered one of the main streets of Capernaum. Hungrily, they were eyeing a table full of breads, dried fruits, and cheese. But before the first bites could be taken, however, a band of black-robed men came to a determined stop on the public street.

Their four pairs of darting eyes grew larger just before their four Pharisee-mouths released a volcanic eruption of judgment.

"Why do you allow your disciples to defy the rules of ritual cleansing?" one poured out.

"They're going to eat without washing their hands! And you're going to let them!"

"I bet the pots and pans weren't cleansed before cooking!"

The disciples stopped laughing. From the faces of the host family, radiant smiles fell into the Pharisees' river of molten guilt.

"What do they mean, ritual cleansing?" Pete asked Jesna.

"The Pharisees," Jesna answered, "and most of the Jews, for that matter, would never eat a meal without at least going through the motions of ritual handwashing. Some scrub their hands until their skin is red and their pots until they are thin."

Just then, Jesus stood up and confronted the Pharisees. His eyes were boring into them as he spoke.

"Isaiah was right about frauds like you, hit the bull's eye in fact:
'These people make a big show of saying the right thing,
   but their heart isn't in it.
They act like they are worshipping me,
   but they don't mean it.
They just use me as a cover
   for teaching whatever suits their fancy,
Ditching God's command
   and taking up the latest fads.'"[26]

"Congratulations," Jesus continued with a sarcastic ring in his voice. "You are masters of getting rid of God's true commandments and replacing them with whatever suits you, whatever establishes you as superior and in control."

By this time a small crowd had gathered on the street. Jesus elevated his voice so all could hear. "Listen to me, all of you. It's not what you eat that poisons your life. What you digest with your stomach and what passes through you is not important. It's what you are down deep inside that matters. It's what comes up and out of your mouth (not what goes down the other way) that tells if you are truly clean. And you can't scrub your hearts clean—only God, your Father, can do that."

Jesus returned to his hosts and began eating with dirty hands and a clean heart.

The Pharisees slithered away, their hands much cleaner than their souls. One of the disciples said to Jesus, "I don't get it. Please say it more simply."

"Yeah," said Pete, "put the hay down here where us goats can get it. If I don't ever have to wash my hands again I want to know it."

"Interesting choice of metaphor, my little *kid* billy goat, I mean *brother.*"

"Don't you see," Jesus began to explain. "It's not what you swallow and passes through you that makes you clean or dirty. Food passes through your stomach, not your heart. It's what comes out of you—from your heart—that tells the story:

" ... obscenities, lusts, thefts, murders, adulteries, greed, depravity, deceptive dealings, carousing, mean looks, slander, arrogance, foolishness—all these are vomit from the heart. *There* is the source of your pollution."[27]

"OK, OK," Pete said. "They're getting it, but I'm not sure I do. It's not what you eat, but what you *spit out* that's important?"

"Pretty close, Pete," Jesna said. "Your physical body is made from the earth you walk on, right?"

"Yep. That's what Priscilla says, anyway."

"And food you eat is made from minerals and water from the earth. Right?"

"Yep, Priscilla says we're 198 percent water."

"And," Jesna continued, "after you eat food it eventually returns to the earth."

"Ummmm. Yep. Just goes to waste."

"Well, while your body is good and made by God, it's not what makes you clean or dirty. It's your soul's hygiene that really matters. And we know if a soul is clean or dirty by what comes up from it, what you say with your mouth."

"Then what do souls eat to stay alive, Jesna?"

"They eat soul food—the 'Bread of Life'—Pete. Jesus is food that cleans you."

"Sort've like *STP Gas Treatment* for the soul?"

"Sort've, Pete."

FAMILY DISCUSSION

1. Do you think it's possible to be clean on the outside and dirty on the inside? How could that be?
2. Since Jesus says that your mouth (the tongue) is connected to the soul, why not ask him to make your soul squeaky-clean? It's much more effective than eating a bar of soap.

SCENE 104
THE SYROPHOENICIAN WOMAN[28]

The next day, Jesus left town. All he told his disciples was, "It's time to move on. We're going to spend some time in the region of Tyre and Sidon." They picked up and followed without question. These guys were finally learning.

As we drove along beside them, Jesna gave us a geography lesson. "Tyre and Sidon are trading centers on the coast of the Mediterranean Sea. They are both located in the area your geography text books refer to as 'Lebanon,' which is north-west of Galilee."

"How long will it take us to get there?" Pete asked.

"Sidon is about fifty miles from Nazareth and a little closer to Capernaum. Tyre is not far from there. It will be a beautiful walk up and over the mountains and down to the Mediterranean seacoast. And no, Pete, we're not there yet."

"Will there be any trouble-making Pharisees in either of those cities, 'Tired' or 'Cider'?" Pete asked.

"Nope," Jesna said, "unless the Sanhedrin sends a few spies along. The region we're going to is a gentile (non-Jewish) area. Most of the people there speak Greek and are really into trading and making lots of money."

"Ha-uh," Mr. Pilgrim laughed out loud.

"What's so funny, Dad?" Priscilla inquired.

"Well, I guess Jesus is still trying to get that vacation he's been after for a while. Maybe he figures the only way he can is to go into the 'world' to get some rest. You know, like a bear going into the city for a vacation."

"You're weird sometimes, Dad," Pete said.

"Thank you, son," Mr. Pilgrim said cheerfully.

It took three Bible-time days to complete the trek to the coast. But the breathtaking view of the Mediterranean Sea was worth every step. You could put a hundred Seas of Galilee in it.

It didn't take Jesus long to find someone who owned a home and was willing to put him and the disciples up for a few days—for a fee. It seemed odd that no one knew who Jesus was. But that feeling didn't last very long. Before Jesus had a chance to sit down, a woman burst into the house and threw herself at his feet.

"Lord, help me," she cried. "I have a daughter who has been taken over by a demon. She throws herself to the ground and shrieks like an insane wildcat. I'm afraid she's going to kill herself!"

"Insane wildcat" sounded redundant to me. But as I was pushing the thought aside, Jesus said something that really seemed strange—for him.

"Stand in line and take your turn. The children get fed first. If there's any left over, the dogs get it."[29]

One of the disciples choked. The tension in the room was palpable. Priscilla checked her pulse to see if she was still alive. Pete just got bug-eyed and said, "Did you hear that? I've never known Jesus to have a bad-mouth day before. You must've been right, Dad, about him needing a vacation. Boy howdy! That was rude."

I noticed that Jesna was straining to keep a straight face and I suspected that something was up.

The woman herself was the only one in the room that didn't seem taken aback by Jesus' remarks. She said: "Of course, Master. But don't the dogs under the table get the scraps dropped by the children?"

Now she was talking my language! Jesus was obviously impressed with her answer too. The corners of his mouth turned heavenward.

"Oh, woman," he said, "your faith is something else. What you want is what you get![30] This very moment your daughter is set free!"

The woman sprang to her feet and ran out the door as she let fly with a series of "thank yous." She didn't hear what Jesus said in return.

"You are very welcome. I only wish that my brothers and sisters in Israel could muster your faith and enjoy your daughter's freedom from the evil one."

FAMILY DISCUSSION

1. Most of us don't quite understand the reason for Jesus' hard words to this woman. Can you still love Jesus if he says hard things to you?
2. Have you ever asked Jesus for something that he didn't seem to want to give you?

SCENE 105
JESUS HEALS A DEAF MUTE[31]

Following a little rest and recreation in Tyre, Jesus said it was time to go back to Galilee. We took the scenic route through Sidon and after a few days of travel arrived in the district of the Decapolis ("Ten Towns").

"So this is 'Metropolis,'" Pete said, shortly after our arrival. "I wonder if we'll see Batman here."

"Decapolis, Pete, Decapolis," Priscilla corrected. "Not Metropolis."

"Oh. What's Decapolis?"

"The Decapolis, Pete, is an area, something like a county, that has ten cities in it," Jesna began to explain.

"'Deca-,' Pete, 'Deca-.' It means 'ten,'" Priscilla inserted impatiently.

"Oh, is that so, Prissy. Well I guess that 'dec-or-ate' means that you ate ten things then."

"Call me when you get a brain, little brother."

Jesna continued, unfazed, "The Decapolis is a region that borders the southeastern shore of the Sea of Galilee. The land was originally given to the tribe of Manasseh. But now mostly Greeks live in the ten cities. The area is pretty independent, although still under the Roman Empire."

We started up a steep hillside overlooking Lake Galilee to find a campsite. Pete asked Jesna another question. "Jesna, why does Jesus need to take vacations sometimes? I mean he *is* God and everything. Does God get tired, too?"

"No, God doesn't get tired—I don't think. But humans do, and Jesus is not only fully God, but fully human, as well."

"Jesna?"

"Yes, Pete."

"Why did Jesus want to give up being God—I mean as a full-time job—to come down here where he'd get tired and sweat and be made fun of by the religious folks he created?"

"Because, Pete, being human is the only way he could know exactly what you feel. Otherwise, he'd never know how hard it can be to be "Pete." If you really love somebody you want to know absolutely how he feels, so you will know what he needs."

"But he made us," Priscilla interrupted. "Couldn't he just look it up in the owner's manual, under 'feelings'?"

"Yes, he could have done that, but which way do you think you would learn the most about swimming, by reading a book about it or by jumping in the lake?" Jesna asked as she motioned toward Lake Galilee.

Priscilla answered the question by slowly nodding her head.

"Plus," Jesna continued, "he came to do more than learn what it's like in the water. He's also here … "

"To save as many of us drowning rats as he can? Right, Jesna?" Pete interrupted.

"You got it, Pete." Jesna said with a giggle.

Before the disciples could get camp set up, a small crowd had gathered. Jesus had to leave campfire-building to his friends. It was time for him to punch the clock and get back on the job. After a few stories, some people from the crowd brought a man before Jesus. His face was frozen sad.

When Jesus reached a stopping point in his talk, one of the men standing in front of him said, "This man cannot hear nor speak. Will you heal him? He's a good man with a wife and a small child. But something has taken his voice."

"Probably a cat," Pete whispered to Jesna. "I hear they'll get your tongue."

"And his ears and his spirit," another said.

Yep, I thought. *Sounds like a cat to me.*

But Jesus was more concerned with cure than diagnosis. He escorted the man away from the crowd. He put his fingers in the man's ears. Then he spat, touched the spit, and then put his finger to the man's tongue. After that Jesus threw his head back and looked up into a twilight sky and sighed a heavy prayer. Then he commanded, *"Ephphatha"* ("be opened").

The world became silent for several seconds. Jesus and the man for whom he had prayed were studying each other's faces as if each belonged to an alien. Then the silence was broken by the song of a bird who warbled in a tree overhead. The man's stone face was cracked by a broad smile. He pointed at the feathered performer and clapped his hands with the excitement of a two-year-old child and plainly said, "Thank you. All glory to you, Master."

As the man was returning to his giddy friends, Jesus said to him, "Tell no one."

But, as we found out later, he might as well have been saying "sic 'em" to a German Shepherd. The man became a motor-mouthed messenger.

FAMILY DISCUSSION

1. If you had lost your hearing for a long time, and then were suddenly healed by Jesus, what would be the most pleasant thing that you could imagine hearing?
2. Would you want to tell someone? Why?

SCENE 106
THE PHARISEES SEEK A SIGN[32]

We stayed encamped on the hilltop for a number of days. At certain times each day, the view of the Sea of Galilee down below was breathtaking. At other times, it was merely spectacular. The crowd of listeners swelled in sized to a throng of several thousand. When Priscilla said she counted exactly four thousand, I believed her.

During this hilltop time, Jesus' teachings and prayers for the people were very intense. For one three-day period the people had become so enthralled, so spiritually minded, they forgot to eat.

At the end of the three days Jesus was overcome with compassion for the people. He fed them all with the rations of one small family's seven loaves of bread.

Pete, in particular, was amazed. He commented, "Jesus can put out more food than a drive-through window at McDonald's."

And he was right. This time there were only seven basketfuls of leftovers—down from twelve. Pete complimented Jesus on his getting better at estimating how much an army of people could eat.

After all four thousand people were served, Jesus was

talking to his disciples—some of whom were still shoveling in the Jesus-made bread. He said to them, "Beware of the leaven of the Pharisees."

When Peter asked him what that meant, Jesus seemed a little impatient. But he responded, "The yeast of the Pharisees is hypocrisy. In contrast, the yeast from heaven—that raises enough bread to feed multitudes of four and five thousand people," he said while scanning the crowd, "is selfless love."

Jesus' comment left more heads being scratched than nodding.

Not long after this we left the hilltop campsite and traveled to the fishing village called Bethsaida. As we entered the dusty little town some people came toward us leading a blind man by the hands. Immediately, they began to beg Jesus to touch him. Jesus took the blind man by the hand and led him back outside the village.

There, just outside the city-limit line, Jesus did something very strange. He put spit in the man's eyes, laid his hands on him and asked, "Do you see anything?"

The man slowly moved his head from side-to-side as he squinted his eyes. He was straining hard to do what most of us take for granted—just *see*. Before he could answer, Pete blurted out, "What's the business with all the spitting?"

No one answered. I'm not sure that even Jesna knew.

Then the man said, "I see men; but they look like trees, walking."

At that Jesus laid his hands on the man's eyes again. When he took his hands away this time the man strained once more to see.

"I see perfectly, now!" he exclaimed. "I see better than I ever have in my whole life."

Before Pete could say "what trees?" Jesus sent the man

home. He told him not to go into the village, but to head straight home.

As the man went away, his head was in constant motion—drinking in the sight of the countryside like a thirsty camel lapping up water. Jesus returned to his disciples as if nothing unusual had happened.

"Jesna," Priscilla said.

"Yes?"

"That's the third or fourth time Jesus has told someone he just healed not to tell anyone. Why does he tell them that? And why do they never do what he asks?"

"Jesus is walking a pretty thin line, Priscilla," Jesna responded. "He wants to do as much good as he possibly can while he's on earth. But he knows that if he gets too popular the Romans or the Jewish religious leaders will try to shut him up."

"So," Pete said with a knowing nod and a rub of the chin, "he wants to keep a low profile."

"That's right," Jesna said, then continued. "So the reason he wants to do as much good as possible without receiving any credit is because he's God. The reason folks keep blabbing even after he's asked them not to … "

"Is because they ain't," Pete said.

"Oh, Pete," Jesna said. "You keep getting wiser every day."

FAMILY DISCUSSION

1. Tell how you would feel if you'd been blind for a very long time, and all at once you could see.
2. Jesus said, when he first began his public ministry, that he had come to "restore sight to the blind." Since that time he has healed many who were physically blind. Can you think of any other way that Jesus might have meant that particular announcement?

3. Do you have any ideas about why Jesus used his spit sometimes to heal people? (It's OK if no one knows for sure.)

SCENE 107
MANY DISCIPLES TAKE OFFENSE AT JESUS[33]

After a brief stay in Bethsaida, Jesus announced that our
next journey would be to a place called Caesarea Philippi.

"What? A town with a last name?" sputtered Pete.

Jesna explained that the two-name town was a peaceful little village nestled into the southern slopes of Mount Hermon,
about midway between the northernmost tip of the Sea of
Galilee and the coastal town of Tyre. The next morning they
set out—with the six of us in our amusement-park-mobile
bouncing along behind.

Jesus' entry into the remote village quickly revealed what
was becoming apparent throughout the region of Galilee—
Jesus was now a celebrity of movie-star proportions. Within the
span of a hundred dusty paces, his walk down Main Street
turned into a parade. When he sat down for an evening meal,
a whole churchful of people instantly appeared for second
helpings of parables and miracle desserts.

And, in spite of the fact that he had limited the number of
"daily disciples" to twelve, a band of additional followers was
growing in size—following him everywhere. Many of them
had come from Bethsaida with us. Mr. Pilgrim referred to
them as "those gospel groupies."

Jesus' fame, however, was completely unsolicited. He did
not ask for it; he did not seek it. And it was a two-edged sword.
While it meant more people were hearing his invitation to live

in the kingdom, it also stirred the pot of the Pharisees' hatred. On second thought, perhaps it was a three-edged sword. His popularity also brought out of the woodwork more and more "disciples"—some of questionable motive.

It was during this stay in Caesarea Philippi that a hot discussion broke out among these "additional disciples." I had been hearing murmurings from this group ever since Jesus had said that he was the "Bread of Life." And that his "flesh and blood" were the "real food and drink." Their prattle intensified after the latest group of Pharisees had stormed off into the sunset in response to those remarks by Jesus.

"What you said, Jesus, about being 'bread and drink' ... "

"Yeah," another interrupted, "and having been sent here by God...."

" ... whom you call your Father!" said a third.

"And that we have to eat and drink *you* to live forever," the last interrupter said while shaking his head from side to side.

"We just don't get it," the original speaker summarized. "This teaching is too tough for us to swallow. You could get killed for saying stuff like that and us along with you."

Jesus looked very sad. He scanned the twenty-four eyes of his closest followers before speaking to the concerns of the fringe group. Only two eyes of the twenty-four looking at him seemed to reflect any sympathy for his questioners.

Jesus then said:

"Does this throw you completely? What would happen if you saw the Son of Man ascending to where he came from? The Spirit can make life. Sheer muscle and will power don't make anything happen. Every word I've spoken to you is Spirit-word, and so it is life-making. But some of you are resisting, refusing to have any part in this."

(Jesus knew from the start that some weren't going to risk themselves with him. He knew also who would betray him.) He went on to say,

"This is why I told you earlier that no one is capable of coming to me on his own. You get to me only as a gift from the Father."[34]

When Jesus finished saying this, the sadness on his face intensified. He looked at the ground and said no more. It was as if he were a parent who had done and said all he could. Now it was up to the children. The ball was in their court, the car keys in their hands.

The next morning a lot of his disciples left for home—never returning to follow Jesus. Before breakfast, that eerily-quiet morning, Jesus turned to the twelve who remained and asked: "Do you want to leave?"

Before anyone could answer Pete blurted out, "How can they do that? How can they walk away after all they've seen and heard?"

"Because," Jesna said soberly, "the journey of a true disciple is much easier to start than to finish. Finishing requires both God-given faith and human willingness—being willing to die to all that is of this world. Those men chose not to die. It's a free choice that means they will never truly live.

"In the end," she continued with stone-face seriousness, "we all become our choices."

FAMILY DISCUSSION

1. What keeps you on the path of being a true disciple?
2. What does it mean to say that we "become our choices"?
3. How do you think Jesus felt when some of his followers left?

SCENE 108
PETER'S CONFESSION[35]

Jesus' question, "Do you want to leave?" was still hanging heavily in the morning air. Pete, who had been sitting cross-legged on the ground, stood to his feet and began to walk toward Jesus.

As he stepped off the distance between them, Simon Peter, unaware of Pete's march (because he couldn't see the little hologram), also stood. He said to Jesus, "Lord, to whom shall we go? You have the words of eternal life."

Pete stopped by Jesus' side and put a small hand on his shoulder. Jesus smiled at Pete and patted his hand. Then he shared the same smile with Simon Peter as he said to the remaining twelve disciples, "Who do men say that I am?"

"John the Baptist," one said. "Elijah or Jeremiah," said another.

"But who do you say I am?" he asked.

There was a moment of awkward silence.

Pete whispered, "I know who you are."

This returned a smile to Jesus' face. But then he put the lines of his mouth straight again. Simon Peter was sucking in air and shuffling his feet.

"You are the Christ, the Son of the living God," he finally blurted out.

Jesus closed his eyes and enjoyed a deep sigh before he said, "God bless you, Simon, son of Jonah! You didn't get that answer out of books or from others. My Father in heaven, God himself, let you know this secret."

Then he continued, looking directly into Simon Peter's eyes:

"And now I'm going to tell you who you are, *really* are. You are Peter, a rock."

"The name 'Peter' means rock," Jesna quickly whispered.

"This is the rock on which I will put together my church, a church so expansive with energy that not even the gates of hell will be able to keep it out.

"And that's not all. You will have complete and free access to God's kingdom, keys to open any and every door: no more barriers between heaven and earth, earth and heaven. A yes on earth is yes in heaven. A no on earth is a no in heaven."[36]

Peter, the Rock, stood in frozen amazement. His future had just been spoken into being by the Maker of Time.

Jesna whispered very reverently, "Just as Peter's ancestor, Abraham, had faith that gave birth to a whole nation of people, Peter's faith will do the same. It only takes a spark of pure, God-given faith to flame into a burning nation or a blazing church."

Then Jesus did what was almost becoming a custom; he swore the disciples to secrecy and made them promise they would not tell anyone that he was the Messiah.

As they were nodding their agreement, Pete was speaking softly into Jesus' ear. With the best of my doggy-hearing I could barely make it out.

"Jesus, I won't tell anyone either," Pete said reassuringly.

"Oh, yes, you will my littlest disciple. Just like your namesake there, you will tell the world."

Pete's face blushed with pride.

"What's wrong, Pete?" Jesus said. "You didn't think you came on this ride uninvited, did you?"

"No, Sir, Mr. Jesus, I sort of thought it was you that invited us to come along."

Jesus threw back his head and laughed (which must have looked pretty strange to the disciples), "Do you know who told you that, Pete?"

"Yep, I sure do. It was your Daddy."

FAMILY DISCUSSION

1. What's the last thing Jesus' Daddy told you? If you haven't heard from him in a while why don't you close your eyes and ask him the question—"God, what do you think of me?"
2. Have you ever thought that maybe God wants you to tell others about him? If so, what has happened to make you think so?

SCENE 109
JESUS FORETELLS HIS PASSION[37]

Priscilla's face was downcast as she raked at the ground with the side of her shoe. Jesna was the first to spot her mood change.

"What's wrong, Priscilla? You look like all the cares of the world are on your shoulders."

"It's not that. I just wonder what's wrong with me sometimes. I try to do everything just right, you know, I'm real, uh,… "

"Calculating?" Jesna offered.

"Yeah, I guess you could say that," Priscilla said, blushing slightly. "At least I put a lot of thought into things, try to figure them out, before I act. And, well.... "

"You're wondering why it is that Pete is getting special attention from Jesus when he's so ... "

"Hyper and bratty!" Priscilla said with a pout.

"Well, actually I was looking for words like *impulsive* and *emotional.*"

"Oh—I guess he's those things too."

Then Jesna's face became very serious. She reached out and took Priscilla's hand and said, "God made each of his children different for a reason. And each one of them has a special role to play in building his kingdom on earth. The cautious help to keep the impulsive in line. The emotional help to keep the heady ones from being too serious."

"Or too boring," Priscilla inserted.

"And the thinkers keep the feelers from following their hearts right over a cliff. The kingdom is built the fastest and the strongest when everyone is using the special gifts the Father gave. Or you could say the kingdom is a song, a symphony, and every note is important."

Just as Jesna finished her sentence, Priscilla jumped with a start.

"I'm sorry," a soft, clear voice said, "I didn't mean to startle you."

Priscilla turned to see whose hand was on her head—and whose voice was in her ear.

"Jesus!" she said. "How long have you been there?"

"I just walked up," he said.

Then, in a low whispering voice he said, "I really need your help, Priscilla. I'm about to tell everyone something very difficult and, well, things might get a little emotional. I'll handle the disciples, but I need your level-headedness to help your family try to understand."

"You need my help?" Priscilla asked in a high-pitched voice.

"That's right. I need you to help them comprehend what I will be saying. You know, Priscilla, you were knitted together in your mother's womb in a special way so that you could help the kingdom grow, by helping people understand. Pete will help them feel, but you will help them know. Will you help me with this, Priscilla?"

"You got it, Jesus! You know, I'm pretty good with numbers, too," she said, beaming like a lighthouse.

"I know," Jesus said as he began walking back to his disciples. "I remember putting that gift inside you, too."

Jesus returned to where his friends were milling around. He called them together and asked them to sit down. Then he sat down with them.

"Since you now know who I am, it's time you knew something more."

He stared at the ground and let several seconds pass in silence. "Soon, it will be time for us to make another trip ... south ... to Jerusalem."

More time passed in unearthly silence. "It will be our last trip there together."

"What do you mean?" a disciple asked. "You know that we go there at least once each year for Passover."

"Oh, we'll be there together for Passover this year. In fact we'll be in and around Jerusalem for several months before Passover. But this will be the last time that we travel south together—to Jerusalem. You will return in the future—but I will not be with you—at least not like this."

"What do you mean," Peter asked, "your 'last trip'?"

"Because of who I am, it is now necessary for me to go there, to submit to an ordeal of suffering at the hands of the religious leaders, and.... "

A long silence passed. It was longer than Peter could stand.

"And what, Jesus?" he asked. "And what?"

"And be killed."

What I had mistaken for silence had not been silence at all, for it was loud noise compared to the deafening quietness that followed those unfathomable words.

"No!" Pete Pilgrim exploded, at the same time that his namesake, Peter, was shouting the same word.

"Yes," Jesus calmly said, "but then on the third day after my death my Father will raise me up from death. Then the world will know I am who I said I am ... who Peter has said I am. Then the world will know that my offer of abundant life is as authentic as the Messenger who brings it. That will be the final measure" (and he gave a knowing glance to Jesna before finishing the sentence) "to the song that I have been sent here to write, the song that each of you will sing."

"No!" both Pete and Peter shouted in discordant harmony.

Immediately, Jesus shot Peter a laser-look and said, "Yes! Get out of my way, Satan. You have no idea how God works!"

Pete was undeterred by Jesus' harsh words to his number-one disciple, Peter. He sprang to his feet and was two steps into a mad dash to Jesus when he was tackled by his older sister.

"No, Pete!" she said as they tumbled to the ground. "It must happen the way he says. He's God's Son, Pete. He knows what he's talking about."

"But ain't nobody going to kill by friend, Jesus. Nobody! Do you hear me?"

Priscilla was now parked on top of Pete's chest and was in the process of pinning his arms to the ground with her knees.

"I hear you, little brother. But you have to put your feelings back in their holster. This isn't the time to be shooting them off. Jesus knows what he has to do. We have to try our best to believe and understand." Slowly—and after a few more unsuccessful struggles to get out from under his sister—the angry, red color began to drain from Pete's face.

"I know you're right, Prissy. I know you're right. I'll just have to believe that Jesus knows what he's doing. So do you mind doing me a favor?"

"What's that?" Priscilla asked.

"Do you mind getting your knee off my Adam's apple? I'm about to choke on all the cider you're making."

"Interesting choice of words," Jesna mused to herself as Priscilla dislodged her knee from her brother's throat. "I'll have to think about that one. 'Adam's apple,' hmmm.... "

FAMILY DISCUSSION

1. How would it feel for you—if you spent the last few years traveling around with Jesus—to hear Jesus say that he had to die?
2. Would you be handling the news more like Pete or Priscilla?

SCENE 110
"IF ANY MAN FOLLOWS ME ... "38

Priscilla crawled off Pete's shoulders. Unpinned, he went to sit on his mother's lap. Priscilla followed and stood by his side.

"He's not really going to die, is he, Mom?" Pete asked.

"You know, Petie, that's the way it is in the Bible—the way it was taught to you in Sunday school," she said while stroking Pete's hair.

"Yeah, but this is a whole lot more realer than that. This is realer than movies. It's almost like real life."

"It *is* real life," his mother said. "We just have the privilege of seeing it in person."

"I'm not sure it's a privilege anymore. I think I might want to go back home."

Jesna stared into space. She looked very concerned.

"You don't want to go home now, Pete," Priscilla said. "Look at my watch. It's 1:30 and 58 seconds. We'll be back in less than two earth-seconds, anyway.

"Plus, Pete, you heard what Jesus said," Priscilla continued. "He said he'd be raised up on the third day. Then you'll get to see what Easter is really like."

"You mean back before the Easter bunny?"

"That's right, Pete. The very first Easter ever."

Their conversation was interrupted. Jesus was speaking to all of his disciples—including his youngest two.

"If any man would come after me, let him deny himself and take up his cross and follow me. For whoever would save his life will lose it, and whoever loses his life for my sake will find it. For what will it profit a man, if he gains the whole world and forfeits his life? [39] ... For I will come with the angels in the glory of the Father, and then I will repay every man for what he has done.

"Truly, I say to you, there are some standing here who will not taste death before they see that the kingdom of God has come with power."[40]

"What does that mean?" Pete asked. "I want to follow Jesus but I don't know where to buy a cross."

"It means ..., " Jesna and Priscilla both began at once.

"No, after you, Priscilla," Jesna said politely.

Priscilla was blushing as she offered her interpretation.

"I think Jesus is saying that truly following him means living like he lives and doing what he does. And while that may not mean that we have to die like he will—on a cross—I think it does suggest that we will have to be willing to sacrifice everything that keeps us alive in the world. It will be a death to life as we have known it."

"You're exactly right, Priscilla. The way to finding yourself—your true self that longs to live in the kingdom—is a way of suffering and self-sacrifice. But it's also the only way to abundant life."

"Abundant death?" Pete asked.

Jesna and Priscilla were both nodding their heads "yes."

FAMILY DISCUSSION

1. What are the most difficult things you have had to give up in order to follow the path of Jesus?
2. What does it mean to you, personally, to pick up your cross and follow Jesus?

SCENE 111
A MOUNTAINTOP EXPERIENCE[41]

About a week had passed since Jesus had let us peek into the future—telling us that our next trip south would be his last. We had spent that time in Caesarea Philippi listening to him teach and watching him perform miracles. He was beginning to give his disciples a bigger part to play in his kingdom work. Their performance was a lot like that of Peter attempting to walk on water—sometimes breathtaking, sometimes floundering.

Then one morning Jesus invited Peter, James, and John to go for a walk. It turned out to be more a climb than a walk.

When Jesna said, with great excitement in her voice, "You don't want to miss what's about to happen," we bolted for the car like rats after cheese, even though we were bone-tired. We had come to trust Jesna's suggestions.

Jesus led the three disciples on a long hike up a high mountain—which Jesna informed us was Mount Hermon. Hermon's face was so scraggly and treacherous that Jesna had to put our car in flight mode for most of the trip and I was glad for that. It would have been a bumpy ride if we had gone on the ground. When they finally arrived at the top, Jesus told his three friends he wanted them to pray together. All four settled on the ground for a long prayer. We all did the same.

After a while Pete broke the silence with a whisper. "This is weird. I feel like I should go over and say this prayer in Jesus' ear—instead of bouncing it off heaven."

"Shhh," Mr. Pilgrim said, "it all ends up in the same place."

After a longer period of silence passed, Pete broke that one too.

"Whoa, what's that bright light? It's shining right through my eyelids."

This time Pete had spoken for everyone. When I opened my eyes I saw a bright, white light, brighter and whiter than I had ever seen before in all my dog-life. It was warm, too. But the most amazing thing was that in the center of the light, Jesus was standing. His face and robe glistened.

"Look at that!" Pete shrieked. "Jesus is eclipsing the sun! I'm going to need some Jesus sunglasses if he keeps that up for very long."

"But it's not hurting my eyes," Priscilla observed.

"Mine either," said Mrs. Pilgrim.

"Hey, wait a minute," Pete said. There's Peter, James, and John over there. So who are those two torches standing beside Jesus?"

"Moses and Elijah," Jesna said, very reverently. "They're talking with Jesus now, but pretty soon they'll say something to his disciples."

"Wow!" said Pete. "Now that's a Holy-gram! That Jesus is some pray-er. Nothing like this *ever* happens to me when I say my 'Now I lay me down to sleep.'"

"Well," Jesna giggled, "he's had a lot more time to practice."

Then, all of a sudden, voices began to come from the middle of the radiating light. Moses and Elijah began prophesying that what Jesus had predicted about his death in Jerusalem was true. After that, in calm voices, they began to reassure the disciples, telling them not to give up hope when things seemed dark.

As the two Old Testament prophets talked, the light that shone from them seemed to be radiating joy as well as streams of brilliant whiteness. Even my doggy-heart felt it. Peter must have felt it too, because as soon as they finished speaking he blurted out:

"Lord, it is great that we are here; if you wish, I will make three booths here, one for you and one for Moses and one for Elijah."

Peter was still speaking when a bright cloud, gleaming with even more light than Jesus, Moses, and Elijah had generated, engulfed us all. Peter's words stuck in his dry throat. Then a voice from the cloud said:

"This is my beloved son, with whom I am well pleased; listen to him."[42]

When the disciples heard this they fell to the ground and covered their heads with their arms. Then, as suddenly as it had appeared, the light was gone, and Moses and Elijah with it.

Jesus walked over to where his friends lay trembling. He said, "Don't be afraid. Get up."

The three disciples, lifting their eyes up from their arms, looked like ostriches pulling their heads out of sand. They saw only a flesh-and-blood Jesus where moments before the kingdom of heaven had been ablaze with glory.

"Wow!" said Priscilla. "Some of his disciples really did see the kingdom in their lifetime—just like Jesus predicted."

"Yeah," said Pete. "And did you hear God? He's got the deepest voice I ever heard, deeper than Darth Vader in *Star Wars*. And," Pete went on, "he said the same thing as before when Jesus was baptized by John in the river. He must be pretty proud of his Boy," Pete said. "Pretty proud!"

FAMILY DISCUSSION

1. How would you feel if a bright cloud appeared in front of you and God's voice came booming out of it?
2. What are some ways (other than out of clouds and bright lights) that God speaks to you?
3. How does it feel to know that you can hear from God when you pray?

SCENE 112
JESUS HEALS A BOY POSSESSED BY A SPIRIT[43]

Not long after Jesus' face had become sunlight, we were on our treacherous way back down the mountain. Once again Jesna found it easier to fly than to drive. She landed our "birdmobile" in the middle of a crowd gathered at the base of the mountain. Jesus' other nine disciples were in the eye of a peoplestorm—a huge crowd of Caesarea Philippi townfolks.

Directly in front of the disciples was a quartet of black-robed men. Just to their right a man sat holding a boy about Pete's age. The boy was foaming at the mouth and flailing his arms and legs as wildly as his father's tight grip would allow.

The disciples and the black-robed men seemed oblivious to the horrible drama being acted out at their feet. Men talked at the top of their voices. They exchanged shouts. It was as if they were having a courtroom fight—outdoors.

"Those are the mean ol' Pharisees over there, ain't they, Jesna?" Pete asked rhetorically.

"Technically, Pete, those men in black are scribes," Jesna answered.

"Why are the scribes dressed like Pharisees?" Pete asked.

"Scribes are sort of like lawyers … "

"Do you want to hear a lawyer joke?" Pete interrupted.

"Save it, son," Mr. Pilgrim inserted forcefully. "Several of my friends are lawyers.… "

"Maybe they'd like to hear it.… "

"Scribes, Pete," Jesna continued, "are about half lawyer and half secretary. They are a highly educated group that make their living studying Jewish law and telling others what it means. While a lot of scribes are Pharisees—in every bad way possible—the two are not one and the same. Being a Pharisee is more like being a member of a political party. Being a scribe is a job."

"Such as being a lawyer and being either a Democrat or a Republican?" Mr. Pilgrim asked.

"Exactly," Jesna said.

Just at that moment a shout of "Jesus!" went up from the crowd of onlookers.

Many broke from the pack and ran to meet him. As they were escorting him to his ambushed disciples, he asked, "What's going on? What's all the commotion about?"

The man holding the convulsing boy tried to rise from the ground. He cried out to Jesus, "I brought my son to you. I think he's possessed by a demon." He staggered a few steps toward Jesus and said, "When you weren't here, I asked your disciples to help me. They prayed for my boy but he became worse."

Nine sets of disciple-eyes immediately focused on the ground.

"Then," the man continued, "these scribes came up and

started arguing with your friends, telling them that there is no place in Scripture that said they had the right to pray for my son. But look at him, Jesus. I can't believe God wouldn't want to heal him—even if they can't find it in their scrolls. It's awful. Whenever the demon seizes him, it throws him to the ground. He foams at the mouth. Look! Like right now. He grinds his teeth and gets as stiff as a board. Can you please help him? Please, Jesus?"

"What a generation this is," Jesus said as he gazed at the nine. By now they had kicked at the ground until they had dug holes deep enough to plant corn. "When will you learn what I've tried to teach you these past three years?"

"Bring the boy to me," Jesus commanded.

As the father came within a few paces, the boy convulsed with a violent seizure.

"The demon saw Jesus," Jesna whispered.

"Man!" Pete said. "Those demons don't like Jesus any more than the Pharisees do."

That captured Jesna's attention but she did not respond.

"How long has this been going on?" Jesus asked the boy's father.

"Ever since he was very small, barely walking. Lots of times it pitches him into a fire or the river trying to kill him. If you can do anything, have pity on us and help us."

"'If you can?!... '" Jesus said to him, with emphasis. Then he looked at his disciples as he said, "All things are possible to those who believe."

Immediately, the boy's father cried out, "Then I believe. Help me with my doubts!"

Jesus looked at the boy with great compassion and said: "You dumb and deaf spirit, I command you, come out of him, and never enter him again."

At once the boy cried out—like a cat with its tail under a rocker. The crowd took three giant steps backward without saying, "Mother may I?"

The boy thrashed about for a few seconds as his father held on for dear life. Then the boy became stiff, his skin ghostly white.

"He's dead!" shouted one of the scribes.

"Did you hear Jesus call that demon, 'dumb'?" Pete asked.

"It's your faith that's dead," the father sobbed. "My boy's not dead."

Jesus walked over and took the boy by his stiff, white hand as his father lowered his son's feet to the ground. Color returned to the little fellow's cheeks and he stood on his own—as calm and composed as an altar boy.

The scribes were the first to go home. Jesus left, too. He motioned for his disciples to follow. All twelve did so. Nine of them, however, followed sheepishly at some distance. When all had arrived at the home where they were staying, one of the braver of the nine asked, "Why couldn't we throw the demon out?"

"The energy of the kingdom," Jesus said, "is pure faith and undiluted love."

"And they all needed recharging. Huh, Jesna?"

"Shhh, Pete," Mr. Pilgrim said.

"How do we get that?" another disciple asked Jesus.

"By taking long talks with your heavenly Father," Jesus said. "That is to say—by prayer and by fasting."

"And by avoiding talks with the law scribblers?" Pete managed to say through his father's fingers. "Huh, Jesna?"

"You got it, Pete."

FAMILY DISCUSSION

1. What do you think the disciples will need to do differently to be able to muster the faith Jesus is describing?

2. How would tomorrow be different for you—if you took with you the faith Jesus gives you into each moment?

SCENE 113
JESUS FORETELLS HIS DEATH AGAIN[44]

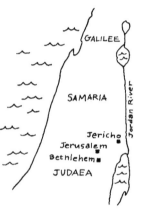

Before long, we left Caesarea Philippi. "We're heading back through Galilee to Capernaum," Jesna informed us. Instantly Pete's face flashed excitement. It was only a matter of nano-seconds before his mouth had put his enthusiasm into words.

"Do you mean we're going to walk through the Sea of Galilee, just like Abraham did?" he asked.

"No," Jesna began to explain. "We're going back through the *province* of Galilee, not the lake. And, as you may remember from your bird's-eye view of the situation, *Abraham* didn't walk through the Sea of anything. It was *Moses* that walked through the *Red* Sea, not Abraham."

"Well, I get all these bearded guys mixed up," Pete whined. "Thanks for 'splainin' 'em to me."

"Sure," Jesna said. Her quick smile was evidence that she loved to teach.

"Palestine is a country made up of three provinces—sort of like America is made up of fifty states. Galilee is the northern-most province. It wraps around the western side of the Sea of Galilee.… "

"Is that the left side—if you are in a space shuttle?" Pete asked.

"Yes, Galilee runs from the left side of the Sea of Galilee west,… left, toward the Mediterranean Sea. But it runs into Phoenicia before it gets there."

"That's where Tyre and Sidon are, right, Jesna?"

"That's right, Priscilla."

"The province of Galilee is also bordered by the Jordan River both to the north and the south of the Sea of Galilee," Jesna continued.

"Just south of Galilee is Samaria.… "

"Where the woman by the well lives?" Pete asked.

"Yes, Pete, and a few more people, too. You two are learning very quickly."

I gave a sharp bark. Jesna patted me on the head. "Yes, you too, girl." If I'd had been a cat, I would have purred.

"South of Samaria is the province of Judea. Jericho, Jerusalem, and Bethlehem are all in that province."

"And," Pete interrupted, "there's the wilderness where John the Baptist was dunking folks."

"Right again, Pete," Jesna said.

"I don't think there was one blade of grass growing anywhere in John's wilderness."

"You're very observant," Jesna said.

"So," Pete continued, "the three provinces of Palestine are Galilee (it's got Nazareth and Capernaum in it), Samaria, and Judea."

"And," Priscilla said, "the Decapolis is a province that isn't part of Palestine."

"Right," Jesna said, "the Decapolis is east.… " Pete was cocking his head. "I mean to the *right* of the Sea of Galilee."

"Jesna?"

"Yes?"

"Thanks."

"You're welcome, Pete."

Along the way to Capernaum, after the geography lesson, Jesus told his disciples (the third time for three of them) about the upcoming trip to Jerusalem.

> "The Son of Man is about to be betrayed to some people who want nothing to do with God. They will murder him. (But) three days after his murder, he will rise, alive."[45]

From the puzzled looks on many of their faces it seemed that most still did not understand what their teacher was talking about. Peter's and Judas' faces were notable exceptions.

After hearing Jesus prophesy about his death, Pete got very quiet. After a mile of walking, he finally said what was on his mind.

"Jesna, if Jesus is going to die, I might want to go back home. I don't think I could stand to see that. I'd have to try to stop it."

Jesna was surprisingly quiet for a long time before responding.

"I understand, Pete. It's not something I want to see either. I've decided that before any of those horrible scenes take place we'll all go back to the amusement park. There you can decide if any of you want to come along for the final earth-seconds of the ride, or not."

FAMILY DISCUSSION

1. Why do you think that Jesus has begun to talk so much about his final trip south?
2. What would you want to do, if you were in Pete's shoes? Would you want to see Jesus killed?

SCENE 114
PAYING THE TEMPLE TAX[46]

"What do you mean, Jesna?" Priscilla asked with a look of grave concern on her face. "Aren't we going to finish the ride?"

"This is not an ordinary ride," Jesna responded.

"You can say that again," Mrs. Pilgrim said.

"What I mean is, you can only stay on it as long as you really, really want to. In that way it works just like God's kingdom. Up to this point you have all wanted to be here more than any other place you could imagine. But if that changes—if you want to be somewhere else instead of here—then that's where you'll be.

"Pete is having a very understandable change of heart. My best estimate is that these feelings will intensify about the time things begin to heat up for Jesus—during his final visit to Jerusalem. So, instead of Pete just disappearing with a poof and you all wondering where he is, I've decided we will all go back to the amusement park before Jesus' most difficult trial begins.

"You'll have a chance to breathe some air that's two thousand years older than this, eat a hot dog if you want, and then all decide (as a family) if you *really* want to complete the ride. After all, throughout history it has been the anguish of the two crosses—that of Jesus and our own personal cross—that has caused the majority of 'pilgrims' to abandon their journeys further into God's kingdom."

"But," Mr. Pilgrim said, "what if Pete still wants to stay at the amusement park and.... "

"... the rest of us want to come back here?" Priscilla finished for her dad.

"Then there's only one option. While the return trip will take less than one amusement-park second … "

"It takes me longer than that to sneeze," Pete said.

"That's for sure," Priscilla said in quick agreement. "He always goes three 'ahs' to the 'choo.'"

" … remember that whoever went back would only be away for a second. Even then I still could not leave Pete alone—not even for a fraction of a moment."

"And neither could I," Mrs. Pilgrim said emphatically. "What if something broke down with the ride?"

"Or," Priscilla offered, "what if the time thing got mixed up and we went back for just a few Bible seconds and when we came back Pete was a grandfather?"

Mrs. Pilgrim looked as if she were about to faint. Pete looked a little queasy too.

"Well," Jesna said, "while none of those things can happen, I'm not allowed to leave anyone alone, even for one earth-second."

"So if Pete's heart keeps him at the park, someone will have to stay with him."

"And if all of our hearts, except Pete's, want to be back here with Jesus?" Priscilla asked.

"Then Pete and I," Jesna said while tapping herself on the chest, "will have a second hot dog while you're away. Or, at least the first bite."

"I can do a hot dog in a second … "

"But, but … "

"We'll talk about it later," Jesna said, firmly. "Let's all be fully here, until we go back there—there's much to see between now and then."

It wasn't long until we were breathing the dust of the streets of Capernaum once more. Jesus sent all of the disciples except Peter on various errands—the most important of which was to find a place to spend the night.

He and Peter walked to the synagogue. As they were standing together just outside the front door of the building, I got the feeling there was something Jesus wanted to say to his star pupil. But if there was, it got postponed.

A man wearing a colorful robe came marching up to where Jesus and Peter stood. His steps and his speech were clipped and controlled.

"Does your teacher pay the Temple tax or not?" the man asked in a burst.

"Why doesn't he ask Jesus directly?" Pete asked.

"I don't know," Jesna shrugged.

Peter answered, "Yes."

"Then you'll both need to pay before you can go inside," the tax taker said. "It'll be a half-shekel each. That's one shekel altogether."

"Wow!" Pete quipped. "That was some fast math."

"We don't even have shekel dust in our pockets right now," Peter said. "Can we go in today and pay you later when we have the money?"

The man just shook his head from side to side as he pooched out his lower lip and made craters in his chin. "Come back when you can pay the tax," was all he said before he let his chin go smooth, turned his back, and walked away.

"Do you want me to go get the money from Judas?" Peter asked.

"No Peter, that won't be necessary. You'll be able to pay the tax in a little while—out of your own pocket."

Peter looked as confused as a bushy-faced man can look.

Jesus continued. "Simon Peter, what do you think? When a king imposes taxes, who pays them—his children or his subjects?"

"His subjects," Peter quickly answered.

Then Jesus said, "His children don't have to pay, right? You are a child of the greatest King. And this building is one of his houses."

"They're going to crash the synagogue party, ain't they?" Pete said with great relish.

"Shhhh."

"But we don't want to upset anyone needlessly. So go down to the lake; borrow a hook and pull in the first fish that bites. Open its mouth and you'll find a coin. It'll be enough to pay the tax for both of us."

"I've got to see this!" Pete exclaimed.

I think that's how we all felt. In fact, Priscilla was the first one out of the car.

As Jesus sat down and relaxed against the nearest wall, Peter turned and jogged off toward the lake—with Priscilla and Pete skipping along behind. I raced along in front of them circling around and around. The rest of the crew took a more civilized pace.

Peter knew almost everyone in Capernaum; so it didn't take him long to borrow a hook. It took even less time for the line to start zipping back and forth across the face of the lake like a water bug. Peter gave the line a quick yank, and then a long steady pull. The fish broke out of the water, and Peter pulled it in to where he stood. He wasted no time in putting a couple of fingers in the fish's mouth to retrieve his hook.

"Oh my!" he exclaimed. "A shekel."

FAMILY DISCUSSION

1. Do you think Jesus still does fish tricks today?
2. When is the last time you were on the receiving end of a special gift from God?
3. Is there something special you need from God right now?

SCENE 115
TRUE GREATNESS[47]

Peter's mother-in-law had once again agreed to let her house be home base for Jesus and the disciples during their time in Capernaum. One afternoon Jesus was outside in the courtyard playing with children. His disciples had gone to the village. Jesna gave us a choice of staying with Jesus or following the disciples. The vote was quick and unanimous. We stayed behind.

We were all mesmerized by the way Jesus played with the children. It was as if nothing else in the universe existed except the three-to-five-year-old kids that hovered around him like bees around a honeycomb. When he talked to them he would get down on the stone  floor and speak eye-to-eye. His speech was gentle, but not condescending. He spoke to them with respect. It was almost as if he expected to learn from them as much as he taught.

As the afternoon progressed, they rode on his back, took turns sitting in his lap, and tugged at his beard. They sat quietly while he told them stories and sang songs.

They seemed to especially like it when he carved a simple toy out of wood as he told a story. Hours passed quickly. Just before sunset, the disciples returned and tromped their way through the playground. From the looks on their faces it was obvious they had been in a heated disagreement and were just trying to hold it in until they got past Jesus. Not one even

looked at him as they walked right through the middle of one
of the few active kingdom outposts on earth.

Not long after the disciples entered the house, hot words
began to pour out through an open window. It didn't take
many escaping sentences to discover the plot. They were arguing about which of them would be the greatest in the kingdom of heaven.

Jesus' countenance quickly sank. His face looked like Mr.
Pilgrim's did once, when a lightning storm cut the power off
and caused him to lose everything he had stored on his computer for a big presentation.

Jesus gathered the children around and asked them to go
into the house with him. They eagerly complied. I think they
would have eaten spinach for him if he had asked. Upon
Jesus' entry with his retinue of small followers, the disciples
immediately went silent.

He moved to the center of the room and sat down. Seven
children played a fast game of musical chairs with the two
benches of his lap. Five lost and had to sit by his side on the
floor.

"If any one of you truly desires to be first in the kingdom of
heaven," Jesus began, "he must be last of all and servant of
all."

Each disciple looked as if he had been caught with his hand
in the cookie jar. Then Jesus asked one of the children who
had lost the musical lap game to stand up. "Do you see this
child?" he asked.

"Unless you turn from your wrong ways of thinking and
become like her you will never enter the kingdom of heav-
en. Whoever humbles himself like this child is the greatest
in the kingdom of heaven. Whoever receives one such child
in my name receives me."[48]

After a long silence the standing child turned and dove into Jesus' lap, tumbling out the other children like giggling bowling pins.

"I don't understand," one of the disciples said over the noise of the laughter. "How are these children more suited for your kingdom than we are?"

"Oh," Jesus sighed, "that's an easy one. These children have all of the 'kingdom credentials' already in place. They are humble; they live simply. All they want from life is love for their souls, bread for their bodies, interesting activity for their minds, and they are oblivious to the kingdom of darkness that is this world. Not to mention that while you were off fighting about who will get the best chair in glory, they were rolling around on the ground with me—the Prince of Glory."

"Well," Jesna said as we surveyed a room full of downcast disciples and upbeat children, "the dividing lines between kingdoms doesn't get any clearer than this."

FAMILY DISCUSSION

1. How would you say, in your own words, what it means to enter God's kingdom by being like a child?
2. Is entering the kingdom of God something you want to do? *(Parents: Here is a wonderful opportunity to pray with your child for salvation.)*

SCENE 116
THE STRANGE EXORCIST[49]

After another long silence, John spoke up. "Jesus, while we were walking, we saw a man using your name to cast out demons. But we stopped him because he wasn't in our group."

"Boy," Pete said, "that John is being pretty obvious about trying to get back in Jesus' good graces."

"Or at least in changing the subject," Priscilla offered.

If either of them were right, it didn't work. Jesus' face became stern as he said to John. "You shouldn't have stopped him. No one can use my name to do something good and powerful and in the next breath insult me. If he's not an enemy, he's an ally. Anyone, even by giving someone an ordinary cup of cold water in my name, is on our side, and he will not lose his reward.

"On the other hand, if he or you…" (Jesus looked each disciple in the eyes before continuing) "… causes one of these simple children to sin, well, it would be better if you were dropped into the Sea of Galilee with an anchor tied to your neck."

"If your hand or foot gets in God's way, chop it off and throw it away. You're better off maimed or lame and alive than the proud owner of two hands and two feet, godless in a furnace of eternal fire. And if your eye distracts you from God, pull it out and throw it away. You're better off one-eyed and alive than exercising our twenty-twenty vision from inside the fire of hell."[50]

"Jesna," Pete gasped. "Is Jesus serious? Would he want me to chop off my hand if I were ever tempted to use it to steal, uh, let's say, a cookie?"

"Yeah," said Priscilla, "tell me he was just being hyperbolic."

"What?!" Pete asked with a contorted face as he pointed in the direction of his sister. "Don't listen to her, Jesna! She didn't mean to say that Jesus was being *hyper*—and I've told her a million times how mad it makes someone to be called that. Just tell me if I need to cut my hand off or not."

Jesna was chuckling right out loud. "Pete, to be 'hyperbolic' means you are exaggerating for effect, that you don't really mean it literally. So," she continued, "the answers to your questions are 'no' and 'no.'"

"'OK' and 'OK'—but what do you mean?" Pete asked.

"I mean," Jesna continued, "that, 'no,' Jesus doesn't want you to cut off your hand. And, 'no,' he wasn't being hyperbolic. The kingdom of heaven is so much better than what we know in this world (not to mention the fact that it lasts forever), that it would be better to give up everything of this life rather than have it interfere with entering into life in the kingdom.

"But," she continued, "I think his strong statements were addressed more to the disciples' pride than to their appendages."

"Jesna?"

"Yes, Mr. Pilgrim."

"What Jesus was saying reminds me of a story."

"Tell it, please."

"Well, I don't remember exactly how it goes, but it's something like this.

"It seems that there was a monkey who slipped into a house."

"Was it a big monkey or a little one, Dad?" Pete interjected.

"I don't know, son. It was just a run-of-the-mill monkey. But inside the house, it found a couple of full cookie jars. The jars had narrow necks with openings just large enough for one cookie at a time to slide out. The monkey smelled the cookies and thrust his hand into one of the jars and wrapped it around one of the cookies. But when he tried to pull his hand back out, he couldn't. There wasn't room for a cookie and a hand to come through the opening at the same time. But the monkey wouldn't let go of the cookie. After a while, the monkey put his hand in the other jar to get a cookie, and got the same result with that hand."

Mr. Pilgrim stopped talking.

"Well go on, Dad," Pete said, salivating, "what happened to the monkey?"

"Oh, he starved to death."

"Dad," Priscilla said, "that story is gross!"

"But, Priscilla, it's a great way to understand what Jesus is saying to his disciples. Don't hold onto anything in the world so tightly that it could cost you your life—real life—in the kingdom of heaven. You can't slide both yourself and any piece of the world through the opening to God's kingdom."

"Way to go, Dad!" Pete said. "And you aren't being hyperbolic, either."

FAMILY DISCUSSION

1. Are there any "cookies" in your life that you would have a hard time letting go of if Jesus asked you to?
2. What are they?
3. What are your "diet plans"? How will you try to keep from indulging in things God doesn't want you involved in?

SCENE 117
THE PARABLE OF THE LOST SHEEP[51]

I can't be completely certain; but I'm pretty sure Jesus paused for a second or two to listen to Mr. Pilgrim's monkey story. The wink and nod he gave when Pete's dad finished the story were unmistakable. Quickly, however, Jesus turned his attention back to the disciples and the giggling, squirming little parables that were crawling all over him.

"Watch that you don't treat a single one of these childlike believers arrogantly. You realize, don't you, that their personal angels are constantly in touch with my Father in heaven?"

"Wow," said Mrs. Pilgrim, "that's a saying you don't hear preached about in church very often."

"You're right, Mrs. Pilgrim," Jesna said, "but the next one sure is."

Jesus continued:

"Look at it this way. If someone has a hundred sheep and one of them wanders off, doesn't he leave the ninety-nine and go after the one? And if he finds it, doesn't he make far more over it than over the ninety-nine who stay put? Your Father in heaven feels the same way. He doesn't want to lose even one of these simple believers."[52]

"And," Jesus continued, "he wants all of his sheep to be as simple and childlike in their relationship with him as these little lambs right here. These are the greatest in the king-  dom. And you," he said— smiling for the first time since he entered the house— "are some tough old rams that still have a lot to learn from them." Then, as the smile slipped from his face, he added, "and not much time left to learn it in."

"Hey, Dad," Pete said in a low voice while tugging on Mr. Pilgrim's sleeve.

"Yes, son."

"Do you remember that time I sort've got lost from you and Mom in the mall—for almost an hour?"

"Do I remember it? I still have nightmares about it."

"And remember how you said you forgot about shopping for your new golf clubs and you and Mom and even Priscilla started looking everywhere for me.

"And do you remember how they were calling my name out on the loudspeakers all over the mall so everybody could hear that I had lost my parents—although I didn't know I had.

"And you found me trying to talk the man at the cookie store into selling me some chocolate chip cookies for a penny. And you grabbed me right up out of my shoes and started hugging on me; and then Mom started squeezing me while you bought me a cookie that was so big you could have used it for a sled. And you didn't even lecture me about staying with you in the mall—until we were home."

"Yes, Pete, I remember all of that very well," Mr. Pilgrim said.

"Well, it's good to know that my other Dad feels the same way about me—and that you sometimes get more of a cookie than you could even dream about."

FAMILY DISCUSSION

1. How does it make you feel to know that the Creator of the entire universe would drop everything and go looking for you, if you got lost?

2. If you've ever been lost, tell what that felt like. Were you scared and homesick? Do you think that if someone really realized that the kingdom was their true home, they would feel just that homesick for it, if they were lost?

SCENE 118
WHAT TO DO WITH AN
ANGRY FRIEND[53]

Later that Capernaum evening—after the house had become empty of children and a score of stomachs had been filled with Peter's mother-in-law's finest fixings—one of the disciples asked Jesus for a private conversation. Twelve sets of inquisitive ears followed them out into the cool night air.

"Jesus," the disciple began. "I'm having a little problem getting along with one of your students."

Jesus' eyes asked to hear more.

"It started when we went out together. You know, when you sent us out in pairs to preach and minister. Well, I don't think he realizes what he's doing but, very often, he treats us arrogantly. We're insulted. It's like he thinks he's more like you are, or something. And (the disciple glanced around before continuing in a softer voice), I think he does the same thing to people he's supposed to be ministering to. I need some advice. I'm having a difficult time not getting mad every time he opens his mouth."

Jesus waited, apparently wanting to make sure his friend had said all he wanted to say.

"And," Jesus began, "you believe that your actions toward him have been motivated by love?"

"My actions, yes. I can't say the same thing for all my thoughts."

"Then this is what you should do. When someone hurts

you, the first thing to do is to try to work it out—just the two of you. If he listens, your feelings of friendship will return and deepen."

"And if he doesn't?" the disciple inquired.

"If he rejects your good intentions—refuses to listen—then you should take one or two others along (so that the presence of witnesses will keep things honest) and try again.

"If that doesn't work, then you need to bring the matter before us all."

"And,…" the skeptical disciple was saying.

"And," Jesus said, "if that doesn't work, neither of you are off the hook."

"What do you mean, Jesus?"

"If your friend is wrong in his attitude and his heart remains hard, life will give him scores of other confrontations—scores of times to repent and become soft-hearted and receptive to love. But, the opportunities are limited in number. You know what the proverb says about a man who hardens himself after much reproof."

"Yes," the disciple said soberly. "He will suddenly be broken beyond remedy."[54]

"That's right. A person can allow his or her heart to become so hard that it grows brittle to the touch."

"But what about me? How do I get off the hook?"

"All that I have told you to do for your brother—confronting him and bringing him before others—is for his benefit. Forgiving him is what you do for your own benefit. Regardless of your brother's response you must always forgive and offer God's healing love."

"This is a very hard teaching, Jesus," the disciple said while slowly shaking his head from side to side.

"Only," Jesus said, "if your desire is to hold on to a white-hot coal of anger while it sears your flesh (for that is the cost of unforgiveness). And only if your brother chooses to keep burning coals of self-righteousness in his belly (instead of cool springs of living water). It's your choice," Jesus said, as he stood and patted his student on the shoulder before turning to walk back inside.

FAMILY DISCUSSION

1. What do you suppose Jesus meant by "the cost of unforgiveness"?
2. Ask your parents if they can give you first-hand examples of the cost of unforgiveness in their lives.
3. What have the costs of not forgiving others been in your life?

SCENE 119
WHERE TWO OR THREE GATHER TOGETHER[55]

"But, but ... " the disciple was saying to Jesus' back as he walked toward the front door of the house. Jesus turned in the doorway and replied.

"Take this most seriously: A yes on earth is yes in heaven; a no on earth is no in heaven. What you say to one another is eternal. I mean this. When two of you get together on anything at all on earth and make a prayer of it, my father in heaven goes into action. And when two or three of you are together because of me, you can be sure that I'll be there."[56]

While Jesus was still facing him, the disciple found the nerve to ask one more question. "How many times must I forgive someone who has hurt me? Seven times?"

"No, not seven times," Jesus said.

"Whew!" sighed the disciple. "That's a relief."

But his relief didn't even live as long as a fruit fly, because just before entering the house, Jesus completed his thought:

"... not seven, but seventy times seven."

The disciple let his head fall to his hands and he sat very still. He looked somewhat like a picture of a statue I saw in one of Priscilla's textbooks (named the "Thinker") as he contemplated the cost of discipleship.

"You mean," Pete gasped, "I have to forgive Priscilla seventy-seven times when she makes me mad!"

"No, not seventy-seven, but seventy *times* seven. That's four hundred and ninety times, my math-deficient little brother."

"Did you hear that?" Pete exclaimed. "She called me a math-deviate. That's another time I have to forgive her! I bet that was the four hundred and ninety-first time, too. That means it's OK for me to put some white-hot coals in your hand, right now," Pete said while looking around on the ground. "If I can just find one, you'd better prepare to sizzle."

Jesna dropped down on her knees in front of Pete and intercepted his downward gaze.

"Pete. It doesn't matter if you have been hurt seven times, seventy-seven times, or four hundred and ninety-one times. Jesus' teachings aren't about retaliation. They are about reconciliation."

"Huh?"

"You *never* get to hurt back. Never! As one of Jesus' disciples, the only thing you are allowed to return for hurt is love and forgiveness."

"But what about Priscilla?"

"Those are her only two options, as well."

"But I can never be like that. I could never do nice things for people who hurt me."

"I know, Pete. No human being can—not all the time. But that's where the Holy Spirit comes in. The Holy Spirit is sort of like a brother or sister that lives inside you and makes it possible for you to obey the teachings of Jesus that seem impossible to obey.

"Jesus' teachings are designed to both excite people about how good life in the kingdom can be and to cause them to drop to their knees and pray, 'Lord, I can't obey; please cause your Holy Spirit to love through me.'"

"Every Christian," Jesna continued, "must eventually say along with Jesus, 'not my will, but yours, Father, be done.' That's the secret password that causes the gates of the kingdom to swing wide open and the holy cavalry to gallop to your defense—to do through you what you can't do yourself."

Pete didn't say a word. He just inched his way over to where Priscilla was standing and gave her a hug around the waist.

"Would you look at that," Jesna said. "Pete's standing just a few feet away from that 'Thinker' disciple there, but he's miles further down the road toward the kingdom than the disciple is."

FAMILY DISCUSSION

1. Who is the person you most need to forgive? Say his or her name in silent prayer, and ask Jesus to pry the hot coal of unforgiveness from your hand. Then use your now-freed hand to write that person a kind letter or to phone him or her for a chat.

2. Make up a story about what happens when someone refuses to forgive.

SCENE 120
THE PARABLE OF THE UNFORGIVING SERVANT[57]

The "Thinker" joined Jesus. Both sat down inside on the clay hearth. We had followed at his heels and then spread out around Jesus—invisible to all but him. A lazy fire of orange and yellow flames glowed behind him. Dinner smelled wonderful as Jesus cleared his throat to tell a story to the ring of disciples around him.

"The kingdom of God," he began, "is like a king who decided to have all of his servants pay up everything they owed him. One servant had amassed a debt equal to five years' wages. The servant couldn't pay, so the king ordered that the man, his wife, his children, and all of his goods be sold at the slave market. The man threw himself at the king's feet and begged for mercy. The king's heart became soft and he canceled the servant's debt. All of it! The servant left, whistling a tune. But he was no sooner out of the king's presence than he came across a man who owed him the equivalent of *one day's* wages. He grabbed the debtor by the neck and demanded that the sum be paid in full, 'Now!' he cried. The poor debtor threw himself to the ground and begged for mercy, just as the servant himself had done only moments before. But the king's servant hardened his heart ..."

"He'd better be careful," Pete inserted. "Those things can break on you, y'know."

"... and had the man arrested and put in jail until the debt was paid. When others saw what he had done they became outraged and reported the event to the king. The king immediately summoned the servant and said, 'You wicked man! I forgave you all the debt because you pleaded with me; why would you not let that same mercy flow down to the one who owed you?' The king's fury grew. He had the wicked servant put in jail."

Jesus studied the fire-lit faces in the room, as each person's guilt began to pour out like wine.

"And that is how my Heavenly Father is going to treat each of you who doesn't ask for his forgiveness and then *share it freely* with anyone who asks you for mercy."

Except for a few fire-crackles the room was silent for several minutes.

"That was an incredible story, Jesna," Mr. Pilgrim finally whispered. "I mean it's exactly how things are on earth. God forgives us all—daily—for not trusting him fully and not living according to his desires. But the first time someone offends us, we, or I should say, 'I,' act like I've got the right to be his judge and jury. That was a truly eye-opening story!"

"And a heart-softening one, too. Huh, Dad?"

"And," Jesna added to Pete's commentary, "every time we sentence other people, it's actually *us* that ends up doing time."

FAMILY DISCUSSION

1. Make a list of everyone who has offended you. Be very thorough. Now have Mom and Dad help you as you hold it over the kitchen sink and set it on fire. Jesus will help you hold the match. Forgive each person in your heart.

2. How does it make you feel to see the list of debts go up in smoke? How does it make you feel to know that God holds a match to the list of your offenses each day?

SCENE 121
HEADING SOUTH[58]

Later that Capernaum evening—as the fire was going down and out, Jesna said it was time for us to be going up and over. We followed her across the courtyard to where our car was parked and piled in. She told us that the next recorded scene in Jesus' life didn't occur for three more Bible days—three days into his journey south to Jerusalem.

As we were ascending through the night air, Capernaum was shrinking to half the size of a postage stamp. Just before it became gnat-sized, Jesna began poking at the buttons that caused time to race past us with all the colors of a kaleidoscope.

Seconds after the world came back into focus we began a rapid descent. "Whee!" Pete screamed. "That's tickling my stomach like when I'm on the swings at school."

Like most dogs, I'd never been on a swing but I was getting a pretty good tummy-tickle, too.

When I found the courage to look over the side of the car, I could see the River Jordan. It appeared as a thin, blue life-carrying artery running down the center of the holy country. The heart-shaped Sea of Galilee was to the north, and the Dead Sea appeared as an oversized kidney, lying due south. All three organs were growing rapidly in size. The Mediterranean Sea was an infinite blue mass to our left, and an endless sea of sand stretched eastward.

"Wow!" exclaimed Pete. "This must be what it's like to land the space shuttle."

"Yeah," said Priscilla. "Assuming you're landing it in the mountains of Samaria—over 1900 years ago."

"Right," Pete said. "But how do you know that's Samaria down there? It could be Kalamazoo for all I know."

"New York City could be Kalamazoo for all you know, little brother."

"You mean there really is a Kalamazoo?"

"Yes," Jesna interrupted. "And there really are Samaritan villages. We'll be touching down on the main street of one of the larger ones in about 5, 4, 3, 2, uh, now."

With our landing gear down we rolled to a sand-grinding stop.

"It's Jesus! Look!" Pete exclaimed, " ... there in the crowd."

Jesna began to fill us in on what had happened. "Jesus and his disciples had left their home base on the northwest shore of the Sea of Galilee three days ago. They've been traveling south to this Samaritan village. And now he's about to meet up with a couple of his disciples whom he had sent on ahead as advance scouts. He wanted them to make arrangements for their meals and lodging in this village."

"Let's listen," Pete said.

We stayed in the car and Jesna eased it closer.

"Master," one of the disciples said to Jesus, "it's no use here. When the villagers found out that eventually we would be traveling on south to Jerusalem to celebrate the festivals, they refused to take any of us into their homes."

When two of the disciples, James and John, heard this, their faces flared with anger. One of them said, "Jesus, do you want us to call a bolt of lightning down out of the sky to burn them to a crisp?"

"Hey," said Pete. "Now we're cooking! Bolt 'em, boys!"

But Jesus answered them with a thunderbolt of his own. "Of

course not! Your angry flames will only cause their coals to burn hotter. If you have no cooling water with you, we will simply travel on."

As the disciples fell in line behind Jesus, Pete asked, "Where would somebody find cool water in this hot, dusty place?"

"From deep, inner wells of living water, Pete. And there should be at least one Samaritan woman along the way who still remembers how to draw it up."

FAMILY DISCUSSION

1. Do you remember (from Book One, Scenes 30 and 31) why there is tension between the Samaritans and the people in and around Jerusalem? (Hint: It has to do with a divided kingdom.)
2. What are some ways you can learn to draw up "living water" from inside of you?
3. What is this living water?

SCENE 122
COMMISSIONING THE SEVENTY[59]

As things turned out there were many along the way who wanted to get a body full of "living water." It seemed that for every village that rejected Jesus and his disciples there were two that took them in. For every person who ridiculed him and his message there were two who wanted to join his caravan and help him preach.

We were headed to Jerusalem at a slow, meandering pace. During the cool of the day we traveled—usually south. In the heat of the day we sat under shade trees and listened to Jesus teach. Nights found us in the homes of friends or under the stars.

Jesus' core of twelve disciples kept a tight orbit around God's Son. But there were also others who had left all behind to follow Jesus. These, too, were with Jesus every day. While they revolved around the Son at greater distance than the twelve, the gravitational pull of his words kept them close.

Jesus never seemed to be recruiting disciples. Indeed, Pete often commented that he seemed to be chasing them away. When people would step out from the crowd and declare their allegiance to Jesus, it was common for him to respond by saying things like: "If you want to follow me you must realize that your only business is the urgency of the announcement of God's kingdom"; or "No backward looks if you follow me— God's kingdom won't wait for tomorrow."

Once, when a particularly well-dressed young man told Jesus that he wanted to follow him, Jesus said, "Are you ready to rough it? We're not staying in the best inns, you know."[60]

When Pete heard this he laughed out loud and said, "I'll say! Jesus doesn't stay in the best motels. It's the 'Econo-Log' one night and 'Motel-Sand' the next."

"Or maybe the 'Holy-Day Inn,'" Priscilla offered with rare wit.

The young man didn't hear Pete or Priscilla, but he heard Jesus. He left the next morning—rubbing the kinks out of his back as he went.

Lots of people seem to find it difficult to sleep like a dog. But it has always been easy for me.

Then, one day, Jesus went around tapping people on the shoulder. He was inviting some of his followers to a special meeting. He tapped all the close orbiters and a whole bunch of distant ones, too.

The meeting time came and found Jesus standing in the middle of the by-invitation-only crowd. He began to talk to his followers as he strolled through their midst. A few paragraphs into his talk with them, Priscilla leaned over and whispered that she had counted the exact number of invited listeners—it was seventy. Pete yawned like a crocodile.

As he continued to speak, Jesus began to pair the audience into groups of two as he walked. This caused Pete to ask if there was going to be a Flood. That caused Jesna to smile.

With the large group of disciples sitting in twos, Jesus continued with his instructions. From his words it became clear that he was going to send them out on an evangelism crusade for a few days, as he had sent out the twelve a few months before. He said:

"When you enter a town and are received, eat what they set before you, heal anyone who is sick, and tell them, 'God's kingdom is right on your doorstep!'

"When you enter a town and are not received, go out in the street and say, 'The only thing we got from you is the dirt on our feet, and we're giving it back. Did you have any idea that God's kingdom was right on your doorstep?'[61]

"The one who listens to you listens to me. The one who rejects you, rejects me. And rejecting me is the same as rejecting God, who sent me."[62]

When Jesus finished speaking, the seventy stood as one 140-legged man, exchanged sober glances with their partners, and then dispersed to all of the directions of the compass. They were to return in a few days to a place Jesus had designated.

While the departing disciples were still within view, Pete asked: "How can Jesus say that if somebody rejects one of these guys, they are rejecting him? I mean, he is God's *only* Son, y'know."

"Because, Pete," Jesna answered, "the measure of true discipleship is always true Christ-like-ness."

Pete stared inside his own head and then nodded his understanding.

FAMILY DISCUSSION

1. Did you know that there were more than just twelve disciples?
2. Why do you think Jesus keeps sending his followers out on field trips?
3. If you are a Christian, did you know you are on one of Jesus' field trips right now? How does that influence the way you act?

SCENE 123
THE SEVENTY RETURN SINGING[63]

After the seventy left, Jesus withdrew to a lonely place deep in the heart of Samaria. He set up his prayer camp by a grove of miniature trees and spent the next few days strolling through the meadows and spacious valleys that surrounded his camp.

Mrs. Pilgrim was the first to comment about how different the countryside looked now in the fall of the year, as opposed to our last springtime trip to Jerusalem. The carpets of flowers that had covered the valleys and green hillsides were gone. They seemed to be replaced primarily by a bumper crop of thorns and thistles. A gentle and sometimes cool wind rustled across dry weeds and brittle leaves in the trees, turning up the white undersides of the olive leaves of an abandoned grove.

The rustlings of these early autumn days made much more noise than Jesus himself did. In fact, days went by without an audible word passing his lips. The same was not true for Pete.

"Isn't he going to eat?" Pete asked one morning. "I haven't seen him eat for days! I'm afraid he's going to get weak or sick or something."

"It's just the opposite that's happening, Pete," Jesna responded. "You know that Jesus usually spends the early morning hours talking with God—every day."

"Yeah," Pete said. "But this is getting ridiculous."

"He talks with his father every day to stay strong and confident in his mission—to let the world know about the kingdom of heaven. But when he is sure that he'll be facing a particularly difficult trial—such as what lies just ahead—he spends even longer times alone, fasting from what attaches him to his world and feasting on his Dad's words. He does this so that his obedience will grow strong. Pretty soon he will need to be able to stare death right in the face and not back down."

"Just like a gun fighter in the ol' West, huh, Jesna?"

"Very much like that, Pete. So, for him, two things are very crucial."

"What two things?" Priscilla asked.

"To be strong in his father's love," Jesna answered, "and to know that his disciples will be able to carry on after, uh.... "

"After he's dead," Pete whispered as he gazed down at the line his foot was carving in the sand. "Jesus is gonna die. I wasn't born yesterday, y'know."

Hearing his name, Jesus walked right up to Pete. Everyone but Jesna took a giant step backwards.

"That's right, Pete. You weren't born yesterday. You were born just a little over eight years ago on a chilly Easter morning, at Northeast Regional Hospital. I was there. And I was just as proud as were your mom and dad. Just as proud as when I saw Priscilla born."

Priscilla's mouth sprang open. "Jesus, *you* were there when I was born?" she gasped.

"Wouldn't have missed it for the world. I haven't missed a birth since those of Cain and Abel. But it's the new birth you are all experiencing now that I'm most excited about. That's why I'm here in Samaria. I'm here to make it possible for any of you who want to have a second birth to help yourselves to life in my Father's kingdom."

Jesus put his hands on the sides of Pete's and Priscilla's astonished faces, tenderly. Then, after a pat to the backs of their heads, he turned and walked away.

But before he had gone far, he looked back and said, "Oh, I was talking to my Father just a while ago. He wanted me to thank you all for coming along for this ride. It means a lot to him."

It didn't take Pete long to shatter the sacred silence that followed. "Tell him I wouldn't have missed it for the world," he shouted to the back of Jesus' head.

Then Pete turned to face his parents and said, while shaking his face from side to side, "He was *there* when I was born! Wow! I can't believe that." Then pointing his face toward his parents, he said, "Hey, were you guys there, too?"

Before Mr. and Mrs. Pilgrim had recovered from a mutual guffaw, the horizon line suddenly sprouted a chorus line of laughing, dancing, returning disciples. "Come on," Jesna said as she began to tug on Pete's hand. "You've all got to see this."

We caught up with Jesus just as one of the disciples was saying with exuberance, "Master, even the demons dance to your tune!"[64]

"I know," Jesus said, "I saw Satan fall, a bolt of lightning out of the sky. See what you have been given...No one can put a hand on you. All the same, the great triumph is not in your authority over evil, but in God's authority over you and presence with you. Not what you do for God but what God does for you—that's the agenda for rejoicing."[65]

Then Jesus led the rejoicing by throwing his head back and laughing from his belly.

"Both goals have been accomplished now, huh, Jesna?" Pete asked.

FAMILY DISCUSSION

1. How does it make you feel to know that Jesus cares enough about you to have been present when you were born?
2. What does it mean to you that when you are "born again," he is there too, and that he takes care of you with more attention than a mother cat gives her new kittens?

SCENE 124
A FATHER THANKED AND DISCIPLES BLESSED[66]

When Jesus had finished filling all the hills and vales of Samaria with peals of loud, Holy-Spirit-inspired laughter, he began to speak to the heavens.

"I thank you, Father, Master of heaven and earth, that you hid these things from the know-it-alls and showed them to these innocent newcomers. Yes, Father, it pleased you to do it this way.

"I've been given it all by my Father! Only the Father knows who the Son is and only the Son knows who the Father is. The Son can introduce the Father to anyone he wants do."[67]

Then, lowering his face, he began to speak directly to the disciples:

"Fortunate the eyes that see what you're seeing! There are plenty of prophets and kings who would have given their right arm to see what you are seeing but never got so much as a glimpse, to hear what you are hearing but never got so much as a whisper."[68]

After saying this Jesus wrapped a holy neck-lock around two disciples who were within arms' reach. He tucked one under each arm and led a processional to his campsite. It didn't take him long to break his fast during the impromptu victory celebration that followed.

An hour or so into the merriment Jesna asked, "Do any of you know where you're standing right now?"

"Right here on this big rock," Pete quickly shot back.

"Anyone else?" Jesna said, ignoring Pete's attempt to balance himself on one foot while holding his arms like wings.

"Yes," said Mrs. Pilgrim. "We're in Samaria."

"Right," Jesna said.

"And," Priscilla added while punching at her wrist computer, "we are north-by-northwest of Jerusalem, about equidistant from both the Mediterranean Sea and the Jordan River."

"And what do you remember about the land of Samaria?"

"I remember," Priscilla began, "that the people down south around Jerusalem think the Samaritans stink. And that the Samaritans think the, uh, the uh.... "

"Judeans?"

"Yes. Thank you, Jesna. The Samaritans think the Judeans are snobs."

"You have a good memory, Priscilla. And a very keen sense of direction, too."

"Psst, Jesna," Pete whispered. "It's her computer that does most of the hard work."

Jesna continued. "Samaria occupies the same territory that was occupied by the ten tribes of Jeroboam—the northern kingdom of Israel that was taken into captivity by the Assyrians in 722 B.C."

"When did they come back?" Pete asked.

"The northern tribes never came back. The were lost in time, like wheat seeds in a windstorm. While a few of the seeds never left this land and a few more blew back home, most became scattered across the globe. Many people in Samaria have Jewish heritage."

"Because of the few seeds that stayed behind?"

"Yes, Pete," Jesna said, and then continued, "the Judeans to the south think of them as impure and unclean."

"What does Jesus think?" Pete asked.

We all looked over in time to see Jesus enjoying another belly laugh while listening to one of his disciples' mission trip stories.

"Perhaps," Jesna said thoughtfully, "he thinks that there is no better place to send out a search party for your lost children than from the place where they were last seen." Then she allowed a long pause for reflection. "Perhaps," she finally continued, "he feels that his lost children are now everywhere, scattered throughout the entire world."

"Even in my hometown?" Pete asked.

"Even in your hometown, Pete. Even in your home."

"Maybe that's why he was there when I was born."

"And," Jesna added, "why he's often pacing around in the waiting room anticipating his children's second birth—their homecoming back to the Promised Land."

FAMILY DISCUSSION

1. Think about the "Samaritans" you might know today. Who are the people at your school who are the victims of prejudice and who are treated as outsiders by the "in-crowd"?
2. How do you think Jesus feels about the "outsiders"? How do you suppose he would treat them if he were a student at your school?

SCENE 125
THE PARABLE OF THE GOOD SAMARITAN[69]

After a while, the joyful noise from the victory party began to diminish in volume. Now waves of laughter had calmed to an occasional ripple. Jesus began to tell stories. As usual, his narratives had a special way of capturing a truth and causing it to be stored in a permanent file in the back of the hearer's mind.

His most memorable story went like this:

"There was once a man traveling from Jerusalem to Jericho. On the way he was attacked by robbers. They took his clothes, beat him up, and went off leaving him half-dead. Luckily, a priest was on his way down the same road, but when he saw him he angled across to the other side. Then a Levite religious man showed up; he also avoided the injured man.

"A Samaritan traveling the road came on him. When he saw the man's condition, his heart went out to him. He gave first aid, disinfecting and bandaging his wounds. Then he lifted him onto his donkey, led him to an inn, and made him comfortable. In the morning he took out two silver coins and gave them to the inn-keeper, saying, 'Take good care of him. If it costs any more, put it on my bill—I'll pay on my way back.'

"What do you think? Which of the three became a neighbor to the man attacked by robbers?"[70]

"The Samarian, the Samarian!" Pete shouted.

"That's Samari-TAN, little brother. Aren't you ever going to do anything about your wax build-up problem? They've invented washcloths now, y'know."

"It's just hologram wax, sis."

"But," Jesna intervened, "Pete knows what he means. It was the Samaritans, the ones the Judeans considered to be no better than trash, and not their exalted religious leaders, who understood the importance of compassion. And compassion and love are the air and water of God's kingdom on earth. If you're not taking them in and giving them out, well, you're dead."

"Man," Pete said, "that Jesus sure has a way of turning the inside of your head into a movie theater, doesn't he?"

"He sure does, son," Mr. Pilgrim said. "And what did you learn from the film you just saw?"

"That those seventy disciples there should feel pretty good about going out and preaching to the Samaritans. Because the Samaritans are just as valuable to God as any of his children. I mean, they *are* his children."

"And...," Mr. Pilgrim prompted.

"And," said Priscilla, "that it's love that makes you a real neighbor and a real friend of God."

"And," Pete inserted, "that since the Samaritans and the Judeans already live right next to each other, they should be more neighborly. Because if you ain't breathing love in and out you're DOA in God's K-I-N-G-D-O-M."

FAMILY DISCUSSION

1. Whom would you rather have as a next-door neighbor, the Samaritan or the priest in this story?
2. What can you do tomorrow to be a better neighbor?
3. Is there anyone on earth who is not your neighbor?

SCENE 126
ON TO MARY AND MARTHA'S HOUSE—BY WAY OF JERUSALEM[71]

The next morning Jesus and the seventy disciples broke camp and headed south, on foot, for Jerusalem. We bounced along behind.

Jesna told us they were going to set up Jesus' southern headquarters in the home of three of his friends in the town of Bethany, and to celebrate the Feast of Tabernacles. She told us we would be in Jerusalem for the entire seven-day celebration—and in the south for several Bible-time months.

"Jesna," Pete said, "it seems like Jesus is always headed to a feast or a fast. Do you think he has an eating disorder? I know I saw once on Oprah … "

"Enough already, Pete," Mr. Pilgrim interrupted. "Jesus might be offended."

"Oh, that's OK, Mr. Pilgrim. I'm sure all the feasts get confusing. Plus, Jesus isn't nearly as touchy as you may think. Do you want me to tell you about the feasts and sacred festivals that are part of the Jewish religion?"

"Sure!" Pete blurted out. "I always like to hear about people pigging out. Almost as much as I like doing it myself."

"Well," Jesna began, "not counting the 'Feast of the weekly Sabbath' in which all Sabbaths are celebrated and kept holy.…"

"Like when we go to church each Sunday?" Pete inserted.

"Yes, Pete. Except that the Jewish Sabbath begins on Friday at sunset and lasts until sundown the following day. Anyway, not counting that, the first feast of the Jewish sacred year was Passover."

"That's the most important one, isn't it, Jesna?"

"That's right, Priscilla. Most people would consider it the most important. It was the first one they began to celebrate. And it commemorates their deliverance from Egypt."

"What does 'commiserates' mean?"

"'Commemorates,' Pete, not 'commiserates'!" Priscilla chided.

"Oh, good. 'Commiserates' sounds like two people being miserable at the same time. So what does that other word mean?"

"'Commemorates' means to remember with honor."

"That's very good, Priscilla," Jesna said, then continued.

"Passover begins on April 14th and lasts until April 21st."

"That's real close to when we celebrate Easter," Pete inserted. "What's the next one?" he asked, without taking a breath.

"It's extremely close to Easter, Pete—in time and in deepest meaning. The next feast is the Feast of Pentecost. Sometimes it's called the Feast of Weeks."

"Wow! How many weeks does it last?"

Jesna said, "It's celebrated on June 6th and it only lasts for one day."

"They should call it the 'feast of day,' then."

"Perhaps, Pete. But it's called 'Feast of Weeks' or 'Pentecost' because it comes fifty days (about seven weeks) after Passover."

"'Penta-' means fifty, little brother."

"Duh! And 'deca-' means I'm about to 'hita youa,' Priscilla. I'm not an idjut, y'know."

"Umph-umm!" Mr. Pilgrim said, clearing his throat warningly.

"The third feast is the 'Feast of Trumpets,' or 'New Moon.' It's held on the first day of October. Sometimes you hear it called, uh, *Rosh Hashanah.*"

"Geshundheit, Jesna."

"As I was saying …It marks the beginning of the Jewish civil year and it is like our New Year's Day."

"Does that mean everybody stays up late, kisses the first person they see, and then stays home and watches football the next day?"

"Not exactly, Pete. But they do celebrate all day, from morning to evening, blowing horns and trumpets."

"Then, the fourth special day is called 'Feast of the Day of Atonement.' That isn't a feast time. It's really more of a fast than a feast, and it's celebrated on October 10th. Its purpose is for God's people to bring to him all their sins of the past year and to ask for forgiveness."

"Hum," Pete mused. "It's usually about ten days after New Year's that Mom and Dad are feeling pretty lousy about breaking their resolution to lose their Christmas pounds."

"You're about to lose your ability to sit down, son."

"Sorry, Dad."

"Jesna."

"Yes, Priscilla."

"According to my calculations it's October 14th right now. Didn't we just miss the last feast, the Day of Atonement?"

"Nope. Jesus was observing the Day of Atonement during his extended fast. And we're heading for Jerusalem for the celebration of the next feast, the Feast of Tabernacles."

"That's what got you started on all of this whole, *loooooong* spiel, huh, Jesna?"

"Right, Pete. But I didn't tell you, yet, that the Feast of Tabernacles always begins five days after the Day of Atonement (October 15th). It's a celebration that marks the completion of the harvest. Its primary purpose, though, is to remind the people of how their forefathers wandered in the wilderness for forty years—living in booths or tents."

"I guess Jesus' coming to town is a way of offering the people another chance to live in the Promised Land—the 'kingdom' he talks about so much."

Jesna's eyebrows looked like the McDonald's Golden Arches. She looked *very* impressed. "That's exactly right, Mr. Pilgrim. Everywhere he goes he is offering people a chance to leave their wilderness wanderings, cross over the Jordan, and settle down in the Promised Land."

Mrs. Pilgrim looked pretty impressed, too. Pete was just looking. But he was the one who broke the silence.

"Is that all the pigging-out times of the year?"

"Well, those are the feasts—six counting the weekly Sabbath—which were given by God before the divided kingdoms went into captivity. Two more have been added since."

"Why not?" Pete said. "I'd add as many as I could get away with."

"The 'Feast of Lights' is observed for eight days, beginning on December 25th."

"Hum. Why does that day seem to stick in my mind?"

"Maybe it has something to do with a certain Jolly ol' Elf," hinted Priscilla.

Pete was scratching his head.

"And, finally, the 'Feast of Purim' is kept on March 14th and 15th—the last month of the religious year. Both of the last two are joyous celebrations."

"Christmas! That's it. Christmas."

Pete's mental sleuthing was ignored by all the Pilgrims. A few silent minutes passed, except for the sand-crunching of seventy pairs of sandals, before Priscilla asked in a very serious voice.

"So will this be our last trip to Jerusalem?"

"No, Priscilla. Jesus will be teaching in and around Jerusalem until the time of the Feast of Lights, and right up to the time of Passover."

"She already said we'd be around Jerusalem for a few months," Pete corrected smugly. "Then what happens?" he added, before catching himself. "Oh," he said as the air went out of his smile. "Never mind."

We came to a stop just outside the magnificent walls of Jerusalem. We watched just as Jesus and his disciples were entering through a city gate. Pete said, "Hey, aren't we going to follow them inside?"

"Nope," Jesna said. "The Bible doesn't provide much information about what happens, until later this evening when they are at Mary and Martha's house. So," she said, playing the panel of buttons like a piano, "tonight we'll be meeting again with Jesus in Bethany."

And with that we were off into the future—only a few Bible-hours of it this time.

When the colors stopped spinning, we were parked in the middle of a large room. The walls were stacked square stones. Soft light from the evening sun slanted in through two high windows, making shadows. The dancing flames of several thick candles were already doing their part to help the failing sunlight.

Jesus was sitting in the middle of the room on a roughly-hewn, wooden bench. A woman, about the same age as Jesus, was sitting on the floor at his feet. She was looking up at him with warm admiration.

As we watched, Jesus told story after story. The woman, Jesna said, was named Mary, and she lapped up every syllable that fell from his mouth. Her eyes were glued to Jesus in rapt attention.

The only intrusion to Jesus' teachings was the wonderful smells of herbs, spices, and roasting meat that poured out of the kitchen area. Pete was swallowing his swallows. Me, too.

Occasionally, a woman's head would appear in the doorway and flash a menacing gaze at the back of Mary's head. Jesna told us that was Martha. Every time, as quickly as she poked her head through the doorway, she pulled it back angrily. Then we would hear an explosion of kitchen-utensil-rattling and sometimes loud mutterings.

Finally, a body followed Martha's head right through the doorway. Mary was still glued to Jesus' words. Martha walked over and squeezed in between Mary and Jesus. She gave Jesus a close-up view of her hot face.

"Master," she fumed, "don't you care that my sister has abandoned me to all the preparations? Tell her to lend me a hand."[72]

Jesus reached out and took hold of Martha's wet hand. "I'll give you my hand," he said. Then he continued, "Martha, dear Martha, you're fussing far too much and getting yourself worked up over nothing. One thing only is essential, and Mary has chosen it—it's the main course, and won't be taken from her."[73]

Jesus gently guided Martha to a seat on the dirt floor beside her sister, Mary.

"But the bread!" Martha exclaimed.

"*I* am the Bread, Martha. Now sit here and let me serve you."

Martha stayed seated, ending her wilderness wanderings just before the Feast of Tabernacles. She was several courses into Jesus' feast before the smell of burning bread began to penetrate the room. It was *Mary* who got up and hurried out to the bread oven. Martha didn't even notice.

FAMILY DISCUSSION

1. Have you ever felt like Martha while she was still doing all the work?

2. Tell about the last time you felt like Mary while she was listening to Jesus?

SCENE 127
THE PARABLE OF THE RICH FOOL[74]

After finishing his stories over a tableful of Martha's abundant cooking, Jesus spent the night there in the home of his friends, Mary, Martha, and Lazarus. In fact, the trio invited him to use it as a home base while he was in the south near Jerusalem. His disciples were staying with an assortment of friends, relatives, and saints-in-the-making.

His friends' home was in Bethany, a community nestled into the eastern slope of Mount Olivet, about two miles southeast of Jerusalem. Jesna told us that some people would now begin to refer to Bethany as the Judean home of Jesus, and Capernaum as his Galilean home.

"But the truth is," she said. "Jesus has been homeless from the day he gave Mary and Joseph a goodby hug in the middle of a dusty Nazarean street. His only permanent home," she continued, "is in heaven with his Father and in the hearts of his friends."

The next morning, as was his custom, Jesus arose early. After a long chat with his Dad, he set out for the two-mile hike to Jerusalem—but not before Martha could fill a cloth sack with fresh-baked bread. She told him that she and Mary and Lazarus would make the trip later in the day.

We drove along behind Jesus as he prayer-walked his way to the Holy City. "I thought he already did his morning prayers," Pete observed.

"To live in the kingdom," Jesna said, "does not only involve breathing love, but it also involves being in constant dialogue with your heavenly Father."

"That sounds sort of boring," Pete blurted out.

"Pete!" said Mrs. Pilgrim. "I can't believe you said that."

"Oh, that's OK," Jesna quickly said. "Most people think that it would be boring to talk to God all the time. That's because they've never taken the time to really get to know him—to learn that he's not some stern, white-bearded grandfather who constantly searches for flaws in his universe and looks for excuses to punish you."

"He's not?" Pete asked.

"NO!" Jesna said. "When you really get to know him, you discover that talking with God is like talking with your best friend, a parent that you haven't seen in a long time, and your fiancé, all rolled into one. Remember, he is the architect of Eden, the Promised Land, the kingdom of God, and heaven!"

"Hmmm," all four Pilgrims mused, before Pete put their thoughts into words. "I may have to give another chance to hanging out with him."

Jesus didn't stop walking, but he did flash a thumbs-up sign over his head.

Once inside one of the city gates, Jesus made his way through the throngs of celebrating people to the courtyard of the Temple. While he was more famous in the north than in the Holy City of Jerusalem, he was the focal point of several pointing fingers and "Hey, isn't that...?" murmurs.

After a little walking and looking around, Jesus took a seat in a remote corner of the Temple courtyard. Most of his inmost circle of twelve friends had already found him by this point, as had a small constellation of the curious.

After an impromptu session of crowd-questions and Christ-answers, someone spoke from the crowd, "Teacher, if you have so much authority, why don't you make my brother give me the fair share of the family inheritance."

Jesus immediately responded, "What makes you think that

is any of my business—to hold family court for you?"

Then while looking at the questioner and speaking to everyone, Jesus said, "Be very careful! You must protect yourself against even a small seed of greed. Your life is so much more than what you own."

Then he told them this story: "The farm of a certain rich man produced a terrific crop. He talked to himself: 'What can I do? My barn isn't big enough for this harvest.' Then he said, 'Here's what I'll do: I'll tear down my barns and build bigger ones. Then I'll gather in all my grain and goods, and I'll say to myself, "Self, you've done well! You've got it made and can now retire. Take it easy and have the time of your life!"'

"Just then God showed up and said, 'Fool! Tonight you die. And your barn full of goods—who gets it?'

"That's what happens when you fill your barn with Self and not with God."[75]

As most of the small crowd nodded their understanding of Jesus' story, the man who had asked the question quickly turned and made a foot-stomping exit.

"I guess he's afraid that if he leaves his barn door open for too long his 'Self' might get out. Huh, Jesna?"

"I think you're right," Pete's dad said, answering for Jesna. "Or maybe that God might get in?"

FAMILY DISCUSSION

1. Why do you think greed is such a problem for most people?
2. As a family read Philippians 2:5-11 (the "Hymn of Christ") and discuss how you might be able to follow Jesus' example of self-emptying.

SCENE 128
WHAT TO DO IF YOU GET LOCKED OUT[76]

During the next seven days we were with Jesus and his friends as they celebrated the Feast of Tabernacles, taught in the Temple courtyard or on grassy slopes just outside the city, ate common meals, and enjoyed cool, crisp evenings together.

On a few of the feast evenings, Martha would prepare a spread of food for Jesus and as many of his friends as he could round up. He was usually able to collect a herd of them.

Mrs. Pilgrim said that, just from *watching* all the food being eaten, she felt she needed to sign up for a Jenny Craig weight loss program.

Other feast evenings found Jesus camped out under the stars. At one point Jesna told us, "The Bible isn't crystal clear on the events of the next few months. But we've put the ride together as best we can."

"What do you mean?" Pete asked.

"Well, don't get me wrong," Jesna began to answer. "It is wonderful that God chose such special correspondents, Matthew, Mark, Luke, and John, to cover the greatest news event in the history of the world. But their intentions were not to, uh.... "

"Build a Bible Ride," Pete offered.

"To tell the events of Jesus' time on earth in precise chronological order," she finished.

"Huh?"

"To build a Bible Ride, Pete."

"Thanks, Mom."

"So," Jesna continued, "all that we really know is that Jesus spent the time from the feasts, until Passover, in and around

Jerusalem. We'll be doing our best to keep up with him during these times—even though some scholars might quibble about what follows what."

"Why are you telling us this, Jesna?" Pete asked. "I'm not a scholar."

"I think she had you down for 'quibbler,' little brother."

"She's preparing you, son, in case you ever go to seminary."

"Why would I ever want to go to a cemetery to study *about* Jesus when I'm spending all this time *with* him right now?"

From the still faces and raised eyebrows, it was clear that Pete had stumped the panel. The silence was finally broken by the sounds of buttons being pushed and the rush of racing colors and Jesna's whisper, "Who can argue? *With* is always better than *about*."

When we came to a stop Jesus was just a few feet in front of the bumper and the heads of two seated listeners were sticking up casually through the hood of our hologram car. "Ooops!" Jesna said, and backed up a few feet.

Jesus was sitting under a twisted pine tree. His subject was the kingdom of God, Jerusalem was his backdrop, and his listeners were mesmerized.

But it wasn't long before the spell was broken by one of the listeners. The man began to shuffle his feet in the sand as he twisted himself in such a way that his body resembled the pine tree behind Jesus. Mercifully he finally gave his body relief by blurting out these words:

"Master, will only a few be saved (to live in your Father's kingdom)?"

Jesus answered,

"Whether few or many is none of your business. Put your mind on your life and God. The way to life—to God!—is vigorous and requires your total attention. A lot of you are going to assume that you'll sit down to God's salvation banquet just because you've been hanging around the neighborhood all your lives. Well, one day you're going to be banging on the door, wanting to get in, but you'll find the door locked and the Master saying, 'Sorry, you're not on my guest list.'

"You'll protest, 'But we've known you all our lives!' only to be interrupted with his abrupt, 'Your kind of knowing can hardly be called knowing. You don't know the first thing about me,"[77]

"Whoa!" Pete moaned. "That's pretty scary."

"It is scary, Pete. And it's precisely why it's so much more important to know Jesus by being *with* him than to only know *about* him. The kingdom is a place for friends, not acquaintances."

"Is that why Mary, Martha, and Lazarus have already been invited to live in the kingdom of God? Because they are Jesus' friends?"

"Everybody is invited to live there. But first you need to invite Jesus to live with you."

"To be 'buds'?"

"You got it, Pete."

FAMILY DISCUSSION

1. How do you think you might feel if you discovered you had been locked out of God's kingdom?
2. You may want to discuss the differences between knowing *about* Jesus and being *with* him.

SCENE 129
ABOUT HUMILITY[78]

Jesus continued his teachings within earshot of the festivities in Jerusalem, as the number of his listeners grew and shrank, shrank and grew, like the tides of a miniature ocean.

After more than an hour had passed, Mr. Pilgrim tapped Jesna on the shoulder. He asked Jesna a question that must have been developing in his mind for some time.

"I'm not sure I get the difference between knowing about Jesus by being with him versus knowing about him by reading his story in the Bible. I mean, if it weren't for being on this ride, I'm not sure I'd ever know how to be *with* him at all."

"I understand your confusion, Mr. Pilgrim."

"Yeah," Pete inserted. "And Jesus made the stakes pretty high for making sure that we *know* about all the *knowing*. Know what I mean?"

"I sure do, Pete."

"Good," Pete said. "Then you can 'splain what I mean to me and Dad."

"I'll try," Jesna said. "You see, for the people in Jesus' time the word 'know' was understood much differently than it is for the people in your modern world. For Jesus' listeners here today to 'know' means that you have gone far beyond knowing *about* someone. It means you *really* know them."

As Jesna was dragging out the word *r-e-a-l-l-y* her face seemed to blush with just a tinge of embarrassment.

"When Jesus and these folks here talk about knowing someone, it means you have spent time with the person. It means that you are *very* intimate with him or her. That type of intimacy can produce new life—babies."

Now everybody but Pete was blushing. Perhaps it was good that he wasn't the one to ask the next question.

"But Jesna," Mr. Pilgrim said, "he can't be saying that, uh...."

"He's saying, Mr. Pilgrim, that he wants a close and personal relationship with you and with all his friends. A living, active, vibrant relationship."

"I think I get it," Mrs. Pilgrim said. "You know, Hon, I've still got all of the love letters you ever wrote me. I keep them in a shoe box, and once every year or so I get them down and read some of them. It's a real nice feeling to do that; but I enjoy going out on a date with you a whole lot more. And sometimes on our dates you update some of those old, yellow letters by telling me 'I love you,' face-to-face."

"Let's not get any of that face-to-face stuff going," Pete said. "I haven't eaten in over thirty Bible years and my stomach can't take it."

"I'm saying," Mrs. Pilgrim continued, ignoring Pete's stomach-clutching, "while your letters are *very* important to me, they pale in comparison to the joy of being with you." Mr. Pilgrim put his hand on his wife's and smiled at her with his eyes.

"I'm warning you ... ," Pete intoned.

"You are exactly right, Mrs. Pilgrim. Jesus offers both love letters (Scripture) and his presence. His real friends will want to be with him and learn more about him by doing what some of his longtime friends have called 'practicing his presence' and 'learning to listen to his voice.' It's developing a special intimate relationship—so special and intimate that, like its physical counterpart, it can produce brand-new life."

"So," Pete said while keeping his back turned to his overly affectionate parents, "it's just like my friend Jesus said—knowing with your heart is better than knowing with your head."

"As usual, Pete. You are exactly right."

At that moment our attention was called back to Jesus. He had finished his last story and appeared to be in the process of leading his listeners back into the city.

"Let's tag along," Jesna said. "He's been invited for a big dinner party at the home of one of the top Pharisee leaders."

"Sounds like there could be a fireworks display afterwards," Pete quipped.

"Yeah," said Priscilla. "It sounds like it could be a trap."

As things turned out, both Pete and Priscilla were prophets.

When we arrived at the Pharisee's home it was already a beehive of activity. In the central room of the home a huge table was in the final stages of preparation.

"Look at all the caterers," Pete said.

Jesus was escorted to a place of honor just to the right of the host's seat.

"Do you think Jesus himself could have made that big table in the carpenter shop?" Pete asked Jesna.

"I don't know," she said. "But I know he made the tree it came from."

Then Pete asked, "What is this? Musical chairs? Look how everyone is elbowing each other out of the way. They all want to sit next to the host guy."

Long after the music had stopped, everyone finally found a chair. But only those close to the host were wearing smiles.

Not long into the meal, Jesus began to tell a story at the invitation of the host. It turned out to be more of an observation.

"When someone invites you to dinner, don't take the place of honor. Somebody more important than you might have been invited by the host. Then he'll come and call out in front of everybody, 'You're in the wrong place. The place of honor belongs to this man.' Red-faced, you'll have to make your way to the very last table, the only place left.

"When you're invited to dinner, go and sit at the last place. Then when the host comes he may very well say, 'Friend, come up to the front.' That will give the dinner guests something to talk about! What I'm saying is, If you walk around with your nose in the air, you're going to end up flat on your face. But if you're content to be simply yourself, you will become more than yourself."

Then he turned to the host. "The next time you put on a dinner, don't just invite your friends and family and rich neighbors, the kind of people who will return the favor. Invite some people who never get invited out, the misfits from the wrong side of the tracks. You'll be—and experience—a blessing. They won't be able to return the favor, but the favor will be returned—oh, how it will be returned!—at the resurrection of God's people."[79]

"Because," Pete began to interpret, "that will be when God will tap you on the shoulder and invite you to a place of honor right next to his seat."

"Yes," Jesna said, "the place reserved for his truest friends, the people who took the time to get to know him by being with him."

FAMILY DISCUSSION

1. What are some ways you can get to know Jesus?
2. Did any of the ways you listed involve spending time with him, listening to his voice?
3. Would you rather get a letter from Jesus or go out and play with him?

SCENE 130
THE STORY ABOUT A LOST LAMB[80]

"I don't think some of those folks liked Jesus' story—about how you shouldn't box a guy out if he's going for the best seat at the table," Pete said.

A quick survey of the room revealed that Pete was right. While a few were rubbing their chins and nodding their dark heads in apparent agreement with Jesus, most had steam pouring out of their ears, as if their faces were bright red tea kettles. (Well, not really, but it made me think of that.) No one in the preferred seating section had offered to give up his place.

The frozen silence was broken by Jesus standing to his feet. He began walking around behind his black-robed, still-seated, still-steaming host, while the rest of the guests observed with hostile eyes. Jesus surprised them by passing through the stone passageway to the kitchen. Within seconds he had emerged, escorting one of the cooks—a young girl—as if they were walking down the aisle of a fancy wedding. They stopped by his vacant place.

"She's a servant in this house," Jesna said quietly.

"Uh-oh," Mr. Pilgrim whispered.

The girl, confused, gave a quick inspection of the table set-up, perhaps wondering if she had made some grave error. The host looked indignant.

Jesus smiled at the girl and then indicated with a gesture of his hand that she was to take his place at the table. She shook her head "No." But not with as much energy as the host, who shook his whole bejowled face with disbelief.

"Look at that," Priscilla said. "If that man at the head of the table isn't careful he's going to give himself whiplash."

"Yeah," Pete agreed, "or slap himself in the ears with his cheeks."

Jesus emphasized his intent by gently guiding the servant girl into his empty spot with a hand on each of her shoulders. "May I serve you?" Jesus asked the girl. Her servant-mask face cracked with a shy smile. "Sure," she giggled.

With that Jesus carved off an oversized hunk of meat for her.

"And how about you, sir?" Jesus said to the host.

The host was silent with outraged astonishment, but the hush was short lived. A loud fist came crashing down somewhere toward the center of the long wooden table. Clay dishes and brass cups leaped into the air to escape, but lost their half-second battle against gravity and came crashing back down.

"This is just what I've been telling you about," thundered a black-robed man from his position at a less preferred position of the table. "He makes a habit of taking in sinners. He eats meals with them and treats them like old friends."

A chorus of sympathetic grumblings followed and grew in volume. Jesus raised his hands over his head and said, "Peace" in a loud and deep voice. The storm became silent. Then continuing:

"Suppose one of you had a hundred sheep and lost one. Wouldn't you leave the ninety-nine in the wilderness and go after the lost one until you found it? When found, you can be sure you would put it across your shoulders, rejoicing, and when you got home call in your friends and neighbors, saying, 'Celebrate with me! I've found my lost sheep!' Count on it—there's more joy in heaven over one sinner's rescued life than over ninety-nine good people in no need of rescue."[81]

A thoughtful silence followed.

"The trouble with some people is," Pete said, "they've been lost so long that they've quit being homesick sheep and turned into wolves."

FAMILY DISCUSSION

1. Why do you suppose the shepherd in Jesus' story would go after any one of his lost sheep?
2. How do you feel knowing that he would do the same for you?

SCENE 131
THE PARABLE OF THE LOST COIN[82]

The dinner party at the rich Pharisee's house ended with only one sheep being brought home—the servant-girl. But her bright-eyed gratitude went a long way toward making up for all the black-robed sheep of God's family who chose to stay out in the wilderness of self-sufficiency.

During this sojourn in and around Jerusalem, Jesus had never once appeared to be in a hurry, not like most other humans I have observed. Nevertheless, his voice was beginning to ring with a growing tone of urgency. I suppose he knew how few grains of time remained in his earthly hourglass.

The next day, a particularly bright blue one, found Jesus sitting on one of the few patches of soft grass in the sandy "suburbs" around Jerusalem. The thick stone walls of Jerusalem rose behind him like a fortress. His audience was a small crowd of the city's castaways as he began to tell a series of parables we had not heard before. Jesna told us they would become known as some of his best stories.

" … imagine a woman who has ten coins and loses one. Won't she light a lamp and scour the house, looking in every nook and cranny until she finds it? And when she finds it you can be sure she'll call her friends and neighbors: 'Celebrate with me! I found my lost coin!'"[83]

"Wait a minute," Pete inserted. "What's all the excitement about a finding a lost coin? I've seen Dad drop a coin and not even bend over to pick it up. He told Mom that it would cost more to get the kinks out of his back than the coin was worth."

"If that happened, son, I'm sure it was a penny. And I'm even more sure I was in a hurry."

"I know, but that's what I mean. When I picked it up you didn't throw a party for all your friends. But you did ask for it back, come to think of it."

"Well, Pete, from the woman's reaction you can be sure that the lost coin was very valuable to her and that she was very poor. The ten coins—they weren't just pennies—probably represented her life savings."

"Yeah," Priscilla chimed in, "and they don't have banks on every corner here, you know."

"They don't have many corners."

"Uh-hmm," Jesna cleared her tiny throat. "As I was saying, for her, putting the coin in a safe place may mean the difference between life and death at some point in her future. That's why she threw the party. Something *very* valuable had been found."

As Jesna was finishing her sentence, we heard Jesus conclude his story.

" ... Count on it—that's the kind of party God's angels throw every time one lost soul turns to God."[84]

"Wow, Dad! If I fell out of Jesus' pocket it sounds like he would bend all the way down from heaven to pick me up."

"That's right, son. And I bet that's because he knows what I know."

"What's that?"

"That you are more valuable than a whole truckload of silver and gold coins."

Pete was beaming. "And I'm not nearly so hard on the back."

FAMILY DISCUSSION

1. Did you know that you are more valuable to Jesus than anything else in the world?
2. How does it make you feel to know that the angels in heaven threw a big party the day you gave your life to Jesus?

SCENE 132
THE STORY OF
THE PRODIGAL SON[85]

A gentle breeze began to play with Jesus' hair as a small child began doing the same with the bottom of his dusty robe. Yet Jesus was undistracted from the telling of his next story.

"Once there was a man with two sons. One day his youngest boy approached him with a demand. 'Father, I want all that's coming to me. I want it right now.'

"While this broke the father's heart, he knew that he wanted sons who were bound to him by love and not by law. So, he gave his boy half of all his possessions. The young man sold the belongings, packed the silver and gold along with fine clothes, and left home. He went far away to a distant country. There he wasted no time in spending his inheritance on wine, women, and song.

"After he had squandered everything, a drought swept through the country and left him completely destitute. He had to take the only available job—assistant pig-slopper. It wasn't long until he became so hungry that he envied their diet of corn cobs and mush. But he couldn't even afford to pay for that for himself.

"The young man's pain finally brought him to his senses, like pungent smelling salts. He reasoned that even the farmhands working on his father's farm had three meals a day—while he was slowly starving to death.

"The youngest son decided that he would return home and plead with his father, saying, 'I have sinned against God and against you. I am no longer worthy to be called your son; please let me return home and become one of your hired hands.' He got up from the muck of the pig pen and set out for home, his face caked with mud and his body covered with rags of shame.

"While he was still a good distance away his father saw him, and was flooded with compassion. He ran to meet him. As the boy attempted to stammer out his rehearsed speech about being unworthy to be his son, the father interrupted the confession by covering his face with kisses. He ordered servants to bring out the best robe in the house.

"The father draped his son with the fine purple robe the servants brought, put his best ring on the boy's finger, his best sandals on the boy's bleeding feet, and ordered a great feast.

"'We're going to have a wonderful time,' the father said. 'My son that was dead is now alive! He was lost and now he is found!'"

Jesus' story was met by a mixed response. Many were nodding their tear-streaked faces. Others, though, had stone faces, as if they were disappointed that the runaway son had not been punished.

"I remember that story from Sunday school," Pete volunteered. "The story of the prodigal son and the prodigal pigs is one of my favorites."

"Why do you think you like it so much, Pete?" Jesna asked.

"I don't know. Maybe because I thought the prodigal father was going to give him a whipping; instead he gave him a party. It just makes me feel good."

"You have good taste in stories, Pete, even though you don't know what 'prodigal' means. This story may be the most important one in the Bible, not counting the story that Jesus is living before your eyes right now."

"Why do you say that?" Priscilla asked. "There are so many."

"Because," Jesna began without pausing for a breath, "this story summarizes all of the great themes of Scripture—from Genesis to Revelation and from the Garden of Eden to your local church."

"What do you mean, Jesna?" Mr. Pilgrim inquired.

"Well, if you were to take a ride through any book in the Bible ... "

"You mean there are other rides?" Pete exclaimed.

"Sure there are, Pete. Don't you remember parting Moses' hair with our car? But as I was saying ... anyplace that you could possibly choose to stop on those rides, anyplace at all, as on this one, you would be able to look around and see four themes, right before your eyes. Relationship. Inheritance. Rejection of God. His relentless pursuit of his runaway children."

"Huh?"

"Anywhere you look," Jesna continued, "the Bible is telling you how much God wants to be in relationship with his children and telling you about the special inheritance he has prepared for them (and you) to enjoy.

"But unfortunately Scripture is also telling the story of how," she swallowed hard, "his children always reject the grace-filled offers of relationship and inheritance and leave their intended home."

"And then, anywhere you look, the Bible is full of stories

about the final theme—how God, our real Father, waits with robe and ring in hand for his children to come back home."

"I'm not tracking with you," Pete whined.

"The kingdom of God," Jesna said patiently, "the place that Jesus has spent the past two and a half years telling runaway sons and daughters about, is a place of relationship with God."

"Like his being with Adam and Eve in the Garden of Eden?" Priscilla asked.

"Like that. And like his being in the midst of his people by his presence in the Temple, or like now, his being willing to live in the temple of your hearts. God wants to be *with* you, in relationship with you. That's a primary theme of Scripture."

"But what about the inheritance?" Pete asked.

"The Garden of Eden, the Promised Land, the kingdom of heaven. They are all different names for the inheritance. They're more similar to each other than they are different. They are all places where the rules of the King are the rules his children live by."

"I think I'm starting to see," Mr. Pilgrim said. "While God, our real Father, is offering relationship and inheritance, people ... uh ... I ... that is, keep leaving home ... his presence ... taking half our possessions with us—our minds, hearts, senses, and freedom to choose."

"Stop it, Dad, you're sounding like a preacher about to shift into high gear!" Pete cautioned.

"A pretty good one, Mr. Pilgrim!" Jesna said over a giggle. "But the story doesn't end there. Throughout history God keeps offering ways for his children to come back home. He offered his Covenant to Abraham, his Law to Moses, fiery messages from his prophets, and finally, his very own Son sent from heaven as a messenger of love, a shepherd in search of lost lambs. *'Come on back home. Your Father still loves you and wants to treat you like a son.'* That's the message of Jesus' parable, and that's the message of his life here on earth."

A long moment of silence passed, and eight smooth cheeks began to glisten with tears. Pete explained what was happening best.

"I think that's the first time I ever really heard that story. It's about *me*, ain't it?"

"Yes, Pete," Jesna said. She motioned toward the Jerusalem celebration with her head. "And how appropriate for it to be told as Israel is celebrating the end of the wilderness wanderings."

FAMILY DISCUSSION

1. If you had seen the Prodigal Son sitting in the pig-mud what would you have said to him?
2. In what ways do you think the father's farm, Eden, the Promised Land, and the kingdom of heaven are alike?
3. How does it make you feel to know that the Creator of the universe has named you as an heir?

SCENE 133
THE STORY OF THE STREET-SMART CROOK[86]

After Jesus finished telling the story of the lost son, he began to answer questions from his listeners. It wasn't long, however, before he was interrupted by the rhythmic sawing sounds of a snoring disciple.

Jesus looked in the direction of his cat-napping follower and began to slowly shake his head from side to side. Peter quickly gave his colleague a wake-up call in the ribs.

"Suddenly," Jesus said, as the startled disciple snorted,

"another story comes to mind."

"Once there was a very rich man. He was so rich that he had a full-time manager to handle all of his business affairs. But the rich man began to receive reports that the manager was a crook—running up huge personal expenses and paying them off with his employer's money."

The sleeping disciple was now wide-eyed awake.

"The rich man called his manager to him and said, 'You are fired. I have heard reports of how you have stolen money from me. I want a complete accounting of all your records by morning.'"

"Man, that's low," Pete said. "I just bet that manager has probably made a bunch of 900-number phone calls and charged 'em to his boss, too."

"Something you'd like to get off your chest, son?"

"No, Dad. Let's just listen to the story."

Jesus continued. "The manager cried, 'What can I do, now that I've lost my wonderful job? I'm not strong enough to work in the fields, and I have too much pride to beg.'

"Then, the crooked manager got an idea. He decided to call in all of his former employer's debtors and make friends for himself—friends that might take him into their homes when he was out on the street.

"As they filed in one by one he said things like, 'Take your bill, sit down quickly and change the number of pots of oil from one hundred to fifty.'

"To another he would say, 'And how much do you owe? Shhh. Make it half that amount.'

"Now here's the surprise: The master praised the crooked manager!" [The crowd gasped.] "And why? Because he knew how to look after himself. Streetwise people are smarter in this regard than law-abiding citizens. They are on constant alert, looking for angles, surviving by their wits. I want you to be smart in the same way—but for what is *right*—using every adversity to stimulate you to creative survival, to concentrate your attention on the bare essential, so you'll live, really live, and not complacently just get by on good behavior."[87]

"W-w-wait a minute," Priscilla said. "That's the first time I ever remember Jesus saying anything like that."

"That's right," Pete chimed in. "And Priscilla has a memory like a steel trap. If he had ever said that we could be *dishonest*, she'd have caught it by the tail."

Ouch, I winced.

"I gotta confess, Jesna," Mr. Pilgrim added while shaking his head. "That is not the way I thought that story would end either."

"That's right," Mrs. Pilgrim chimed in, "What about those four Bible themes you were talking about. Is Jesus saying, 'Stay on out there with the pigs—just learn to be a good pickpocket so you can keep on eating?'"

"Oh, no!" Jesna said laughing. "But I understand why you would be confused. Jesus was telling that story to wake up a sleeping disciple—in more ways than one."

"You see, there are many reasons why God's faraway children don't come back home. One of the biggest is that they become complacent where they are."

"English, Jesna, speak English!" Pete protested.

"'Complacent' means self-satisfied—with no energy to change."

"That's English?"

"'Lazy,' Pete," Priscilla said. "They've gone to sleep in the pig pen and aren't even thinking about getting up and walking back home."

"Oh," Pete said. "They've started snoring like that sleeping disciple. Jesus is saying 'wake up and smell the pig manure!'"

"Well," Jesna said, "to put it just a little more delicately, Jesus is saying, 'Wake up and take hold of life in the kingdom with all of your energy, all of your wit.' That life is more important than your earthly life, so seize it! Hold on to it with at least the same energy that the street-wise manager held onto his plans for meal tickets."

"Exactly," said Pete. "That's what I said."

FAMILY DISCUSSION

1. Why do you suppose the Pilgrims were so surprised by the ending of Jesus' story? Were you surprised too?
2. What are some of the thoughts and efforts you put into holding onto your new life in God's kingdom? Name some choices you try to avoid.

SCENE 134
THE PHARISEES ARE PUT IN THEIR PLACE[88]

While Jesus hadn't been listening to Jesna's explanation of his crooked manager story, it quickly became obvious that they both were singing from the same hymnal.

"The story isn't about rewarding dishonesty," Jesus said. "It's about how much you should value and strive to hold on to the real life—life in my Father's kingdom—that is being offered to you. Don't be complacent."

"There's that delightful word again!" Pete sang.

"This is life and death—and don't be content with anything less than abundant life and total victory over death. But as you enjoy that life—here and now—you'll begin to respond in ways that are the exact opposite to how the crooked manager acted. Because ...

"If you're honest in small things,
    you'll be honest in big things;
If you're a crook in small things,
    you'll be a crook in big things.
If you're not honest in small jobs,
    who will put you in charge of the store?
No worker can serve two bosses:
    He'll either hate the first and love the second
Or adore the first and despise the second.
    You can't serve both God and the Bank."[89]

Three oversized, black-robed Pharisees surged to their feet at the same time. Each dismissed Jesus with a downward wave of a hand, turned their backs to him, and began to march toward Jerusalem to the tune of a hundred coins jingling in their money-pouches.

"What upset *their* applecart?" Pete asked.

"The Pharisees, at least most of them, are pretty taken with money. They like to believe that you *can* serve both God and the bank," Jesna said as she kept her eyes focused on the unfolding drama.

Departing with only pursed lips was too little for one irate Pharisee. After about a dozen dirt-kicking steps he spun back around and faced Jesus like a gunfighter in the old West.

"You're hopelessly out of touch with life in the *real* world, you would-be king," he fired. Then, holding up his bulging pouch of coins. "You can't build temples without these. Hmmpht! You can't even eat without them."

Then, as he surveyed the crowd for sympathetic eyes, he continued his speech. "You *can* serve God and the bank. I keep his laws—to perfection. And," he said while purposefully shaking his coin purse, "I don't have to sleep out under the stars with a band of bums."

Jesus' face was creased with sad lines as he slowly raised his invisible gun from its holster and reluctantly pulled the trigger: "You are masters at making yourselves look good in front of others, but God knows what's behind the appearance.[90] And he knows that what is glorified among those who belong to this world is an abomination in God's eyes. My Father," Jesus continued, "wants you to find the *real* gold—the treasure that is buried in your heart, not in your pocket. Then you'll know the truth—that wherever you sleep is in the arms of God; and whatever you eat is manna from his table."

Jesus fired no more verbal shots. But the three Pharisees were mortally wounded. Only the Great Physician would be able to bring them back to life. It was enough to make a grown dog cry.

FAMILY DISCUSSION

1. What are some things which the world exalts as being very important?
2. How valuable do you suppose those things are in the kingdom of heaven?
3. Describe the price-tags and the time-tags that you yourself have placed on those items.

SCENE 135
THE RICH MAN AND LAZARUS[91]

As the departing Pharisees stormed off toward Jerusalem, Jesus returned his attention to the bewildered crowd. He told them a story about a rich man and a poor man.

"Once there was a very rich man," Jesus began. "He wore only brightly-colored clothes made from the finest and softest fabrics. He ate as if every day were a feast day."

"Ummmm," Pete said. "Maybe we'll get to stay at his house tonight."

"The rich man," Jesus continued, "took a walk each day so others could see his expensive clothes. Each day, as he passed through the gate to his huge estate, he would hear the faint voice of a poor, sore-covered man named Lazarus. Lazarus would call out to him, 'Master. May I have some of your table scraps? It would be a banquet for me.'

"But the rich man would turn his head away from the pleas of his dying neighbor. The only comfort Lazarus got was from the stray dogs that licked his wounds."

Yuck! I thought. *That's enough to make a self-respecting dog spit. And I know I can't even get a good pucker like Pete uses.*

"Eventually the poor man died and was carried by angels to sit in Abraham's lap. The rich man also died, but he went in a different direction. His trip was to the parching pains of hell. One day he looked up from torment and saw Lazarus sitting in the lap of Abraham. He cried out.

'Father Abraham, mercy! Have mercy! Send Lazarus to dip his finger in water to cool my tongue. I'm in agony in this fire.'[92]

"He's still acting like he's better than Lazarus," Pete said. "Like he can boss him around."

"But Abraham answered back,

'Child, remember that in your lifetime you got the good things and Lazarus the bad things. It's not like that here. Here he's consoled and you're tormented. Besides, in all these matters there is a huge chasm set between us so that no one can go from us to you even if he wanted to, nor can anyone cross over from you to us.'[93]

"To this the rich man said, 'then I beg you, father, to send my friend Lazarus to my father's house so that he can warn my brothers—so they will not follow my path to this place of torment.'

"Abraham answered him and said, 'They have Moses and the prophets; let them hear them.'

"'No, father Abraham, that has not worked for them. It will only be if someone goes to them from the dead that they will repent.'"

Jesus' voice cracked with sadness as he said that last sentence. He let a silence grow—as he gazed in the direction of the now-empty horizon. Then he concluded the story.

"And Abraham answered him this way, 'If they won't listen to Moses and the Prophets, they're not going to be convinced by someone who rises from the dead.'"[94]

"Wow," Priscilla whispered. "Jesus is saying that some people have things so messed up that they wouldn't even change the way they act if someone came back from the dead to talk to them. I wonder if he.... "

"Yes, Priscilla," Jesna interrupted, "he probably is thinking about those Pharisees and what his own future holds."

"It must feel pretty futile to him sometimes," Mrs. Pilgrim said as she studied Jesus' sad face.

"Hey!" Pete said. "Do you think people really *fry* in hell?"

"Pete!" Mrs. Pilgrim gasped. "That's a terrible thing to say!"

"Thanks, Mom. But what do you think? Will there be snapping, crackling, and popping down there?"

Mrs. Pilgrim was reeling with shock. Jesna stepped in before Pete got on a roll.

"Pete, the Bible has much more to say about the inheritance God has prepared for his beloved children than it does about the place where those who stubbornly reject him end up. But from what Jesus has just said, you can be certain that it's a place where you wouldn't even want your worst enemy to visit, even for a second."

"I don't know, Jesna. This kid in my class is so mean … "

Mrs. Pilgrim staggered backward.

"Pete," Jesna pressed on, "people in hell have gone so far into their own selfishness that they've created a chasm between themselves and God—a chasm so deep and wide that they can no longer get back across it to be with him."

"Wait a minute, Jesna. Do you mean that a person in hell can't be with Jesus anymore?"

"That's right, Pete."

"Why didn't you say so! I would never have said something so awful in front of my Mama. I wouldn't even say that in front of that mean kid."

FAMILY DISCUSSION

1. What do you think the rich man was thinking when he would pass by Lazarus sitting at his gate?
2. What do you think he was thinking when he later saw Lazarus sitting in Abraham's lap?
3. Does it scare you to talk about hell? What scares you about it?

SCENE 136
THE CLEANSING OF THE TEN LEPERS[95]

One morning, before a crowd had begun to gather around, but after Jesus' morning chat with his Father, we sat watching Jesus enjoy a breakfast of day-old bread and dried fruit with his disciples. He hadn't been able to get back to his home base for fresh supplies the night before.

"I'll never understand." Mr. Pilgrim mused.

"Me neither, Dad."

"What will you never understand, Mr. Pilgrim?" Jesna asked.

"Oh," Mr. Pilgrim said with a start. "I didn't know I was putting my thoughts into words."

"Happens to me all the time, Dad." Pete consoled.

"Look at Jesus there, laughing, talking, enjoying the simple pleasures of eating and being with friends. I mean, he's the Creator of the entire universe. He knows more about DNA mapping than a $1,000-an-hour defense lawyer. He knows exactly what all the chemicals and electrons are doing in your brain when you are thinking.... "

"And if the Cubs will ever win a World Series; and the street address for Santa Claus." Pete chimed in. It was obvious he liked the game.

"So, as I was saying, how can he take all this time to just sit around with a bunch of men who can't even fathom a ball-point pen, and enjoy their company? It's like the world's smartest man spending thirty-three years with a handful of four-year-olds."

"Four-year-olds can be a handful, Dad."

"But if it were the smart person's very own four-year-old children, Mr. Pilgrim," Jesna inserted, "don't you think he would rather spend time playing and laughing with them than … "

" … talking about smart stuff." Pete butted in, trying to be helpful.

"You see, Mr. Pilgrim. God doesn't need our intelligence. He invented our brains. He doesn't need our money. He could turn stones to gold nuggets if he ever needs to buy something. And he doesn't need our strength … "

"'Cause he could lift a horse, huh, Jesna?"

"That's right, Pete."

"But could he make a horse so big that he couldn't lift it? That's what I want to know. … *Ouch*, Priscilla! You could stab somebody to death with those elbows. Put 'em in a holster!"

"You're getting Jesna off track. Shhhh!"

"As I was saying. God doesn't need the things most people scurry around trying to give him—like the Pharisees trying to give him perfection. What he does need and what he can't provide for himself is the fellowship, love, and laughter of his children."

"Right, Dad. Do you think the smartest person in the world would rather write a smart book that nobody else but him could understand, or play on the swing set with his fun kids?"

"I see your point, uh, both of your points."

At about that time Jesna's meaning was coming into focus, so were ten ghastly creatures who had just interrupted Jesus, his friends, and my appetite. Deformed, walking with the help of sticks, some blind—they were closing in on us.

"Eeeeeh!" Priscilla cried out. "Who are they?"

"You mean 'What are they?'" Pete corrected.

I growled through my whiskers.

The walking dead men stopped short of where Jesus and his disciples sat. Well, actually, only Jesus was still sitting. The others had already retreated several paces and looked as if they were waiting for someone to fire a starters' gun.

The group of ten spoke as one. "We won't come any closer. We're lepers who live outside of the village."

"And they're off," Pete teased, looking at poised-to-gallop disciples.

"Please. We know who you are. Jesus, Master, have mercy on us!"

Jesus stood to his feet and studied the men with moist eyes as he took a few steps in their direction. They inched backward.

"Go and show yourselves to the priests," he said.

At that, the ten turned on their heels and sped away. It didn't take the pack long to stop limping and break into a sprint.

With a small smile, Jesus watched them go, then turned and faced his team of would-be track stars. "Their skin will be as whole as yours before they reach the village."

In a few moments, out in the distance, I could see one of the ten drop back from the pack. He turned around and began to establish a world record in the half-mile run as he raced back to Jesus.

As he approached, it became plain for all to see that he was a new man. No longer was he caked with the sores and dead white skin of leprosy. The disciples gasped. I guess you never grow accustomed to miracles, even when they are a daily occurrence.

The former leper approached his finish line and threw himself at Jesus' feet. With a jumble of words and gushing tears, he couldn't seem to thank Jesus enough.

"He's a Samaritan!" one of the disciples shout-whispered.

Jesus finally broke the man's soliloquy of praise and said,

"Were not ten healed? Where are the nine?" [Then facing the disciples.] "Can none be found to come back and give glory to God except this outsider?" Then he said to him, "Get up. On your way. Your faith has healed and saved you."[96]

The man rose to his feet, received a pat on both shoulders from Jesus, and walked away.

"I guess you're right," Mr. Pilgrim said to Jesna as he studied Jesus' smiling face. "Nothing in the universe compares with doing something nice for one of your kids—unless it's seeing them smile back at you and say 'thanks.'"

FAMILY DISCUSSION

1. Why did Jesus tell the lepers to show themselves to the priests? (Hint: look in the Old Testament laws for your answer.)
2. Tell everyone the nicest thing you can remember Jesus doing for you. If you forgot to say "thanks," this would be a good time to do it.

SCENE 137
ON THE COMING KINGDOM[97]

Later that day Jesus had assumed his familiar teaching posture—sitting on the ground and telling stories directly to each person in his audience. It was as if each listener were his only child and he was telling one final bedtime story before lights-out.

Not too many stories had been told that afternoon, however, when some of the "children" became unruly. It was no surprise that the troublemakers were those too-perfect-to-be-true Pharisees.

"I've been meaning to ask you for a few Bible-years, Jesna, why do the Pharisees have snakes wrapped around their heads and down their arms."

Jesna giggled. "Those aren't snakes, Pete." Then, giggling even harder, "The only snakes they have are in their heads."

"Oh. Huh?"

"What you see there is called a *tefillin*, or some in the Greek communities call them *phylacteries*."

"I call them snakes."

"*Phylacteries*, Pete, are little cases, or pouches, made from the skin of certain animals (ritually clean ones, of course). Each of the pouches contains four passages of Scripture taken from Exodus and Deuteronomy. There's a leather strap that connects the pouches and runs down from the forehead and wraps around the left arm. That's what you mistake for a snake."

"Yeah, but why do they wear them?"

"The Scriptures in the two pouches, Pete, contain God's commandments to love him and to fear him. They're worn on the forehead and arm in hopes that they'll sink into a person's thoughts and influence his actions."

"Oh," Pete said. "And why do they almost always have a beach towel over their heads?"

"That's called a *tallith*."

"We call them 'beach blankets' now. Don't we?"

"No. If you saw one today—they're still worn by Jews during morning prayers—it would be called the same thing, a *tallith*—it's a tasseled prayer shawl."

"Oh! Those things hanging from the bottom are *tassels*. I thought they were just old cow tails."

"Nope, Pete. Tassels, not tails."

"Well, why do some of them have longer cow tassels than others?"

"Well, Pete," Jesna continued patiently, "some Pharisees probably wear longer ones to attract attention to themselves. Probably for the same reason they wear their prayer shawls even out here, away from the Temple."

"Yeah, little brother, probably for the same reason you keep your shooting hand over your head for five minutes when a basketball you throw actually goes in through the hoop."

"Oh." Pete said, slowly nodding his head. "But I do have one last question."

"Shoot," Jesna said with a cute laugh.

"Why are they always wearing those black uniforms—under their tail-iths?"

"Pharisees don't always wear black uniforms—or any uniform for that matter. Being a Pharisee is like being a member of a political party. It doesn't affect what you wear."

"Except for the shawls and leather snakes?"

"Right, Pete, except for those things. The rest of what they wear is determined by taste and the amount of money they can afford to spend on clothes."

"But the Pharisees we have seen have always been wearing black." Priscilla inserted.

"Yeah," said Pete. "Have we only been seeing the undertaker-Pharisees?"

"You two are just too sharp," Jesna said. Then she went on to explain. "There are a couple of things done on this ride to help you understand the big picture. First, as we've discussed earlier, you are able to hear the people speak in English instead of their own languages. And secondly, you see the Pharisees dressed in black—to make sure you don't miss the night-and-day contrasts between them and Jesus."

"My goodness!" Priscilla exclaimed as she quickly glanced around. "Is there anything else that's been colorized?"

"That's black-and-whitized, sis."

"Nope," Jesna said, still giggling. "Those are the only two modifications. Otherwise you're seeing, hearing, smelling, and feeling just what everyone else did back then."

"You mean 'back now.' Don't you, Jesna?"

Jesna didn't have time to answer. This small group of "children" was being very loud about not being able to see "the kingdom of God" in black and white.

"If you're so smart, Teacher, then tell us the exact day and hour that the 'kingdom' will arrive."

"Yeah," echoed two others. "Tell us that, then let us see its arrival—with our own eyes—and we might believe all your stories."

Jesus stood to his feet. The band of Pharisees took a step backward. But even a dog could see from Jesus' expression that he meant them health and not harm. He spoke with firm kindness.

"The kingdom of God doesn't come by counting the days

on the calendar. Nor when someone says, 'Look here!' or, 'There it is!' And why? Because God's kingdom is already among you."[98]

The Pharisees must not have liked what they heard. They spun in a cloud of dust and billowed garments and stomped their way back home in a huff.

"Hum," Pete mused. "I guess Jesus is talking in rainbows and they can only see black and white."

FAMILY DISCUSSION
1. What do you think Jesus meant by saying, "God's kingdom is already among you"? Is it still among us today?
2. Do you think that people today still have a tendency to act like the Pharisees? How does it look?

SCENE 138
THE DAY OF THE SON OF MAN[99]

Mr. Pilgrim's face was furrowed with confusion. "What does Jesus mean, 'God's kingdom is already among you'?" he asked.

"Yeah, Dad, I'm having a little trouble with that one too. It's not like there are any knights, or dragons, or any fun kingdom-stuff like that running around here."

"I know you've tried to explain it to us before, Jesna, but I still don't get it, and it seems like it's the main thing that Jesus is trying to get people to understand."

"Well, Mr. Pilgrim, you're right. It *is* the main thing and the main theme. But don't feel badly about not seeing it clearly. It's pretty rare when someone does get it in bright focus."

"Why is it so hard for people to get it, Jesna?" Pete said. "Why would something so important only be computable to the Spocks?" He pointed at Priscilla with his head.

"The problem isn't that people aren't smart enough," Jesna said. "The *problems* are, number one, it's so simple that people often look right past it, and, the really big problem is what it requires of a person to live there."

"You forgot to say, 'number two,'" Pete inserted.

"What does it require, Jesna?" Mr. Pilgrim asked.

"Everything," Jesna answered. "It requires that you give up *everything*."

"My baseball cards?" Pete gasped.

"Not baseball cards. More, much more."

"My Cocoa Puffs?" he squeaked.

"Your *life*. Being a citizen of the kingdom means giving up your life as you've lived it before deciding to follow Jesus and live in his realm.

"The kingdom," Jesna continued after a quiet moment, "is simply the place—any place—where the rules of the King (God) are the rules that his subjects live by. That's it, just that easy. But it isn't easy. Humans are generally only able to do it for brief moments at a time—before straying down the well-worn paths of their fore-parents (Adam and Eve in the Garden, Abraham's descendants in the Promised Land, and modern-day Christians on padded pews)."

"It's like you said before, Jesna," Mrs. Pilgrim said, "We must not only say, 'Your kingdom come,' but also 'my kingdom go.'"

"Yes, Mrs. Pilgrim. That's exactly what Jesus is looking for. That's the hard part. Saying and meaning 'your kingdom come,' a few thousand times each day."

"And that gets a person into the kingdom?" Mr. Pilgrim asked.

"No."

"No?"

"No. That gets a person doing all that they can do. All the rest, the other 99.9 percent, is up to God. But, it's easy for him."

"Sounds like it's about as easy as being willing to take a bullet in the head and then gettin' raised from the dead," Pete said.

"Oh, you are exactly right, Pete," Jesna responded. "Listen to how Jesus says it. He's finishing his talk."

"Remember what happened to Lot's wife! If you grasp and cling to life on your terms, you'll lose it, but if you let that life go, you'll get life on God's terms."[100]

FAMILY DISCUSSION

1. How would you tell a friend what is necessary to live in God's kingdom?
2. As a family discuss what "your kingdom come—my kingdom go" means for each of you.

SCENE 139
THE PERSISTENT WIDOW[101]

After the departure of the disruptive Pharisees, the scene quieted down. The sun was low in the sky. Jesus changed topics. He began to talk about another of his favorite subjects—communicating with his Father.

"I want to tell you a story about how it's important to pray consistently and persistently. I want to tell you about a widow and an unjust judge."

As a warm breeze blew across his words they made a movie inside the heads of his listeners. The film was about a cold-hearted judge in a faraway city who cared nothing for God and even less for the people who came to courtroom.

The star of this cinema, however, was a persistent widow who kept after the heartless judge. Again and again she told him that her rights had been violated. She persistently called out to him for fair and just protection.

At first the judge paid her less attention than he would give to a self-petting cat. He brushed her away. But her pleas would not be so easily shooed away. She was as persistent as a pit bull.

After a while, even though this judge still cared nothing for God, man, or widows, he gave in to her requests. "I had better do something to see that she gets justice or I will never have any peace."

At that point in his movie-making Jesus stopped the projector and let everyone's screen go blank. He let the audience sit in their darkness for a few seconds before telling them more.

"Do you hear what that judge, corrupt as he is, is saying? So what makes you think God won't step in and help? Won't he stick up for them? I assure you, he will. He will not drag his feet. But how much of that kind of persistent faith will the Son of Man find on the earth when he returns?"[102]

The crowd was silent. But not Pete.

"What is Jesus saying? Is God like that mean judge? Does he only answer our prayers because we make pests of ourselves?"

"Oh, no, persistent Pete. That story wasn't about the judge. It was about the widow and how we should not give up when we are praying to God."

"Yes," Mr. Pilgrim said. "I've always thought it's a comforting story. If a hard-hearted judge eventually gives in and does what is right, how much more will a loving Father be affected by our persistent prayers?"

"So if I ask long enough and hard enough, I'll get anything I want?" Pete said with the grin of a bandit.

"I don't think so, son. Remember that the widow was asking for justice and protection, not for video games and candy bars."

"That's right, Mr. Pilgrim. That's another difference between a heartless judge and a loving Father. A loving father knows that good grades and healthy teeth are important and his love might make him say no or wait a long time to answer some of our requests."

Only Pete seemed a little disappointed with Jesna's interpretation.

FAMILY DISCUSSION

1. Is there something inside yourself—deep down in your character—that you feel needs to be touched and changed by God? Be as persistent as the widow in praying for this change for the next couple of weeks and see what happens. Don't forget to report the results to someone.

SCENE 140
THE PHARISEE AND
THE IRS AGENT[103]

The sun completed its downward slide into the grassy hills west of Jerusalem, painting fiery colors across a dark purple canvas before turning out its light for the evening. Jesus and the disciples spent that feast-night under a star-spangled ceiling.

The next morning Jesus was back on his impromptu seminar circuit. An early crowd of listeners was seated all around. He hadn't been speaking long before one of the Pharisees stood to his feet.

"Why's *he* standing up?" Pete asked. "Even when he's sitting, everyone can see that he's the south end of a northbound donkey."

"Pete!" Mrs. Pilgrim exclaimed. "When did you start using language like that?"

"Oh Mom, I've been knowing my directions for a long time."

"That's not what I meant."

"Let's listen," Mr. Pilgrim said.

"I heard about the story you told—the one about the unjust judge and the persistent widow." The sneer on the Pharisee's face let the cat out of the bag—a compliment was not forthcoming.

Things always change for the worst when cats escape, I mused.

"And I just thought you'd like to know that there are none more persistent and consistent with their prayers than we Pharisees. I don't like to brag, you know, but I also think you would be hard-pressed to find another Pharisee that prays more faithfully than I myself." This brought a chorus of grunts from his religious friends.

"So," he continued as he raised both hands in a theatrical gesture, "I just wanted to thank you for the compliment. Maybe others will be encouraged by your story to be more like me."

"Oh," Jesus said. "I'm afraid you misunderstood. That particular story was for folks in another situation: those who lack discipline in their prayer life."

The wind was failing in the Pharisee's self-righteous sails as he responded to Jesus. "But surely you are aware of the disciplined manner in which we Pharisees pray."

"Indeed I am," Jesus answered. "That's why the story was not for your benefit. You don't need to be reminded to have discipline. You need to be reminded to have a heart. I have another story that might hit closer to where you live. It goes like this.

"One day there were two men who went to the temple to pray. One was a Pharisee and the other a tax collector."

The Pharisee in the audience put his thumbs under his armpits and puffed out his chest with satisfaction.

"I don't think he knows how this story ends," Jesna whispered.

"The Pharisee," Jesus continued, "struck a prayer posture and prayed something like this: (Jesus tucked his head in toward his chest and lowered his voice at least one octave as he continued.) 'Oh Gawd, I just want to offer you thanks that I am not like other men—crooks, adulterers, and (may you forever forbid) like that tax collector over there. For you know, Oh Gawd, that I fast two times each week, I give tithes of everything that passes through my hands.'

"Meantime, the tax collector was sitting on the back row and staring at the floor. He was ashamed to lift his head toward heaven, and beat his chest like a sad bass drum. 'God, please show mercy to me, a poor sinner!'"

Then, still staring at the ground, Jesus said in his normal voice:

"This tax man, not the other, went home made right with God. If you walk around with your nose in the air, you're going to end up flat on your face, but if you're content to be simply yourself, you will become more than yourself."[104]

Jesus slowly raised his head from his chest as the boastful Pharisee slowly lowered his nose from the air. Somewhere in the middle, their eyes met. But it wasn't enough to stop the Pharisee from turning and leaving with his companions.

FAMILY DISCUSSION
1. Why do you suppose God liked the tax man's prayer more than the one offered by the Pharisee?
2. If right now you were going to pray like the tax man, how would your prayer go?

SCENE 141
BACK INSIDE THE CITY[105]

The daily departures of disgruntled Pharisees were not without consequence. Messages began filtering back from inside the walls of Jerusalem about the cauldron of anger that was brewing there. Many in the Holy City wanted to see Jesus put to death.

As strange as this may sound, most of Jesus' disciples were anxious for Jesus to go back to Jerusalem. They reasoned that if important people in the city saw and heard Jesus for themselves, they would know that he was not a threat and that his ministry was legitimate. Besides, the Feast of Tabernacles was drawing to a close.

But Jesus did not agree. He told them that his "time" had not yet come. I'm not sure the disciples or the Pharisees knew what he meant. We Pilgrims didn't. Jesus sent the disciples on ahead so that he could be alone to pray.

"He's really got some important praying to do," Jesna said. "He's trying to make sure that his deepest will is the same as the will of his Father. That's the best way to courage and joy, you know, to will the will of your heavenly Father."

After a long time of prayer Jesus found the brave joy that comes only when our wills are perfectly aligned to God's. As soon as he found it we all were able to see it. It slowly spread across his face like a mirror-smooth lake of serenity.

Within moments he was on his way to join his disciples in Jerusalem for the last celebration of the Feast of Tabernacles.

When he arrived, the gala was just past half-time. He walked the narrow stone streets with soft, quiet steps. He wore a shawl pulled far down over his head, hiding his face. We drove along behind in our car. No one was making a sound. Even Pete's stomach was respectfully quiet.

But we heard plenty. Pharisees were stationed throughout the crowded city like secret service agents. They were scanning the throngs looking for the face of Jesus. "Where can he be?" I heard more than one lookout whisper as Jesus continued his march. We knew where he was, and from our knowledge of Jerusalem's geography, we knew exactly where he was headed. He walked straight toward the focal point of the city, the huge Temple and its sprawling courtyard.

As we passed through packed streets it seemed as if every other person was talking about Jesus. "I've heard him teach. He's a good man," some were saying. "No!" others countered. "He's leading the people astray."

Jesus, unfazed by his mixed reviews, continued on to the Temple. He crossed the courtyard and found an open spot in the shade of a high stone wall. Then he let his shawl slip down onto his shoulders. Within minutes of the unveiling, a small crowd had gathered to see this man they'd heard so much about. As he started his first story, the crowd grew to resemble a swarm of bees around a giant hive.

Many in the crowd had never heard Jesus teach—the occasion of the Feast of Tabernacles was only his third visit to the city since beginning his ministry. Their faces soon began to beam astonishment as words of life continued to pass through his lips. "How can any man know so much without being thoroughly trained?" one of the crowd blurted out. "He must be making this up."

Jesus said to the man,

"I didn't make this up. What I teach comes from the One who sent me. Anyone who wants to do his will can test this teaching and know whether it's from God or whether I'm making it up. A person making things up tries to make himself look good. But someone trying to honor the one who sent him sticks to the facts and doesn't tamper with reality."[106]

As Jesus was saying this, the back row of the crowd was becoming thick with black-robed security agents. It was plain to me that it was the security of God's only Son that was in jeopardy.

FAMILY DISCUSSION

1. Why did Jesus hide himself until he reached the Temple?
2. Have you ever experienced the courage and the joy of knowing that you were in the center of God's will? Tell someone about that time and about your feelings.

SCENE 142
MORE TEACHING IN THE TEMPLE[107]

"Uh oh!" Jesna warned. "I think Jesus is filling up with courage right now."

"Yep!" Pete chimed in. "From the looks of those veins on the side of his head, I'd say he's about to blow. Ten, nine, eight … "

"Speaking of not making things up," Jesus began slowly, like a small earthquake clearing its throat, "Moses got the Law directly from God. But no one here in this Temple is living it. No one! So why are some of you calling for my death? I'm simply suggesting that you transfer the Law from stone tablets to the flesh of your hearts."

"You've got demons flapping around in the space between your ears!" someone from the crowd shouted. "There's no one here trying to kill you."

"I'm afraid you're wrong about that," Jesus said as he lifted his eyes for some silent communication with the black-robed security guards on the back row. "I did a miraculous deed a few months ago. I made a man's whole body well on the Sabbath, and because of it many still have anger for me that burns white-hot. You say I have profaned the Sabbath. Yet, if the eighth day after the birth of a male child falls on a Sabbath, you circumcise the baby so that Moses' Law won't be broken. Come on now ...

"Don't be nitpickers; use your head—and heart!—to discern what is right, to test what is authentically right."[108]

"Hey!" someone from the crowd yelled. "Quit talking as if you were the Messiah or something. We are learned people here in Jerusalem. We know that the Messiah will come out of nowhere. No one will know where he is from. Many here know that you are a carpenter from a village up north. (What's the name of that one-camel town? Nazareth?) By obvious logic you are an imposter!"

The back row was nodding a pleased smile. But close to Jesus the tremors of an about-to-be, full-grown earthquake was felt by all with discerning feet.

Jesus exploded in a loud voice,

"Yes, you think you know me and where I'm from, but that's not where I'm from. I didn't set myself up in business. My true origin is in the One who sent me, and you don't know him at all. I come from him—that's how I know him. He sent me here."[109]

"Wow!" Pete exclaimed. "That earthquake was probably a 'ten' on the Richter scale."

"I believe you mean the righteousness scale, Pete," Jesna corrected.

Whatever the rating, it began to split the crowd down the middle. Half were saying things like, "When the Messiah comes will we expect more from him than what this man has already done?", and "Perhaps this is the one we have been waiting for."

The Pharisees were, of course, on the other side. They were in shock, er, *aftershock*, motioning wildly to each other. Some were pointing in the direction of a large stone structure that shared a wall with the Temple. Others went off running in that direction.

Within minutes the departed Pharisees boomeranged back to the crowd. In their company were a few older men with long flowing white beards and longer flowing white robes. Their heads were capped with puffy white hats.

"Look!" Pete exclaimed. "That stone room must be where the Pillsbury Doughboy lives. I bet one of those men is his grandfather."

"No, Pete," Jesna said with a very sober expression on her little face. "Those men in white are from the Sanhedrin, and the big brutes running along behind are their police. I'm afraid Jesus' tremors were felt inside that big protective stone shelter."

The band of black, white, and brute marched right through the middle of the crowd as if they owned the Temple courtyard. The crowd parted before the wedge that was being driven into the fissure Jesus' words had begun.

"You're under arrest!" one of the Pharisees thundered as he thrust his quivering face just a few inches from the courageous one Jesus was still wearing.

Jesus gazed calmly at the assembled brute force arrayed against him. His courage was impressive; it melted their hostility. A few seconds passed in tense silence before Jesus said, "I don't think I'll let you arrest me today. You see,

"I am with you only a short time. Then I go on to the One who sent me. You will look for me, but you won't find me. Where I am, you can't come."[110]

Jesus finished the last word and just walked through the crowd in the same way he had exited through the midst of the lynch mob up in Nazareth a couple of Bible-years ago.

Even a seasoned tour guide like Jesna couldn't help showing her amazement. "Only when your will is one with the Father's," she whispered. "Only then."

FAMILY DISCUSSION
1. What would you have been feeling if you had been in Jesus' sandals, staring at the police who had come to arrest you?
2. Why do you think the Sanhedrin became involved in opposing Jesus?
3. What would you have been thinking and feeling if you had been in the crowd witnessing this scene?

SCENE 143
THE PEOPLE DIVIDED OVER JESUS[111]

For the next couple of days, Jesus' parting words were the talk of the feast. "What could he have possibly meant, 'You will look for me, but you won't find me,' and 'Where I am you can't come'?" a multitude was asking.

"I don't know what will give the Sanhedrin the most grief," Jesna said, "trying to solve that riddle or the peoples' interest in Jesus." Jesna's face was troubled.

Not long after Jesus' departure from the Temple courtyard, Jesna asked if we would like to go inside the "hall of hewn stones" where the Sanhedrin held their meetings, to hear their debate. Pete was all for it. But I think he was still expecting it to be a tasting-tour at the Pillsbury plant.

We drove over the few hundred yards of flat stone that separated us from their meeting place. Then we drove right through its square, rock walls! Even so, Pete seemed very disappointed when the room we entered was empty of any hint of pastries. "Hey," he exclaimed, "where's the giant kitchen where all these doughmen do their cooking?"

"The only thing they'll be cooking for the next few days is Jesus' goose," Jesna replied. How right she was!

The large room they had entered had high earth-tone walls. It was sparsely decorated with beautifully carved wooden benches and cloth-covered chairs. Deep brown lattice work trimmed the top half of the doorways. The collection of benches and chairs framed all four walls but were placed only two rows deep. A lineup of oversized chairs caught our attention. Judging from the number of questions directed to the occupants of those particular chairs, it appeared that those seats were reserved for the leaders of the Sanhedrin.

Pete had been very patient, but finally gave in to ask the obvious question. "Hey, Jesna. What the heck is a Sanhedrin?"

"Thank you for asking," Mr. Pilgrim sighed.

"The Sanhedrin is like your Supreme Court, Congress, and President all rolled into one. It's an aristocratic council of seventy elders, and a president (they call him 'prince'), that is presided over by the hereditary high priest."

"Oh, thanks. That's clear as mud, Jesna," Pete said, scratching his head. "So then, what's 'aristocratic,' 'council,' 'presided,' and 'hereditary high priest'?"

"'Aristocrat' means upper-class, usually people who inherit wealth and position. A 'council' is a group of people who meet together to discuss things. 'Preside' means to be in charge of. And 'hereditary high priest' means the title has been inherited from the tribe of Levi—Joseph's brother—whose descendants acted as priests for the Israelites. Does that help?"

"If the Sanhedrin is a bunch of rich dudes that get together to tell people what to do, and those guys over there in the good seats, are in charge, and everybody here calls their great-great-great-grandfather the same name that's on the back of my jeans, then I got you."

"Uh … OK, Pete. But there are a few more things."

"Psst," Priscilla whispered. "You might want to stay away from any words with more than one syllable."

"Hey," Pete shot back. "I couldn't hear all of that but I resemble anything she said, Jesna."

"Well, in any case," Jesna continued. "The Sanhedrin is a very, very powerful group. It's the final court of appeal, for any questions connected to the laws of Moses."

"That's the Ten Commandments, huh?" Pete proclaimed.

"Those ten and a few hundred more," Jesna said. "And, because this area of the Roman world is relatively unimportant to the empire, the Sanhedrin pretty much governs this area, even in nonreligious matters. Except for collecting the tax, it's rare for Rome to step into the affairs of the people.

"But," Jesna continued on, "after the death of Herod the Great, the authority of the Sanhedrin in civil matters began to shrink."

"Was there a civil war or anything like that, Jesna?"

"No, Priscilla. By 'civil' I mean non-religious matters. I'm saying that during Jesus' lifetime the Sanhedrin's civil power was limited to the region of Judea."

"Is that another reason why Jesus spends most of his time in Galilee?" Priscilla asked again.

"Probably so. It is also why very soon Jesus will be leaving Judea again."

"Is the Sanhedrin lesson almost over?" Pete moaned.

"Almost," Jesna said before continuing. "The members of the Sanhedrin are drawn from three classes: acting high priests (from the tribe of Levi), scribes (many of whom are Pharisees), and elders (tribal and family heads).

"One of the main jobs of the Sanhedrin," Jesna went on as Pete's mouth gaped in a yawn, "is to decid if prophets are really prophets and to rule on charges of blasphemy."

Jesna glanced at Pete who nodded that he did not need a definition of the big word.

"Until just before this time, the Sanhedrin had the right to put someone to death, even without Rome's permission. They can still pronounce that sentence, but they have to get Rome's permission, and Rome's soldiers have to actually carry out the execution."

"You mean the Sanhedrin was crucifying people in Jesus' lifetime?" Pete asked.

"No, Pete. When they were in charge, just a few Bible-years ago, they used stoning as the means of execution."

"Wow," Pete exclaimed for all. "I didn't know how close our church came to not having a cross in it."

Mrs. Pilgrim was looking at her son as if she weren't sure if he were a blasphemer or a thoughtful saint.

Speaking as an objective dog-observer, I've noticed he often has that effect on people.

We spent the next three days listening to the debates that raged in Judea's supreme court. A ruling was finally reached and the politically powerful Sanhedrin sent out its physically imposing police to bring Jesus in for a trial.

An hour passed slowly to the drumming of 568 fingers

before the police squad reported back—empty-handed.

The indignant "prince" of the Sanhedrin asked why they had not brought Jesus with them, and one of the policemen answered, sheepishly, "Have you heard the way he talks? We've never heard anyone speak like this man?"[112]

"What could any man say that would make you risk yourself before us?"

"W-w-well," the man stammered. "Just as I was about to grab him by the wrists, he looked at me, right in the face, as if he were about to hug me, and he said,

"If anyone thirsts, let him come to me and drink. Rivers of living water will brim and spill out of the depths of anyone who believes in me this way, just as the Scripture says."[113]

"Have you lost your mind?" one of the black-robed members of the Sanhedrin spoke out. "Are you as dense as the boneheads who swallow his tripe?"

"Peetuee," Pete spat. "I know what *that* word means. My grandmother ruined the paint in her house by cooking some tripe in her kitchen. That stuff smells just like . . .ouch!"

"You don't see anybody in this room believing him, do you?" the Sanhedrin prince spat. "The only thing that's going to be spilling out of you is your blood—in a river of death!"

"I have something to say," came a voice from a shadowy back row.

"Hey!" Pete exclaimed. "Look who that is! He hasn't said anything this whole time. That's Nicodemus. You know. The man who talked to Jesus by the campfire that night, who almost became a disciple."

Nicodemus said, "Does the law judge a man without first giving him a hearing, learning from him what he believes and does?"

"Are you on his side?" someone shouted. "Are you as slow-witted as that officer there?" another said, gesturing toward the hapless policeman.

Nicodemus sank back into the shadows.

"I guess he hasn't got that courage thing down yet, huh Jesna?" Pete whispered.

"No prophet ever comes from Galilee!" a man shouted from his padded seat of honor. "And that's final."

The meeting broke up after that. But not before Pete had given the final nay-sayer a hologram-kick to the shin, a free diagnosis, and a word of warning. "You're so closed-minded you've suffocated your brain. If your brain was still breathing you'd realize that you just don't mess with your Maker."

Then looking at the frightened policeman, he said, "See. That's how you have to talk to these folks."

FAMILY DISCUSSION

1. Why do you think the Sanhedrin was so concerned about Jesus and his teaching?
2. What would you have said if you had been in Nicodemus' shoes?
3. Which side do you suppose Nicodemus ends up on?

SCENE 144
THE WOMAN CAUGHT IN ADULTERY[114]

A darkness had settled upon Jerusalem like a funeral shroud dropped from heaven. The members of the Sanhedrin walked out into it, mumbling their disgruntlement.

"You know, you could just give up *pretending* to be God and turn your life over to the real One," Pete offered invisibly to one muttering scribe, but to no avail.

Jesus himself took a less-traveled road that evening. While the members of the Sanhedrin were returning to the comfort of their elegant homes, he crossed over the valley to spend the night praying and sleeping under the gnarled trees that gave the Mount of Olives its name. We tagged along, not wanting to miss one breath of his night.

"Jesus must think his life is like these trees sometimes," Priscilla said.

"What do you mean?" Jesna asked.

"Well, look at them, branches all knotted and gnarled, and heading off in all possible directions, close to the Holy City, but outside its walls and boundaries."

"That's pretty poetic, Priscilla," Jesna said.

"Yeah," Pete added, "especially for a computer-packing math-lover."

Jesna went on, ignoring Pete, "Maybe that is why he likes to pray in the middle of olive trees so much; he feels at home here. Besides, it's the olive trees' differences from other trees that make them so beautiful."

"And," Priscilla added, "they'll be around for thousands of years, too—just like his words."

Mrs. Pilgrim nodding appreciatively. Pete was scoping out the tree situation, trying to decide which one would be best for climbing.

The next day, just minutes after the sun woke up and stretched its rays across the sky, we were assembled at Jesus' heels, following him back down the winding path through the olive groves to the city of Jerusalem.

"But I thought the feast was over," Pete yawned. "Why would he want to go back there after all the food is gone?"

"The Feast of Tabernacles is over, Pete," Jesna replied, "but he's going back to the Temple anyway."

"Doesn't he know those Poppin' Fresh guys will be settin' a trap? They'll try to lynch him."

"He knows, Pete. That's precisely why he spent the night talking things over with his Dad."

"Oh."

It was a short walk. The Temple courtyard where Jesus was headed was within a Frisbee-toss of the Mount of Olives. Once Jesus arrived back in the yard of his Father's house, he was immediately surrounded by a small mob of eager listeners. He took a seat and began to teach them about his Dad's other homes—one in heaven and the other in the temple of their hearts.

But in less time than it takes for a Great Dane to eat a poodle-portion of dog food, Jesus' first early morning story was interrupted. Raising a cloud of dust, an unfriendly assemblage of black-robed Pharisees surged forward like a noisy flock of ravens tussling over a tasty morsel. In their midst was an almost-naked woman, her face apple-red with humiliation.

They paraded the woman through the middle of the crowd and spun her around to face the collection of her friends and neighbors.

"This woman!" the lead Pharisee announced in a ringmaster's voice, "this woman has been caught in the very act of adultery."

The woman dropped her head so low that the back of her head was visible even to me.

"Teacher," the Pharisee continued in a sarcastic voice, "*Teach* us! What are we to do here?"

"What's 'adultery'?" Pete asked anyone who would notice.

"Well, son," Mr. Pilgrim said, "Let's just say that she spent the night a whole lot differently than Jesus did."

"Huh?"

"Shhh. I'll tell you more when you're forty."

The Pharisee went on to answer his own question. "I'm sure that *you*, as a teacher of the law, realize that our father, Moses, gave us strict orders that we are to take sinners such as this one and stone them to death. Otherwise, this cancer will spread. What do you say? We'll let *you* make the call.... "

"Surely he knows this is a trap," Priscilla said.

"Of course he knows, Priscilla. One of them must have come up with this plan after last night's meeting. They're just fishing for an excuse to bring him to trial."

"I wonder which one of them caught her in the act of being an adult tree?" Pete mused while making clicking sounds with his mouth. "Must have kept him up all night."

Jesus said nothing. He just knelt down over a dirt patch in the stony courtyard right next to the condemned woman, and stared, downcast.

The Pharisees and half the crowd bent down to find their first stones.

Jesus, however, picked up a discarded stick and began to poke at the ground.

The half of the crowd already packing stones raised them over their heads and began to murmur as they waited for the outcome of the kangaroo court. The other half of the crowd was still looking for convenient rocks.

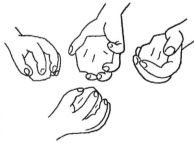

"What's he doing?" Pete exclaimed in a worried voice. Then he darted over to where Jesus knelt for a closer inspection. Also paying close attention to Jesus was the band of Pharisees.

"Hey, what's 'slander' mean?" Pete called back to his parents, as Jesus glanced up from his writing to make eye contact with one of the Pharisees.

Pete didn't wait for an answer. Jesus wasn't giving him time.

"And, what about 'ex-tor-tion'?" Pete asked as Jesus gave another Pharisee a knowing nod.

"My goodness!" Pete said. "He's writing a whole grocery list down here. There's 'pride, gluttony, drunkenness, self-love, lying, dishonesty, envy, anger, hatred, bribery, and lust.'" Pete slowly read, keeping pace with Jesus as he wrote and pronounced individual judgment with his piercing eyes.

When Jesus ran out of space, he slowly stood to his feet and said, "Here's your answer: Let the one among you who is without sin cast the first stone."

The crowd looked at the Pharisees with "all-right-let's-get-on-with-it!" glittering in their eyes. Some had cocked their arms in anticipation of flinging the second wave of rocks—after the sinless Pharisees had fired first.

Nothing happened. The silence extended until all that could be heard was the sound of rocks dropping from fists. One. Two. Three … then a whole hailstorm of them. Without comment, the Pharisees departed, followed by the rest of the vigilantes.

The only sound you could hear was teardrops falling on a stone. Not counting the Pilgrims, there were only two people left standing, and now, neither one was a sinner.

FAMILY DISCUSSION

1. Imagine that some people, who aren't your friends, find out about a secret sin of yours. Imagine that they bring you and the evidence of the sin before your friends. But in the midst of your embarrassment, you hear a voice from heaven that says, "You are forgiven. Go and sin no more." How do you suppose that would feel?

2. If you had been forgiven like the woman in the story, how do you suppose you would feel about sinning in that way ever again?

SCENE 145
THE LIGHT OF THE WORLD[115]

"What should I do now?" asked the young woman with grateful eyes.

"You should go wherever you want, but sin no more," Jesus replied.

As she gathered her scanty clothes tightly around herself, Pete asked, "So, adultery is a sin?"

"It certainly is, son!" both Pilgrim parents responded instantly.

"Is it the only one?"

"No, Petie," Mr. Pilgrim said. "Look over there. Every word Jesus wrote on the ground is the name of a different sin."

"That 'g' word there," Pete said, "'gluttony,' is that the sin we saw King Herod doing, back before he killed John the Baptist?"

"Yes, eating more than your body needs, to the point that you are harming yourself. That's a sin, son."

"I was afraid of that, Dad."

"Exactly how do we know if we are committing a sin?" Priscilla asked with a worried look on her face. "Because if I knew the exact criteria, maybe I could, say, write a program for my computer that would beep or something if I were to do a sin."

"I don't know if God has any exact criteria like that, Priscilla, except for his Ten Commandments, of course. But I'll be glad to tell you my favorite definition of 'sin,' if you like."

Priscilla nodded for Jesna to continue.

"Sin is when you are living your life on your own terms instead of on God's terms. And it always involves making someone or something a substitute for God—as a source of peace, comfort, or security."

"Well how do you know when you're *doing* that?" Priscilla queried.

"Two things can happen when you sin," Jesna explained. "First, your conscience usually 'beeps,' if you get too far away from life on God's terms and, just like with Adam and Eve, you will get embarrassed about being in God's presence—and run even further away from him. Sinners try to hide within themselves. Those who continue in sin retreat from God's light to live in their own darkness."

"Then what?" Priscilla asked.

"Well, duh, sis," Pete mocked. "I guess they get scared of the dark and go running back home. Wouldn't you?"

"That certainly is what God hopes will happen, Pete. And he does everything to grease the skids for their return trip to living life on his terms, in his kingdom."

"Does he ever send up a flare?" Pete asked. "I mean if you get a real, real, long way from home."

"Funny you should ask that, Pete. Jesus is about to send up

a flare right now ... well, in a few Bible-hours. Shall we take a half-day trip through Bible-time to catch up with him?"

Back in the car, Jesna pushed a sequence of buttons to make us travel a few hours in a few seconds. When the day came to a spinning stop, we were in the center of a large room.

"Whoa! What are those big ol' things?" Pete asked. "They look like trumpets a band of giants might play."

We looked in the direction of Pete's pointing finger and saw a collection of strange-shaped baskets against the wall. The baskets were narrow at the mouth and wide at the bottom. Pete was right; they did resemble enormous trumpets. A long line of people was filing by and dropping coins into the baskets.

"We're in the treasury of the Temple, Pete," Jesna said. "Those thirteen 'trumpets' are baskets for people to drop their offerings into. Each basket is for a different offering— trespass-offering, sin-offering, offerings of birds ... "

Priscilla gasped. "People put poor little birds in one of those baskets?"

Without forethought, Pete darted over and hurriedly inspected the mouth of each basket. "Nope. Nil. Nyet. Nada. No birds here. Just big, boring piles of play money."

"You won't find any birds in any of them, Pete. The bird offering basket is for *paying* for the birds that will be sacrificed by the priests."

The long line of people continued to march by in front of us and drop money into the baskets. After depositing their coins they would file into another room. A couple of men sat close by scribbling on parchment which was stretched out on a fancy carved wooden table. They had the look of tax collectors, aloof and self-absorbed, and seemed to be supervising the fee collections. A couple of black-robed Pharisees from the morning's stoning seemed to be keeping tabs on them.

"Hey," Pete said, "there's Jesus."

At that moment Jesus entered the room. He wove his way through the loose line of people, and made his way to the area where the thirteen trumpet-shaped baskets were stationed. The fee collectors and Pharisees looked on in wide-mouthed disbelief.

"He's not going to clear the Temple again, is he?" Pete asked, looking alternately worried and excited. "Is he looking for a whip?"

"No," Jesna said with a firm expression on her face. "He's about to send up a flare for anyone who wants to find the way back to a God-managed life, and," she continued as she gave a nod in the direction of the offering baskets and their supervisors, "he wants to let a few people know that there is more than one way to be unfaithful."

At that moment Jesus spoke in a loud voice for all to hear:

"I am the world's Light. No one who follows me stumbles around in the darkness. I provide plenty of light to live in."[116]

Affronted, the Pharisees lunged in his direction, shouting their objections. "Who do you think you are to say that? You can't just say you're the world's light!"

"I am one with my Father. My words are the same as his. If you really knew him, really spent time talking with him and listening to his voice—being in love with him—you would recognize the Father's words in the Son's mouth. But you don't even know the one you claim to obey." The Pharisees were without a comeback. Jesus continued,

"You're tied down to the mundane; I'm in touch with what is beyond your horizons. You live in terms of what you see and touch. I'm living on other terms. I told you that you were missing God in all this. You're at a dead end. If you won't believe I am who I say I am, you're at the dead end of sins. You're missing God in your lives."[117]

"That Jesus is something else!" Mr. Pilgrim said admiringly. "I bet he would be some chess player."

"Can you explain, Mr. Pilgrim?" Jesna asked with a twinkle in her eye.

"Well, the Sanhedrin and the Pharisees set a trap for him— baited with the woman caught sinning in the dark. Then later, the very same day, he walks right into the darkest part of the Temple, the treasury, and says, basically, 'you, aren't any better than that woman! You've lived on your own terms, seeking money, control, and power. And living that way has taken you so far away from your true partner (God), that you don't even recognize his voice anymore. Now YOU go and sin no more!'"

"Go, Dad!"

Jesna looked as though she shared the youngest Pilgrim's admiration. And she said, "You're right, Mr. Pilgrim. Adultery isn't the only way to be unfaithful."

FAMILY DISCUSSION

1. What does it mean to be faithful to something?
2. What do you think Jesna meant when she said that there is more than one way to be *un*faithful?

SCENE 146
THE TRUTH WILL MAKE
YOU FREE[118]

The line of those dropping coins as they filed by the thirteen trumpet-baskets had slowed to the pace of freeway traffic when there's an accident. Everyone was shuffling at a snail's pace so they could rubberneck at Jesus as he preached to the Pharisees. Suddenly, he startled them by turning his attention to *them*, the people in line.

"Some of you claim to believe in me and what I teach,

"If you stick with this, living out what I tell you, you are my disciples for sure."

("Did Jesus just say 'for sure'?" Pete asked.)

" ... then you will experience for yourselves the truth, and the truth will free you."[119]

People in line began to exchange puzzled glances with each other.

"I can't believe I'm actually hearing Jesus say those words!" Mr. Pilgrim said excitedly. "When I was in college our library had those exact words chiseled in marble above the entrance. Not all of them, just the last few, 'The truth will set you free.' It always made me feel good to know that I was walking under something Jesus had said every time I walked through the entrance to our library, and now I've heard him say them in person. Every time I went into that library I felt that if I studied hard enough, I would be set free."

"It's a real shame your school didn't invest in a little more marble."

"What?"

"As it was, Mr. Pilgrim, they weren't offering you the truth of Jesus but the deception of the Pharisees. If they had spent a little more they could have gotten his whole message, all of what you just heard him say. To take only the last few words is to miss the most important part."

"Go on."

"Jesus put a pretty big 'if' in the middle of that quote. He said, *If* you stick with this, living out what I tell you, you are my disciples.'"

"For sure," Pete said.

"Mr. Pilgrim, the ones who get set free are those who stick so close to Jesus that they become his best friends and do what he says to do. Those who begin to live their lives on his terms and not on their own. Those are the one who get set free."

"Set free from what, Jesna?" Mr. Pilgrim asked.

"Set free from this world, set free from sin, death, and the devil. Set free to do what Jesus asks, to enjoy a life of peace in the kingdom of heaven."

"It sounds pretty confusing, Jesna," Mr. Pilgrim protested while shaking his head. "I'm not sure I'll ever get it."

"I'm not sure those folks in line get it yet, either. But it's as simple as falling in love. Jesus wants friends to be in close, loving relationship with him so they can experience his joy, and so they can share his love with others. Anything less is to still be a slave to the kingdom of the world."

FAMILY DISCUSSION

1. What is your definition of being set free? What do you want to be set free from?

2. What are some things you can do to stay close to Jesus throughout the day?

SCENE 147
ANOTHER GREAT ESCAPE[120]

Jesus had just offered his audience in the Temple treasury a ticket to freedom from the world, the flesh, and the devil. It seemed that most had taken his words as a license to bite back.

"Just who do you think you're talking to?" someone called out from the line, as one of the Pharisees nodded approvingly.

(*That should be, "to whom do you think you are talking?"* Priscilla thought smugly.)

"We are Abraham's descendants!"

"I know who *our* grandparent is," Jesus shot back, "but I keep close company with *my* Father and listen to his words, while you, apparently, have been keeping company with *your* father and doing what he tells you to do."

"Our father is Abraham!" a whole chorus of people said at once. "We already told you that."

"If you were truly Abraham's children you would act like him—showing reverence for God and the willingness to obey him no matter what the cost. Instead, you are plotting to kill me, the One who listens to God and is willing to obey him no matter what he asks. But you refuse to do anything except to live your lives on your own terms. And you keep on doing the works of your *real* father."

"Our real father is God!" the crowd shouted.

"No," Jesus said. "If God were your father,…"

" … you would love me, for I came from God and arrived here. I didn't come on my own. He sent me. Why can't you understand one word I say? Here's why: You can't handle it. You're from your father, the Devil, and all you want to do is please him. He was a killer from the very start. He couldn't stand the truth because there wasn't a shred of truth in him. When the Liar speaks, he makes it up out of his lying nature and fills the world with lies. I arrive on the scene, tell you the plain truth, and you refuse to have a thing to do with me."[121]

At these words the crowd exploded with fury. "Now! Now we *know* the truth, and it isn't *your* truth! You are just what we thought you were—a demon-possessed Samaritan."

"No. I am the very essence of life. I am *being* itself. Long before Abraham was, *I am.*"

This instigated a murderous riot. Jesus somehow slipped away, an escape that would have boggled a Houdini.

"Looks like Abraham's *real* father isn't ready to sacrifice his Isaac just yet," Jesna said solemnly.

FAMILY DISCUSSION
1. What do you think the people in the crowd meant when they said Abraham was their father? What do you think Jesus meant when he said the same thing?
2. Abraham became the "Father of the Jews" by being willing to obey God no matter what the cost. In what way has it been the most difficult for you to obey God?

SCENE 148
JESUS HEALS THE MAN BORN BLIND[122]

"Quickly!" Jesna said. "Back in the car. You don't want to miss what's going to happen next." We scrambled in.

Jesna accelerated, right through the milling Jews. Our exit was as undetected as Jesus' had been, but it wasn't without commentary.

"Run over that loud-mouth's foot," Pete suggested to Jesna.

"He wouldn't feel it, little brother."

"Yeah. Well it would make *me* feel a whole lot better."

Ignoring Pete's unsanctified request, Jesna kept our front bumper at Jesus' heels as he crossed the Temple courtyard and continued out into a section of the city where the cobbled streets were narrow and crooked. We were surrounded by three-story-high stone buildings that kept us out of the sun.

He was joined by a few of his bravest disciples, who appeared from the shadows and rejoined their master. It appeared they still had quite a way to go before perfect love would cast out all their fears.

Jesna threaded through the maze of streets carefully. Suddenly, she slammed on the brakes. Jesus had stopped in his tracks, causing a pile-up of Pilgrims and disciples. He had halted to study a man who was feeling his way down the street with outstretched hands and careful feet. The man's eyes were sealed shut by creased skin.

"Is that man blind?" Pete asked.

Pete's question was answered by one of the disciples.

"Teacher, who was it that sinned? Was it that man's fault or his parent's fault that he was born blind?"

Jesus said,

"You're asking the wrong question. You're looking for someone to blame. There is no such cause-effect here. Look instead for what God can do. We need to be energetically at work instead for the One who sent me here, working while the sun shines. When night falls, the workday is over. For as long as I am in the world, there is plenty of light. I am the world's Light."[123]

No sooner had Jesus said that than he knelt down and spat onto a patch of dust.

"All *right!*" Pete exclaimed, and then he let go with a hologram spit of his own.

Jesus mixed his spit with the dirt and made a mud paste. He stopped the blind man with an outstretched hand and asked him if he would like to see the world that his Father had created. The blind man was too dumbfounded to respond. But his hesitation turned into sputtering shock 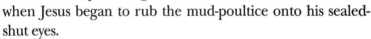 when Jesus began to rub the mud-poultice onto his sealed-shut eyes.

"Help! W-w-what are you doing? Can't you see I'm a helpless blind man?"

"Go now," Jesus said, "and wash your eyes in the Pool of Siloam. You'll leave both your helplessness and your blindness in the pool."

We couldn't tell if he did it out of faith or the desire to get away from a madman who would put spit and dirt on his face, but the blind man obeyed. Even a sighted person wouldn't have been able to see with all that mud in his eyes. It was this fellow's advantage to have groped his way for years; he knew the way to the pool pretty well.

Soon, the man came running back. While his face was still a little mud-streaked, it was studded with two wide-open, deep brown, sparkling eyes. He was literally spinning in circles and scanning the city of Jerusalem like a kid in a candy factory.

Within minutes the whole town was stirring with the never-before-heard news of a blind-from-birth man who had been given new eyes. In no time, Jesus had found an open area and was teaching an eager audience about how they could get new eyes too, the kind of eyes that would let them see their Father's kingdom, a wonderful world that is invisible to those with hard hearts and sightless souls.

The teaching had been going on for some time when, suddenly, Jesus interrupted his own lessons and cried out, "Come over here!"

He was calling to a man who was walking down the street with his face turned down.

"Hey!" Pete said. "Isn't that the blind man Jesus healed?"

It was indeed. As the man slowly shuffled over to where Jesus was standing, Jesus asked him a question to which he already knew the answer. "Why are you so glum?"

"I've come from the Pharisees' inquisition," the man said.

"And?"

"And they say, at least most of them, that you can't be from God, because you healed me on the Sabbath. They said you had a demon."

"What did you say?"

"I told them that I didn't think God was at the mercy of demands from demons. And I said it was more likely that he would only answer the request of someone he really liked. And then I ask them if they wanted to be your disciple; I told them where they could find you."

"What did they say?" Jesus asked with a laugh.

"They called me 'dirt,' and said that I would probably lose my sight again."

Jesus wasn't laughing anymore. He asked the man, "Do you believe that I am God's Son?"

"If you say it's true, I will believe it."

Jesus nodded his response and the blind man received a

second gift of vision in one day. He fell to the ground and began to worship Jesus.

Jesus then said,

> "I came into the world to bring everything into the clear light of day, making all the distinctions clear, so that those who have never seen will see, and those who have made a great pretense of seeing will be exposed as blind."[124]

"I believe," Jesna said, "that there are a lot of people here who are seeing God's kingdom of love for the first time."

Priscilla looked puzzled. She formulated a careful question: "So, which type of 'sight restoration' did Jesus mean the first time he spoke in the synagogue in his hometown, when he said he had come to restore sight to the blind?"

"Both," Jesna said. "Both types of blindness."

FAMILY DISCUSSION

1. In what ways is the blindness of the Pharisees worse than that of the blind man in this story?
2. Perhaps you would like to offer a prayer to God, "Lord please give my heart new eyes to see your vision for my life."

SCENE 149
JESUS IS THE GOOD SHEPHERD[125]

As the formerly-blind man took his place on the front row of the audience, Pete couldn't contain a question.

"When Jesus finishes talking can we drive over and take a look at that 'pool of salami' where the blind man washed his face? It sounds interesting. I might want to bob for some."

"It's a very interesting place, Pete, although the Pool of Siloam has no salami floating in it."

Pete made a disappointed face.

"It's a reservoir located inside the city walls—just down that street and around the corner," Jesna continued. "It's a deep pool of water—a lot longer and deeper than most of your back yard swimming pools."

"But about the same skinniness?" Pete asked, perking back up at the mention of backyard swimming.

"Yes, Pete, about the same width."

"Can we swim in it?"

"I don't think these folks would like that too much, Pete. Would you like it if one of them stuck his grimy toes in a glass of water you were drinking?"

"Depends on whether or not they've had a bath that day," Pete deliberated.

Jesna continued, ignoring Pete's standard of hygiene. "'Siloam' means 'sent.' It was constructed by King Hezekiah…"

"Don't tell me … Didn't he write one of the books of the Bible?"

"No, Pete."

" … Its water comes from the Spring of Gihon (which is outside the city walls), through an underground tunnel. To the people of Jerusalem it represents 'life' sent by God from outside their walls."

"*I* know where you're going with this!" Pete exulted. "You're about to say that Jesus is like the Pool of Siloam because he's 'life' sent by God from outside our world."

Everyone looked at Pete as if he were suddenly holding a Harvard degree in his small hands. Well, everyone but Priscilla. She was looking at him like she had seen a blind-folded monkey type an original sonnet.

" ... Precisely my point, Pete," Jesna finally managed to sputter.

But Jesna's sputters were interrupted. Four Pharisees had followed the healed man's directions. Now they had found Jesus again. Their faces were dark red with exertion and fury.

"Hey!" one shouted first. "We've been told you've been calling us 'blind'!"

"Yeah," said another. "What do you have to say for yourself? Are *you* blind to just who you're accusing?"

Jesus, unfazed by the intrusion said calmly, "I wish that you were all blind."

"Wh-what?"

"If you were blind, then it wouldn't be your fault that you spend your lives stumbling around in the dark. But since you claim perfect vision, you will be held accountable for all of your transgressions, and for all you lead astray."

The anger of the Pharisees was apparently beyond their ability to communicate.

"Is that steam coming out of their ears?" Pete asked.

The eldest Pharisee spun around and began the now-familiar Pharisee-retreat. The others stampeded to follow him. At about twenty angry paces, the lead wolf turned back to the crowd and said, "You had better follow us to safety, or you'll meet the same fate that awaits *him.*"

He was pointing at Jesus with a trembling bony finger. At least half of the crowd arose and followed the wolves.

Jesus watched the exodus thoughtfully, then told this story to the ones who remained.

"If a person enters a sheep pen through the fence instead of through the gate, you know what he is. He's a thief and a sheep-stealer. Only the shepherd can go through the gate. He calls the sheep by their name and they follow him out.

They have spent so much time with him that they recognize his voice. They will not follow a stranger because his voice is strange to them. Let me make that clearer," he said,

"I have come that you might have real and eternal life, more and better life than you ever dreamed of. I am the Good Shepherd. The Good Shepherd puts the sheep before himself, sacrifices himself if necessary. A hired man is not a real shepherd. The sheep mean nothing to him. He sees a wolf come and runs for it, leaving the sheep to be ravaged and scattered by the wolf. He's only in it for the money. The sheep don't matter to him.

"I am the Good Shepherd. I know my own sheep and my own sheep know me. In the same way, the Father knows me and I know the Father."[126]

The crowd was silent. Many still looked confused, but Pete was not one of them.

"I guess you have to spend a lot of time with the Shepherd before you learn to recognize the sound of his voice. Huh, Jesna?"

The very recent Harvard graduate had typed another line of poetry.

FAMILY DISCUSSION

1. Do think that God speaks to you sometimes when you pray? Can you recognize his voice?
2. What are some ways that God's sheep can tell his voice from that of the thief and robber—Satan?
3. How can you tell God's voice from your own thoughts?

SCENE 150
BACK OUT INTO
THE WILDERNESS[127]

Pete didn't ever get to visit the Pool of Siloam, but Jesna did treat him to an aerial view of three other, bigger bodies of water—the Dead Sea, the Sea of Galilee, and the Mediterranean Sea.

Jesna had said to me, "Wisdom, please herd all the Pilgrims back in the car for a trip straight up and across a few days of Bible-time."

I love my work!

It never takes long after we close the car doors. Within seconds of her button-pushing, the ground had dropped so far below us that the city of Jerusalem had shrunk to the size of a child's sand castle on the beach, and the Dead Sea once again resembled a beached whale. Jesna punched a few more buttons, spun a dial, and three days passed beneath us in less time than it takes Mr. Pilgrim to sneeze, which, as with Pete, always involves at least three "ahs" to the one "choo"! Dogs are alert to these things.

Priscilla commented that the sudden flashes of day and night made her think of camera flashes. "Cool!" was the only thought Pete revealed.

When the earth and the sun finally stopped trading places, the brave of heart looked over the side of our time-ship for a view of the Holy Land.

"Wow!" said Pete. "I'd never noticed that big, ugly brown ditch that got dug right down the middle of the country."

Pete was right. From our present elevation it was strikingly apparent that Jerusalem sat at the top of a crest of mountains that ran far to the north and south (that's "up" and "down" for Pete), dividing the country into equal portions of green and brown. To the west ("left") of that crest were sloping, green foothills and plains. To the east was a steeply sloped, barren wilderness; the floor of a deep, hundred mile-long "ditch"; and then a mostly-brown plateau.

"Look at it," Pete instructed. "It looks like a big ol' dragon fell from the sky and made a giant hole. And it looks like it tried to claw and scratch its way up the deep bank it made. Hey, you don't suppose it's still living down … "

"No, little brother. The only real dragons live in your mouth when you get out of bed in the mornings. Shoo-weee."

"That dead and dry wilderness that Pete is describing as a 'ditch' is the wilderness of Judea," Jesna said. "We were all there to hear John the Baptist preach."

Everyone looked sad. I couldn't help whimpering myself when I thought about brave John.

"When Jesus leaves Jerusalem, he will head out into the wilderness for a while."

"Why would anybody want to spend time in that brown gully?" Pete asked. "I'd rather sit through a funeral than spend time out there."

"Well, Pete," Jesna said, "things are getting pretty hot for Jesus back in Jerusalem. And, he's doesn't want there to be, well, uh, a, uh … "

"A final confrontation?"

"Thank you, Priscilla. He's not ready for a final confrontation. It's very important for him to make his last trip to Jerusalem at the time of the Passover Feast. That's still six months away."

"What will we see in the wilderness?" Pete asked.

"Not one blade of grass. That's for sure!" Priscilla answered.

"In the wilderness we'll see that Jesus completes the circle of his ministry—back to the wilderness of John the Baptist, where he was baptized. You'll see that crowds of needy people will still brave the parched desert in hopes of finding water for their dry and barren lives. But you don't have to hear it from me. Let's go see it."

Jesna threw our space-car into a steep descent. This was better than the Dragon Master back home. We let out a chorus of shrieks (and yips) that would frighten a ghost.

Jesna brought us to a stop right on Jesus' left toenail. (I kid you not!) He was in his familiar teaching posture at the front of a new, open-air class of listeners. The crowd was salted with sweat and peppered with Pharisees.

"Oh, no," Pete moaned. "Not more kingdom-crushing Pharisees. They multiply like gerbils."

We had arrived in time to hear Jesus patiently explaining to everyone about how God was their real "Daddy" and how he had prepared a great inheritance for his children to enjoy—now and later.

But this didn't stop one of the Pharisees from interrupting him with an unrelated question. "Uh, Jesus. I have a question for you. Is it legal for a man to divorce his wife?"

"What did Moses command?" Jesus asked back.

The expert of Moses' laws who had posed the question didn't hesitate: "Moses said that a man can fill out a document of dismissal and divorce a wife. But we were just wondering if you were making more changes in Holy Scripture."

Jesus said,

"Moses wrote this command only as a concession to your hard-hearted ways. In the original creation, God made male and female to be together. Because of this, a man leaves his father and mother, and in marriage he becomes one flesh with a woman—no longer two individuals, but forming a new unity. Because God created this organic union of the two sexes, no one should desecrate his art by cutting them apart."[128]

The dark-robed Pharisees flowed toward each other like molten lava, smirking with satisfaction. They knew that what they had heard would help to build the Sanhedrin's case against Jesus. But they froze in their tracks at what he said next.

"Divorce is always a ripping and a tearing that God never wanted for his children, but that doesn't mean that he turns his back on his children who have taken that awful course. Divorce is not an excuse for him to use to cut himself off from them. He never stops honoring *his* commitment to loving union with his children, no matter what. This should make you glad," Jesus said to the grim Pharisees. "Even though you've divorced yourselves from being in loving relationship with him, he'll never give up wanting to be in relationship with you."

FAMILY DISCUSSION

1. How does it make you feel to know that no matter what happens in your life, God's love for you is permanent?
2. Do you know someone with whom you could share this good news?

SCENE 151
JESUS BLESSES THE CHILDREN[129]

The small group of spy-Pharisees divorced themselves from Jesus' presence and departed for Jerusalem. Pete's earlier remarks—about this wilderness looking like dragon-scratchings—came to mind.

After a few more stories, Jesus told those remaining that he was finished teaching for the day. He looked weary. The crowd looked disappointed. But they were sympathetic to Jesus' need for rest and began to file away.

"I still can't get used to God needing to rest," Pete said.

"God doesn't, Pete," Jesna said. "Probably what you forget, Pete, is that Jesus is not only fully God, but also fully a man."

"Yeah. That's the part I keep forgetting. And the part about why he was willing to give up being God."

"He *didn't* give up being God, Pete," Jesna hastened to say. "He took on human-ness at the *same time.*"

"Yeah, but why? Why would he want to have rashes and toothaches and hay fever and stubbed toes and headaches and scratchy clothes and bad breath and bleeding and … "

"She gets the picture, Pete," Priscilla said impatiently.

"So he would know *exactly* what you feel when you experience any of those things. So he would know *exactly* how tough it can be to be human. You know, Pete, even the angels in heaven have great respect for all you humans have to go through in trying to hold on to faith in God and his kingdom in the midst of so much darkness and misery."

"Hey, Jesna! How would you know what angels say to each other, unless … "

Jesna's face suddenly flushed and she began to look like a cat caught with a canary in its mouth.

"W-well, p-Pete," she began to stammer, "I can see that we might as well pile back in the car right now and start pushing those buttons. There's really nothing else to see here for a few Bible-days anyway."

All the Pilgrims obeyed promptly—even Pete. I think they would all rather be licked by a cat than embarrass Jesna. Even I, with my superior sense of smell, had been able to tell from the first sniff that she wasn't like any other human *I* had ever smelled....

When this brief blast through time ended, we saw Jesus sitting on the hard ground, being mobbed by a baker's dozen of children. They were all over him. A couple were playing King of the Mountain on his shoulders. Four more were playing musical chairs with his lap. The rest were doing elasticity tests with different parts of his face and hair. I must say, Jesus was taking it with more patience than a bluetick hound.

"What's going on?" Pete said. "Is Jesus renting himself out as a McDonald's playground?"

"No, Pete," Jesna answered. "Recently people have been bringing their children to Jesus for him to touch them. They think it will be a spiritual blessing for their children to be touched by Jesus."

"OK, OK, that'll be more than enough." One of Jesus' disciples snapped. "Can't you see that our Master needs his rest? It's bad enough that the Sanhedrin is trying to pull him apart without you letting your children do it too." As he spoke, several other disciples began to push and pull the children off of

Jesus. I was beginning to wonder if my herding skills might be needed when I heard Jesus say, "Stop!"

"Don't push these children away. Don't ever get between them and me. These children are at the very center of life in the kingdom. Mark this: Unless you accept God's kingdom in the simplicity of a child, you'll never get in."[130]

The thirteen children were puzzled. Jesus gathered them into his arms one-by-one. Each received a holy hug, a gentle touch to the forehead, and a whispered blessing.

When he had finished, he said for all to hear, "Each of you is a giant in my kingdom. I hope your parents, and my disciples, will follow you all the way to the playground my Father built for all."

FAMILY DISCUSSION

1. What do you think Jesus meant when he said that we needed to accept God's kingdom "in the simplicity of a child"?
2. How does it make you feel to know that the Creator of the universe likes to have children crawling in his lap?

SCENE 152
THE POOR RICH MAN[131]

I think I was the first to notice Pete strutting around like a peacock on a fashion runway. With his thumbs stuck under his armpits, he looked as if he had sprouted wings. Priscilla noticed right away too.

"What in the world are you so proud of, Petie? You're prancing around like a show horse."

"You heard the man, didn't you, Priscilla. You heard him say that unless you accept God's kingdom like *me*, you won't get in!"

"He said, 'like a child,' Pete. Not 'like Pete Pilgrim.'"

"Do *you* see any *other* children in our family?" Pete said with the confidence of a master chess player announcing "check-mate."

"Well ... well ... " Priscilla said. But she couldn't make her mouth say that she was also a child.

"Why, Jesna? Why is it easier for a child to get into God's kingdom than it is for grown-ups like us?" Mr. Pilgrim asked.

"It's not about being young," Jesna began. "It's easy for real old people, too."

"But how come?" Mr. Pilgrim said.

"Because it's often the case that young children and people in their last years of life are less busy and more interested in fun and simple pleasures. They're more likely to say, 'yes,' if someone asks them to play, or to go for a walk, or to have a talk. So when Jesus asks them to hang out with him for a while, they're more likely to say 'yes.' Right, Pete? Pete! Pete! Where did he go?"

A quick survey located Pete. He had gotten tired of talking about the kingdom. He had run off to be a child with Jesus and the other children. "Whaa-hooo!" he squealed, using Jesus' back as a sliding board.

"I think I get it now," Mr. Pilgrim said.

Right then, a man came running up to Jesus—the portable playground—and asked a breathless question. "Good Teacher, what must I do to inherit eternal life?"

From the looks of his fine clothes and flashy jewelry, it appeared that he had already inherited about everything else.

"Who told you that I am good?" Jesus asked through a lap

full of giggling children. The rich young man didn't seem to notice the fun that was going on. "No one is 'good' except God. But, I'm sure you know the Ten Commandments given to Moses. Go and keep those rules if you want to be 'good.'"

"Psssst. Jesna," Priscilla said. "The Pharisees keep all the commandments and I don't think Jesus considers them to be good."

"Oh, no," Pete answered for Jesna. "They're no good at all."

"Teacher," the shiny young man said. "I have kept the law since I was a child."

"I bet he was never a child," Pete said. "Probably was born with a camel driver's license in one hand and a checkbook in the other."

At Pete's comment, a one-syllable laugh escaped Jesus' mouth before he gave the young man a long stare right in the eyes. Both of Jesus' sad eyes were saying that he loved the young man. Then he said,

"There's one thing left: Go sell your possessions; give it all to the poor. All your wealth will then be in heaven. Then come and follow me."[132]

For a long moment the rich young man stared back into the eyes of Jesus, who, wearing his only cloak over his dusty body, was the unfathomably wealthy owner of all of existence. But the young man turned and walked away, grasping instead the gold trinkets that decorated his neck and shaking his glossy hair.

"Poor rich man," Pete said. "I wish he had taken Jesus' present."

FAMILY DISCUSSION

1. What do you believe the rich young man thought was more valuable than being a disciple of Jesus?
2. What would be the most difficult things for you to let go of if you wanted to get a grip on Jesus with both hands?

SCENE 153
ON RICHES AND THE REWARDS OF DISCIPLESHIP[133]

Jesus' eyes stayed glued to the rich young man's back until he was out of sight. For me, it was like watching the story of the prodigal son played backward—a would-be prince comes home, but then chooses to depart, exchanging eternal inheritance for the slop of this world.

Jesus finally broke the silence. He said to his disciples and to anyone within earshot, "You can hardly imagine how difficult it is for rich people to enter the kingdom of my Father." He finally took his eyes from the prodigal prince. Perhaps the smacking sounds of a nearby camel drew his attention.

"You see that camel, there?" Jesus asked.

"That reminds me, Dad. What did you mean when you said a camel was a horse designed by a committee?"

"Shhhh!"

"Well you say it all the time.... "

"It would be easier for that camel there to squeeze through the eye of a needle than for a rich man to enter God's kingdom," Jesus said.

The disciples seemed astonished by their Master's comment.

"Look at those twelve wide-open mouths," Pete instructed. "I can't tell if they are doing baby-bird imitations or just having a hard time picturing a camel jumping through a needle's eye. But I think a camel could do it. It could happen."

"That's not what they're all so gaped-mouthed about, Pete," Jesna said. "They can't believe that Jesus said that it's harder for rich people to get in than poor people. In their culture, the wealthy are considered to be favored by God. Their wealth is supposed to be a sure sign of God's blessing."

If anyone doubted the truth of Jesna's observation, a travel-worn disciple demonstrated it.

"Then who in the world can get into the kingdom, if the rich can't?" one disciple managed to put his lips back together long enough to say.

Jesus answered him,

"No chance at all if you think you can pull it off yourself. Every chance in the world if you trust God to do it."[134]

"So," Mr. Pilgrim said, looking a little relieved, "It's not about money. Getting into the kingdom is about trusting God instead of trusting yourself."

"That's right," Jesna said. "A person might be able to squeeze through the narrow opening of the kingdom with a big fat wallet. But it's impossible to squeeze one iota of self-trust through."

"So," Mr. Pilgrim said. "It sounds like the problem with wealth is that it's easier to trust in *it* than to trust God for your security and peace of mind."

"That's exactly right, Mr. Pilgrim. It's very hard not to make an idol out of your gold," Jesna said. And as she gazed at the rich young man who was now a speck merging with the horizon, she voiced, "It's a crying shame when your hands become welded to things that won't fit through the narrow opening to the kingdom."

"Yep," Pete said. "I bet it would be easier to get a peanut butter sandwich through a closed screen door than to get your checkbook into heaven."

FAMILY DISCUSSION

1. How would you explain what Jesus meant about rich people, camels, and needles?
2. Can you think of any things that you trust more than Jesus for your peace of mind? What are they?
3. If you could think of anything, write it down on a piece of toilet paper and go flush it down the commode. Better *it* than *you!*

SCENE 154
THE PARABLE OF THE LABORERS IN THE VINEYARD[135]

Jesus and his disciples spent the next couple of months in the Judean wilderness. But I don't think they stepped on a single blade of grass. I know I never saw anything green there.

Jesna continued to be quite taken by the fact that Jesus had returned to the same barren "stage" where John the Baptist had delivered his fiery sermons. And like John, Jesus attracted some pretty big crowds. She liked to say that Jesus was harvesting the fruit from the trees that John had planted almost three years before.

Once after Jesna made that observation, Pete said: "Well it's for certain that soul-seeds make out a whole lot better in the desert than grass seeds do."

"Right you are!" Jesna responded. "Desert times cause souls to send their roots deeper—in search of living water. And if they find it—instant oasis."

"But the grass just dries up and blows away," Pete responded to Jesna's smiling approval.

The two months of desert time with Jesus was spent watching him tell stories, make friends, harvest John's deep-rooted soul-crops, and plant new ones.

When our sojourn in the wilderness came to a close, Jesus announced to his disciples that he planned to go back to Jerusalem for the Feast of Dedication. Twelve faces reflected fear for his life.

Later that day, sitting crossed-legged in the shadow of a time-worn hill, Jesus began a story about God's kingdom.

"God's realm is like a farm foreman who went out early in the morning to hire workers for his vineyard. He offered a fair day's wage. They accepted the job and went to work.

"Around mid-morning he left the fields to find more workers. He found some people standing idly in the marketplace and asked them if they wanted to work for the rest of the day. They also accepted the offer of work and the foreman told them he would give them a fair wage.

"As the day progressed, the overseer saw that he needed

even more workers. He left at noon and again at mid-afternoon and rounded up more laborers—giving to them the same offer of decent wages.

"Then at 5:00 P.M., he left the vineyards again. Arriving in town he said to a group, 'Why are you just standing around doing nothing all day?' To which they replied, 'Because no one has hired us.'

"The foreman said, 'You go and work in the vineyard of my boss, too.'

"When quitting time came (at 6:00 P.M.) the owner of the vineyard instructed his foreman to call the workers in and pay them their wages, beginning with those hired last. Every worker was paid the same amount—a respectable day's wage.

"After each had been paid, the ones who had worked for more hours began to grumble and complain. The ones who had worked the longest griped the loudest. 'These last workers put in only one easy hour—the sun was almost down—and you made them equal to us who have worked for you in the scorching heat.'

"He replied to the one speaking for the rest, 'Friend, I haven't been unfair. You agreed on the wage at the beginning of the day, didn't you?'

"' … I decided to give to the one who came last the same as you. Can't I do what I want with my own money? Are you going to get stingy because I am generous?'

"Hear it is again, the Great Reversal: many of the first ending up last, and the last first."[136]

Jesus' story left more than one listener scratching his head. I think Mr. Pilgrim became their invisible spokesperson.

"Jesna, I'm afraid I don't like that story. I mean I'm with the ones who were complaining. That just doesn't seem fair!"

"No, Mr. Pilgrim, you aren't with the ones hired first. You

were hired last—and have received the easiest job."

"What?"

"Some of the first hired would be Abraham, standing over Isaac with a knife, wringing with sweat as he tries to obey God's will without the benefit of a Bible or the life-parable of Jesus' time on earth.

"Or, Moses, trying to obey God's voice while facing down Pharaoh's authority; or, Daniel, mid-air between the king's strong men and a fiery furnace; or, Mary telling Joseph that's she's pregnant and he's not the father; or, Paul, receiving his 39th stripe for the third time, still with no Bible, except for a few pages in his own head, to confirm that he's not insane."

"Jesna, I see your point. I'm one of the last to sign on and my labor has been easy."

"And," Mrs. Pilgrim inserted with a question mark in her voice, "the kingdom isn't about fairness?"

"Those aren't exactly the points. But very close. Jesus is reminding John's converts—who have endured many trials for more than two years now—to resist becoming angry with these new believers who are getting in on the same rewards. He also wants them to understand that the kingdom isn't governed by the world's standards of what's fair and just. It begins with fair and then only gets … "

"Gooder?"

"Right, Pete. It only gets gooder."

FAMILY DISCUSSION

1. How would you have felt if you had been one of the first ones hired by the farm manager when you saw the last hired getting equal pay?

2. How does it make you feel to know that you are getting equal pay with Abraham?

SCENE 155
JESUS AT THE FEAST OF DEDICATION IN JERUSALEM[137]

The following morning we arose and began a trek back to Jerusalem—across the miles of furrowed hills. The wilderness terrain often resembled an endless sea of rock. And at certain times of day the rock waves were turned golden by the sun. In the distance were higher, snow-capped Judean hills.

Mercifully (at least during the daytime) we were making this trip at the beginning of winter. Jesna told us that we would arrive back in Jerusalem on the 25th of December—the day of the Feast of Lights, now called Hanukkah.

"Will Jesus be getting lots of presents from his parents and friends that day?" Pete asked.

"*Gifts* for the Feast of Lights, Pete?" his mother asked.

"Well, it will be his birthday, you know. The 25th of December."

"My goodness, son," Mr. Pilgrim said. "You're right."

"He'll be thirty-three years old," Priscilla proudly added.

"What do you get a thirty-three-year-old who's already made everything?" Pete asked no one in particular.

"I don't know, son. But I like it that you're thinking about gift-giving," Mrs. Pilgrim said.

"Well, he has given quite a lot to me, y'know."

The trip back to the Holy City took a couple of nights and the best part of three days. Along the way Jesna explained that the Feast of Lights, while beginning on December 25th, was observed for eight days. She said that is was one of the newer feasts, and that is was started by Judas Maccabeus in 164 B.C. to celebrate the fact that the Temple—which had been defiled earlier—had been cleansed and rededicated to the service of God.

"Wow," Pete said. "Knowing how much Jesus likes to use meadows for stuff, I bet he has a field day with that holiday."

"Do you mean 'metaphors,' Pete? If you do, you are more right than you know. There's nothing Jesus would like more than for people to have their own temples—their soul hold-ers—cleaned and rededicated to prayer and service to God."

"Maybe that's why he picked the first day of the Feast of Lights for his birthday?" Pete further mused.

It wasn't long before Pete's pondering became a fulfilled prophecy.

Jesus arrived in the city on the evening of the first day of the Feast. The entire city was ablaze with festive lights (lamps and torches). He immediately walked through the city streets—now very familiar to us all—and across a thousand shadows that were dancing on the floor of the Temple courtyard. His disciples were bringing up the rear. They seemed afraid of their own shadows.

Jesus was met and encircled quickly by his countrymen—many of whom had familiar faces and were wearing black. "How long are you going to keep us in the dark?" one asked sarcastically. "If you are the Christ we are all waiting for, tell us plainly."

"Don't bite, Jesus!" Pete cautioned. "It's a trap!"

Despite Pete's warning, Jesus answered anyway. "I have already told you that I am. And I have backed my words with miraculous actions. It is obvious to me that you will never believe who I am, because you do not belong to my sheep.

"My sheep hear my voice (as I hear my Father's) and they follow me. They know me and I know them. I lead them to a reward of eternal life and no one is able to snatch them from my hand.

"But here in plain terms is the answer that you want. I and the Father are one."

An eerie moment of stone silence followed. Then, as the disciples took several steps backward, the encircling crowd fell out of formation and began to pick up stones. As they were raising them over their heads to kill Jesus, all four Pilgrims shrieked, "Noooo!"

Pete tried to take on the largest murderer with a flying tackle to the knees. He flew right through him, and was sliding across the stone courtyard when Jesus yelled:

"I have demonstrated my Father's love and power through many good works. For which of these acts are you going to stone me?"

"For none of the things you have done," one shouted back. "We are going to kill you because you are a blasphemer!"

Pete's second attempt to stop a murder sent him through the same man's back and to a sprawling stop at the feet of Jesus.

"Make me real," he said to Jesus, "and I'll hit 'em where it hurts."

With a hand on Pete's head Jesus said to the mob:

"I'm only quoting your inspired Scriptures, where God said, 'I tell you—you are gods.' If God called your ancestors 'gods'—and Scripture doesn't lie—why do you yell 'Blasphemer! Blasphemer!' at the unique One the Father consecrated and sent into the world, just because I said 'I am the Son of God'? If I don't do the things my Father does, well and good; don't believe me. But if I am doing them, put aside for a moment what you hear me say about myself and just take the evidence of the actions that are right before you eyes. Then perhaps things will come together for you, and you'll see that not only are we doing the same thing; we *are* the same—Father and Son. He is in me; I am in him."[138]

The rabble was frothing at the mouth. "Arrest the blasphemer!" someone shouted. They charged toward him.

Without further comment, Jesus, as we had seen him do on two prior occasions, walked through the midst of the angry horde. He left the city and headed back out into the wilderness.

As we were cruising back through the city gate, Pete said to Jesna, "I guess the Temple was just too dirty with stubborn, dark sin spots to be cleaned and rededicated today."

"Don't worry, Pete. Jesus knows what it will take to make things clean again. And when the time comes, he'll pour it out freely."

FAMILY DISCUSSION

1. Did you know that Jesus' birthday was on the first day of the Jewish Feast that celebrates the reclaiming and cleansing of the Temple?
2. Do you think this has any implications for the "temple" that you own—your body?

SCENE 156
LAZARUS: BACK FROM THE DEAD[139]

The dust seemed to be still settling from our recent trek into town as we retraced our steps back into the wilderness.

The next morning, not long before we crossed the Jordan River, Pete was trying to tug on Jesus' sleeve.

"Jesus."

"Yes, my littlest disciple."

"Well, I just wanted to wish you a happy birthday."

Jesus looked down warmly at Pete, who was trying to match the longer strides of his friend.

"And," Pete continued, "well, uh, I know it's not much of a present but I just wanted to give you this."

As Pete lifted his gift to Jesus on an open palm, Jesus smiled broadly and said, "That certainly is a fine present, Pete. I don't think I've ever seen a nicer rock."

"Well, I know it's just a rock and that you made it and everything. But it's not just *any* rock. I've had my eye out for a special one ever since you walked through the middle of those mean guys in your Dad's house."

"Oh, I can tell it's no ordinary rock. I don't think I ever made a rounder one, or a flatter one."

"That's just what I was thinking. And I thought you might want to see if you could get ten skips out of it—across the Jordan River."

"That would be a lot of skips."

"I know. Eight is my personal record. But with you being God and everything, I thought you might go for double digits."

"Pete?"

"Yes, Jesus."

"Would you mind if I didn't throw it away?"

"No, I wouldn't mind. It's your rock now. You can do whatever you want with it. Turn it into a boulder if you like. Whatever you want."

"Then I think I'll hold on to it for a while. It's the only present I got for my birthday and I'd like to keep it."

"Whatever you say, Mr. Jesus. I'd be real happy if you decided to hold on to it for a while."

And with that Pete gave Jesus two quick pats on the shoulder and dropped back in line beside his parents. He was beaming like a lighthouse.

After a couple of minutes passed he called up to Jesus. "Hey, maybe when I get up to heaven you can show me that rock and we can skip it across something then."

Jesus turned to Pete and nodded his smiling agreement.

True to his word, Jesus didn't skip his present across the Jordan. He kept it with him from that day forward. He kept it as a symbol of simple love.

After we had been back in John's wilderness for three full cycles of the moon, Mary and Martha (Jesus' friends from Bethany) sent word to Jesus that they needed him. Their brother, Lazarus, was sick.

The messenger simply said, "Jesus, Mary and Martha wanted me to get word to you that the one you love is sick."

"Lazarus!" a disciple exclaimed.

Oddly, Jesus did not immediately set off for Bethany. He remained encamped in the wilderness for two more days of teaching.

When a disciple finally questioned him about this, he responded, "Lazarus' sickness is not fatal. It will be an occasion for showing God's glory." Later that same day, however, Jesus informed his disciples that they all would be going back to Bethany.

"No! Not now!" several said. "You know the Jews are out to kill you."

"I guess there's just no pleasing everybody," Pete said.

But Jesus, never worried about winning friends and pleasing people, simply said, "Our friend Lazarus has fallen asleep. I'm going to wake him up."

"Come on," a disciple named Thomas sighed. "We might as well die along with our Master."

By the time we had all crossed the wilderness for the third time, Lazarus had already been dead for four days. Martha (the one who had been more of a chef than a listener) met us at the outskirts of the village of Bethany, weeping.

"Lord, if you had been here, my brother wouldn't be dead. But even now, I know that whatever you ask God he will do."

"Wow!" Pete exclaimed. "She's come a long way since her griper days in the kitchen."

"Have no fear, Martha," Jesus said. "Your brother will be raised up from the dead."

Martha said to him, "I know that he will rise again at the resurrection of the dead, at the last day."

"No," Jesus said in tender tones. "I am the resurrection and the life; whoever believes in me will, though they die, yet they will live, and whoever lives and believes in me shall never die. Do you believe this, Martha?"

"Yes, Jesus," Martha said with awe stretching her face, "I believe you are the Messiah, the Son of God."

After saying those words, Martha's countenance turned upside down. She spun around and raced back down the path to Bethany.

"She can't wait to give her sister the good news," Jesna said.

Within minutes, Mary was running toward Jesus, a crowd of mourners at her heels. She threw herself at his feet saying, "Jesus, if only you had been here, my brother would be living."

"I'm not sure she heard all of Martha's good news," Priscilla said.

Jesus seemed equally puzzled by Mary's simultaneous expression of faith and lack of faith. After he collected himself he asked, "Where did you put him?" He meant Lazarus' dead body.

"Come with me and see," Mary responded, with fresh grief.

Jesus began to weep too, as he followed her to the tomb.

Some from the morning crowd said, "Look how much he loved Lazarus."

But others said, in cynical tones, "If he loved him so much, why didn't he do something to keep him from dying? He's the one who can make the blind see, isn't he?"

Mary led Jesus to the mouth of a cave that had been shut by a huge, round stone. The seal wasn't tight enough to keep the smell of death inside. A stench that would offend the olfactory lobes of a buzzard was emanating from the cave. Whatever was stinking on the other side of that rock needed to be buried deeper. I hoped nobody would ask me to do the job.

Mr. and Mrs. Pilgrim and Priscilla were already holding their noses. So were most of the disciples. Pete looked green.

"Remove the stone!" Jesus ordered.

"Are you sure about that, Jesus?" Pete asked. "I was thinking that maybe you would want to add a few more."

Jesus had both hands raised over his head as he thundered, "Believe and see the glory of God!"

As several men struggled to roll away the stone door to Lazarus' tomb, Jesus raised his face to heaven and prayed for all to hear,

> "Father, I'm grateful that you have listened to me. I know you always do listen, but on account of this crowd standing here I've spoken so that they might believe that you sent me."[140]

Then Jesus thundered, "Lazarus, come out!!!"

A long moment of awkward silence followed. The dust settled in the still air. More silence, broken only by the snickers of the disbelieving.

Then, from the black mouth of the cave, a white mummy appeared and walked stiff-legged through the mouth of death. Mary and Martha sprang across the space that separated them from their brother, the recent cadaver, and began to unwrap their miracle.

Only Lazarus seemed disappointed.

"Wow!" Pete exclaimed. "It's like a Stephen King movie played backward!"

FAMILY DISCUSSION

1. How would you feel if you saw a dead man brought back to life?
2. How does it make you feel to know that your Daddy, God, can bring dead, smelly things back to life—like the decayed parts of a person's heart?

SCENE 157
THE CHIEF PRIESTS AND PHARISEES PLOT AGAINST JESUS[141]

After the jubilation died down (so to speak), we all went over to Jesus' southern headquarters, in Bethany—the home of Mary, Martha, *and Lazarus.*

Even though there was plenty of left-over funeral-food to eat, Martha insisted on cooking up a fresh feast. While she still pulled most of the kitchen duty, she didn't complain this time about the way Mary and Lazarus were in the other room at the feet of Jesus. (On occasion, however, she did say a "Louder, please!" from the kitchen. Jesus was pleased to oblige.)

When the food was brought out everyone ate for about as long as it had taken Martha to cook it. I thought Pete would split laughing when Lazarus said, "That's enough for me! One more bite and I think I'll die." Even Jesus sprayed some crumbs at that one.

It was almost time for the roosters to crow when the last

story was told and the party finally fizzled down to the rhythmic sounds of sleep.

Needless to say, the night was very short. We were all awakened by the sounds of knuckles loudly rapping on the door post. I wasn't fully awake myself when I heard Lazarus exclaim, "Nicodemus! What on earth are you doing here?"

Through the bright crack between door and post I could see Nicodemus. He was wearing his white Sanhedrin robe and a terrified look on his face. His shadow extended across the room to cover Jesus, who was now sitting up.

"I figured we'd be seeing some more of him!" Pete said. "I think he wants to be a disciple, too."

"Quick!" Nicodemus panted. "You've got to get away from here. The high priests and Pharisees called a special meeting of the Sanhedrin last night. They've decided that Jesus must be put to death. They will send men here to arrest him … *this morning!*"

"To whom can we appeal?" Matthew asked.

"No appeal is possible," Nicodemus answered. "It was Caiaphas himself who made the decision. He said, 'It is to our advantage that one man dies for the people instead of the whole nation being destroyed.'"

"What!" the disciple Peter thundered. "How is it that Jesus' love and miracles will destroy the nation?"

"The Sanhedrin is very worried about Jesus' popularity with the people," Nicodemus answered. "They are afraid that Rome will become concerned about a man who draws such a crowd of followers—and that was before he brought a man back from the dead."

"Oh," said Lazarus, cagily, "so you believe that Jesus can raise the dead?"

"Well, according to what everyone is saying, *you* would be the only one who could answer *that.*"

"Oh, you can believe it all right," Pete jumped in. "At this time yesterday, ol' Lazarus there smelled worse than my gym socks."

At that point Jesus stood to his feet and approached Nicodemus. Putting a hand on the Sanhedrinite's shoulder he said:

"You can believe those rumors. And you can believe everything that your heart is telling you about me."

Nicodemus was speechless for the better part of a minute before he said, "Well and good. But you must leave at once. I still haven't heard of a man who could raise *himself* from the dead."

"You will," Pete declared. "You will."

FAMILY DISCUSSION
1. Why do you think the Sanhedrin was so concerned with what Rome might be thinking?
2. If you were Jesus, what would you do next?

SCENE 158
JESUS GOES TO EPHRAIM[142]

His dangerous mission accomplished, Nicodemus gave a slow nod to Jesus and slipped back into the morning. Jesus turned to his group of friends and announced, "My time has not yet come."

We had all heard that before. His disciples sprang from the floor and began to pack their sparse belongings. Before the last "cock-a-doodle-doo!" had sounded outside, they hugged Mary, Martha, and Lazarus goodby, and were off.

"I bet Lazarus will never forget what happened to him," Pete said as he skipped across the courtyard pavement, apparently trying to avoid the cracks.

"And neither will anyone else, for a few millennia," Jesna assured. "But as you know, Jesus is just warming up."

Even though we were a couple of miles southeast of Jerusalem, we avoided the city as we slipped like cats to our destination—Ephraim, a village almost due north of Jerusalem.

When Pete heard the name of our target town he said, "Ephraim, I know I've heard that name in Sunday school."

"I'm sure you have," Jesna said. "Ephraim was the younger of Joseph's two sons, born to him and his Egyptian wife Asenath."

"That reminds me of a question I've always had," Priscilla said. "If Joseph had two sons, then why are there only twelve tribes? It seems like there would be thirteen, right?"

"There *are* thirteen tribes," Jesna answered. "There's Judah, Simeon, Benjamin, Reuben, Gad, Dan, Issachar, Zebulun, Asher, Naphtali, Levi, Ephraim, and Manasseh."

"Then why did our Sunday school teachers lie to us?" Pete said indignantly.

"I'm sure they didn't do that, Pete. Maybe you were listening too fast to hear that Levi, the priestly tribe, wasn't given any land. There were twelve land-holding tribes and also the Levites, the priests."

"So we're going to live with Joseph's youngest son's people for a while?" Pete asked.

"That's right, Pete. We are going just across the border of Judah and Ephraim."

"Well, that would put us in Samaria, wouldn't it, Jesna?"

"Yes, Priscilla. Ephraim and Manasseh make up the biggest part of what is called Samaria. Jesus knows it's unlikely that people from Jerusalem would 'defile' themselves by spending much time in Samaria."

"Yeah," Pete added. "They wouldn't be caught dead with the people they consider worse than toenail dirt."

"And besides," Priscilla said, ignoring her brother's colorful speech, "they wouldn't be very welcome there."

"You're both right," Jesna said.

So we spent the next several days in Ephraim, where Jesus remained in seclusion, until the time of the Passover. As the days passed, the main travel route became a swelling stream of southbound travelers. This let us know that the greatest feast time of the year was rapidly approaching.

All the Pilgrims knew from Sunday school what the upcoming Passover held for Jesus. That made this lull before the storm, a storm that he would not still, all the more special. They savored each moment like a hundred-dollar steak.

FAMILY DISCUSSION

1. If you had a quiet week to spend with Jesus, how would you want to spend it?
2. What are some of the questions you would ask him?
3. You can spend a quiet week with Jesus any time you want to. Why not get started doing things with him and asking your most important questions, almost as if it were your last week with him?

SCENE 159
PREDICTIONS AND SQUABBLINGS[143]

Our week of seclusion came to an end. One morning we awakened to find that Jesus' sleeping spot was empty. Matted grass was the only evidence that he had been there.

The disciples roused themselves in record time and set out

to find him. They could see him in the distance, on the road to Jerusalem. Two brothers, James and John, Zebedee's boys, led the pack. Each of them seemed puzzled and more than a little afraid. Our car followed along behind as the caboose.

By race-walking over the rutted road, the disciples were able to catch up with Jesus a couple of miles out of town. He never explained why he had set out alone. No one ever asked.

Around noonday Jesus directed the band to the shade of a lone tree. No one felt like eating, although some dried fruit and drier bread were passed around. After the travelers felt a little rested, Jesus began to tell them about what to expect in Jerusalem. It wasn't a story any of us wanted to hear.

"Listen to me carefully. We're on our way up to Jerusalem. When we get there, the Son of Man will be betrayed to the religious leaders and scholars. They will sentence him to death. Then they will hand him over to the Romans, who will mock and spit on him, give him the third degree, and kill him. After three days he will rise alive."[144]

"I thought it was *Jesus* that was going to die," Pete said.

"He *is*, you moron!" Priscilla scolded, distressed by the whole thing.

"But he keeps saying it is going to happen to 'the Son of Man.' Who's that?"

"Don't look at me, Pete," Mr. Pilgrim said.

"I think," Jesna began, "Jesus uses that phrase to show how much he identifies with us, and perhaps, to indicate that all people are invited to follow the perfect example he is setting—obedience unto death."

At that point Jesus rose up and continued his collision course for Jerusalem. He hadn't taken very many strides before James and John jogged up to him. James spoke eagerly, "Teacher, we want you to do us a favor."

"What is it that you want?" Jesus asked while continuing his pace.

"When you come into your reward, make it so that John and I will sit at your right and left hand."

"That's the weirdest request I've ever heard," Pete said. "If you're going to ask for a favor you might as well make it a big one. I would have asked for a flying carpet and a pizza that gets bigger as you eat it."

"Hush, Pete!" Priscilla said. "I want to hear his answer."

"You have no idea what you're asking. Are you capable of drinking the cup I drink, or of being baptized in the baptism I'm about to be plunged into?"

"We can do it!" they both chorused.

"Come to think of it," Jesus said, "you *will* drink the cup I drink, and be baptized in my baptism. But as to awarding places of honor, that's not my business. There are other arrangements for that."

"Who do you two think you are?" one of the disciples accused. "You're no better than the rest of us. Drop back in line!"

"Yeah! Maybe not even as good!" another echoed. "The rest of us aren't so power-hungry."

Jesus turned wearily and faced the bickering band. He spoke to them in stern tones.

"You've observed how godless rulers throw their weight around," he said, "and when people get a little power how quickly it goes to their heads. It's not going to be that way with you. Whoever wants to be great must become a servant. Whoever wants to be first among you must be your slave. That is what the Son of Man has done: He came to serve, not to be served—and then to give away his life in exchange for many who are held hostage."[145]

"Whew!" Mr. Pilgrim breathed. "That sure made me feel better about myself."

"In what way?" Jesna asked.

"Well, if after even three years straight with Jesus, the disciples still are wrestling with the need for power and recognition, then I don't feel so bad about my lapses into thinking worldly thoughts."

"You're certainly right that human nature is tough to kill."

"Sort've like a cockroach, huh, Jesna?"

"A lot like a cockroach, Pete. But it still has to be exterminated if you're going to be the kind of disciple Jesus just described—and not just a sinner with a good fire insurance plan."

"I bet Jesus will show them how to squash their cockroaches."

"That's where this road ends, and real life begins," Jesna said soberly.

FAMILY DISCUSSION

1. Have you noticed any parts of your self (thoughts, attitudes, behaviors) that are like cockroaches—hard to kill?

2. Why don't you take a few moments in silent prayer to confess those things to God and ask him to spray some divine "Raid" on them? You've got nothing to lose but your old nature.

SCENE 160
THE HEALING OF BLIND BARTIMAEUS[146]

"Next stop, oldest city in the world," Jesna announced.

"Jerusalem?" Priscilla asked.

"Nope."

"Cairo?" Mr. Pilgrim offered.

"Nope."

"Eden City?" Pete proposed.

"Nope," Jesna said again. "Jericho."

"Jericho?" Pete questioned. "I thought that place got vaporized way back in the Old Testament, when all those marchers blew their noses on it."

"*Trumpets*, Beanbrain!" Priscilla snorted. Jesna continued, undisturbed.

"The first Jericho was destroyed when Joshua led the Hebrew forces against it."

"With a big assist from God," Mrs. Pilgrim added.

"Right," Jesna said. "The Jericho we're going to visit on the way to Jerusalem has been rebuilt on a higher elevation close to the old site. It's still not very high, though—it's about eight hundred feet below sea level."

As Jesna was talking, we rounded a bend in the road. From that vantage point, we had a bird's-eye view of the tops of a thousand palm trees.

"There it is," Jesna said. "The place people call the 'City of Palm Trees.' The world's oldest city."

"Easy to see where the nickname comes from," Pete offered. "I guess they'd call *our* town 'City of Wal-Mart,' because that's the first thing you see."

Jesus and the disciples closed the distance between themselves and Jericho. We tagged along, gawking. As we got down to them, the palm trees seemed to grow before us until they towered over our heads.

As Jesus came to the outskirts of the tropical trade center, Pete spotted a blind man sitting by the roadside. "Poor guy," Pete said. "Can we give him some money or something?"

"He'd have a hard time spending a hologram quarter around here," Priscilla snorted.

Apparently the man heard all the footsteps going by. Staring blankly into the air, he called out, "What's all the commotion?"

A man standing nearby said to him, "Jesus the Nazarene is passing by."

At that the blind man yelled out at the top of his lungs, "Jesus! Son of David! Have mercy on me!"

Some of the disciples in front of Jesus spun around and squelched the man's yelp for help. "Shut up!" they barked.

"That's mean," Pete said. "Hey, you guys were blind once too, if you get my drift!"

"They're probably afraid the blind man's yelling will call unwelcome attention to Jesus," Jesna interjected. "Remember, the Sanhedrin does have a death warrant out for him."

But the disciples' command had no effect on the man who was desperate for his sight. He called out all the louder. "Jesus! Have mercy on me! You can make me see again!"

Jesus stopped and turned to face the man. As he began to walk toward him, Jesus said, "What do you want from me?"

"I want to see again!" the man cried out. "I want to see the faces of my children! I want to see so that I can support my family. I want to see so I am no longer a stumbling clown. Christ, have mercy!"

Jesus was obviously touched by the man's plight, and by his faith. His eyes became pools of tenderness as he studied the two dry wells of eyes that belonged to the beggar. Raising his right hand and pointing at the man he said,

"Go ahead—see again! Your faith has saved and healed you!"[147]

No spittle-mud this time; the man's healing was instantaneous! His random, blind eyes focused on the smiling face of Jesus. He whooped loudly enough to make a sleeping hound dog jump straight up like a startled cat. After that he became a one-man dance troupe following Jesus into town, where the bystanders became a praise-choir.

Once again, wall-shaking shouts were being heard in Jericho!

FAMILY DISCUSSION

1. If you had been blind, and then suddenly received your sight, what's the first thing you would do?
2. Why do you think Jesus agreed to perform such a spectacular healing on Bartimaeus—when he was trying to keep a low profile?

SCENE 161
THE WEE MAN[148]

We followed Bartimaeus' trail into the city of Jericho. Crowds of townspeople hurried to line both sides of the street, barely giving Jesus and his friends enough room to squeeze through.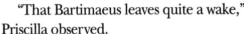

"That Bartimaeus leaves quite a wake," Priscilla observed.

"Who's that?" Pete asked, pointing like a hunting dog. "Is he riding a pogo stick?"

Even in the growing multitude, it didn't take me long to spot the one Pete was referring to. A round, bearded face was making periodic appearances up and over the shoulders of the people in the back row, like a full moon rising and setting every few seconds. He looked like a leprechaun on a pogo stick.

Jesna's pretty short, so she couldn't spot him right away. "Oh," she said after one of his higher bounces, "that's Zacchaeus."

"Zacchaeus?" Pete asked. "I know a song about him! 'The Wee Wee Man.' Here's how it goes: 'Zacchaeus was a wee wee man, a wee wee man was he-uh. He climbed up in a sycamore tree, for the Lord he wanted to see-uh.'"

"Pete," Priscilla said. "You really can't carry a tune."

"Oh yes I can. Hey, I sing good. Just ask Mom."

Mrs. Pilgrim made a point of giving her nails a quick inspection instead of making eye contact with her little monotone songbird.

Jesna came to the rescue. "Pete, Zacchaeus is a publican."

"Well, my dad used to be, too. Now he's a *re*publican."

"A publican, Pete, is an occupation. It's someone who collects money for the Roman government. And Zacchaeus is the chief tax collector for the entire city of Jericho."

"Do you have to be real short to get the job?" Pete asked.

"No!" Priscilla answered impatiently for Jesna. "Matthew was a tax collector in Capernaum and he's as tall as Dad. Remember?" She asked this while knocking on Pete's head as if it were a wooden door.

"Hey," Pete said, ignoring Priscilla's noggin-knocking. "What's ol' Zacchaeus doing now? He's climbing that tree like a monkey."

Just then, Jesus passed under Zacchaeus' perch. He stopped abruptly, causing a minor pile-up of his retinue. He said:

"Zacchaeus, come down. Quickly. Today I'm going to be a guest in your home."

"Hey! That was just like in the song!" Pete enthused.

Before Pete had finished his sentence, Zacchaeus was shimmying down the sycamore tree so fast that he knocked off sheets of bark—half of which landed on his head.

He ran to the side of Jesus and looked up. Way up.

"Master," he began, brushing bark dust from his hair and beard. "I'll give away half of everything I own to the poor. And if I have cheated when collecting taxes, I'll pay four times the damages."

Jesus was smiling down at the diminutive man, but the crowd didn't seem to share his warm feelings. I heard someone say, not very quietly, "Why would anyone want to be seen talking to a sinner like that?"

But Jesus lifted up his voice and proclaimed, still looking into Zacchaeus' pleading eyes.

"Today is salvation day in this home! Here he is: Zacchaeus, son of Abraham! For the Son of Man came to find and restore the lost."[149]

"Yep," Pete said, nodding approvingly. "That's just the way I sing it."

"Yes," Jesna said. "It's not your stature or importance in the community that gets you into God's kingdom. It's your persistence and the size of your faith that counts."

FAMILY DISCUSSION

1. Why do you think Jesus decided to go to Zacchaeus' house?
2. What do you think are some things that Zacchaeus asked Jesus about?
3. If Jesus were going to spend the night at your house tonight, what would you want to ask him? Well, since he is, go ahead and ask him!

SCENE 162
THE PARABLE OF THE POUNDS[150]

While Jesus had the attention of most of the people in "The-City-of-Palms-and-at-Least-One-Sycamore," he told them a story about the kingdom.

As he was just beginning, Jesna leaned over and whispered. "You need to keep in mind when you hear this story that a great expectation is building. The people feel that God's kingdom might appear any minute."

"There was once a man descended from a royal house who needed to make a long trip back to headquarters to get authorization for his rule and then return."

"That's really Jesus, huh?"
"Shhh, Pete."

"But first he called ten servants together, gave them each a sum of money, and instructed them, 'Operate with this until I return.'

"But the citizens there hated him. So they sent a commission with a signed petition to oppose his rule: 'We don't want this man to rule us.'

"When he came back bringing the authorization of his rule, he called those ten servants to whom he had given the money to find out how they had done.

"The first said, 'Master, I doubled your money.'

"He said, 'Good servant! Great work! Because you've been trustworthy in this small job, I'm making you governor of ten towns.'

"The second said, 'Master, I made a fifty percent profit on your money.'

"He said, 'I'm putting you in charge of five towns.'

"The next servant said, 'Master, here's your money safe and sound. I kept it hidden in the cellar. To tell you the truth, I was a little afraid. I know you have high standards and hate sloppiness, and don't suffer fools gladly.'

"He said, 'You're right that I don't suffer fools gladly—and you've acted the fool! Why didn't you at least invest the money in securities so I would have gotten a little interest on it?'

"Then he said to those standing there, 'Take the money from him and give it to the servant who doubled my stake.'

"They said, 'But Master, he already has double...'

"He said, 'That's what I mean: Risk your life and get more than you ever dreamed of. Play it safe and end up holding the bag.'

"'As for these enemies of mine who petitioned against my rule, clear them out of here. I don't want to see their faces around here again.'"[151]

Mr. Pilgrim sighed loudly. "That story is hard to understand. It almost makes God seem like a money-driven capitalist or something. From the way we've seen Jesus live for thirty years, usually without even two pennies to rub together, I know *that* can't be true."

"Well, Mr. Pilgrim, your son was off to a good start in interpreting the story. Jesus is the man who has, literally, 'descended' from a royal house. And if the truth be known, the story is as much for his disciples' benefit as it is for those in the crowd. They are the ten (plus or minus two) servants who have been given something extremely valuable (knowledge of the kingdom of God) and who will soon be told to 'operate with this until I return.'"

"With all of that known, the point of the story becomes simple."

"Better to bet on the horses than stick your money under a rock?"

"No, Pete."

"Jesus is coming back with proof that he is the King's Son?"

"That's part of it, Priscilla."

"Be aggressive in investing what Jesus has taught you about the kingdom into the lives of others."

"*Exactly*, Mr. Pilgrim! Loves always grows if spent on others. But it shrinks if hidden. To not invest it because of fear likely means that you never really had it in the first place. Perfect love casts out fear. Remember?"

FAMILY DISCUSSION

1. What are some ways that you can invest your knowledge and love in the lives of others?
2. What is likely to happen if you do some of those things tomorrow?

SCENE 163
THE ANOINTING AT BETHANY[152]

Jesus and his band of investors awoke bright and early the next morning to continue their journey. All but one had empty moneypouches.

Eleven had hearts filled with a king's treasure. These ones were well on their way to becoming good stewards of real treasure. The twelfth was the group's treasurer. He always kept his valuables hidden, and he was only days away from losing all that had been given to him.

After about an hour of marching, Jesna announced, "It's only a few more days to Passover." No one was excited.

It was a long day's walk that took us up from hundreds of feet below sea level to Jerusalem. Jesna reminded us that we were on the same road the Judean and the good Samaritan had once taken. That information had the unfortunate effect of making everyone begin to look over their shoulders for approaching thieves.

"Hey!" Jesna had to finally say. "Holograms can't get

mugged. Lighten up a bit. Besides, you're in line behind the best Shepherd in the business."

After a few more hours of uphill marching, Pete spoke up. "Speaking for myself, this hologram's legs hurt. And my ears are popping. Why ain't we ridin'?"

"Because I've sent the car on ahead. I thought you'd appreciate *feeling* things, just like Jesus is, for a while."

Several more hours passed. The sun had grown in size and was sitting heavily on the horizon when it became obvious that we were bypassing Jerusalem this time.

Before anyone could ask, Jesna explained. "We're going to Bethany tonight."

"Lazarus hasn't died again, has he?"

"No, Pete. Jesus just wants to spend some time with his friends before going into Jerusalem for Passover."

"I can sure understand that," Mrs. Pilgrim nodded. "He probably needs the moral support."

Just before the last of the sunset colors bled into the night, we all arrived at Jesus' southern headquarters. It seemed strange to see a twentieth-century roller-coaster car parked in the pathway to the house.

Jesus was greeted by the warm embrace of Mary, Martha, and Lazarus. Martha prepared quickly for an additional thirteen ravenous guests.

Martha served and Lazarus kept everyone entertained with tales about his near-life experience, but Mary had disappeared. Near the end of the meal, she re-entered the room, an alabaster jar in her hands. She knelt at Jesus' feet and took off the top of the beautiful container. A million flowers came rushing into my nostrils. I began to wag my tail wildly with joy. Even to inferior human noses, it must have smelled wonderful.

Mary poured a generous amount of oil from the jar onto Jesus' feet and rubbed it in with her fingers. When she finished, she began to wipe his feet with her *hair!*

"You know, Mom, you really should buy these folks some towels," Pete offered. We really didn't quite know what to make of it all.

But Judas did. Suddenly, his hand crashed down on the wooden table, and he thundered, "Why wasn't this expensive perfume sold and the money given to the poor? It could have brought three hundred silver pieces!"

"Hey, man!" Pete exclaimed. "What crawled into Judas' shorts?"

"Well," Jesna began, "you can rest assured that it *isn't* concern for the poor. Judas is in love with money. He's in charge of the group's money box, as you know, and he doesn't mind helping himself to the funds."

Jesus was indignant.

"Let her alone. She's anticipating and honoring the day of my burial. You always have the poor with you. You don't always have me."[153]

Judas was standing to his feet. Martha placed her serving tray on the table and made her way to his side. She touched his shoulder. "Don't be angry, Judas. It wasn't so long ago that I thought as you do."

But her intended balm was not received. Judas jerked away from her and bolted for the door—away from heavenly smells and Divine Anointing.

FAMILY DISCUSSION

1. What do you think Martha meant when she said that she used to think like Judas? Was she talking about money?
2. Are there any ways that you still think like Judas?
3. If there are, why don't you take a moment and ask Jesus to make your heart softer in those areas? Then go and "waste" some time and/or money on Jesus and his friends.

SCENE 164
THE TRIUMPHAL ENTRY[154]

The next morning Jesus roused his disciples and gave a triple embrace to Mary, Martha, and Lazarus. Then he began walking away in the direction of the Mount of Olives. Groggily, twelve silent men followed along behind. Of course, we came too.

While we were all en route, Pete made conversation, "Boy, you can still smell that brute, can't you?!"

"What brute? What do you mean?" Mr. Pilgrim asked, sniffing the air.

"You know, Dad, all that *Brut* cologne Mary was splashing on Jesus. I can still smell it this morning. Don't get me wrong," Pete continued, "but I have to admit I was wondering the same thing that Judas was. Why *do* you think Mary would pour all that perfume on Jesus? He wasn't even going to church or anywhere last night."

There was an awkward silence. Jesna cleared her throat.

"I hate to be the one to remind everyone," she began, "but Jesus *is* headed somewhere. To Death."

Everyone got real quiet.

"And in case you didn't know," Jesna continued, "it's the

custom, here, to wash a dead body and anoint it with aromatic spices in preparation for burial."

Everyone got even quieter.

Mr. Pilgrim finally interrupted the silence. "Do you mean that's what Mary was doing last night. She was saying goodby to Jesus, and anointing him for his, uh,..."

"For his death. Yes, Mr. Pilgrim. That's exactly what she was doing."

"But," Priscilla began, "how would she know that Jesus will die real soon? I don't think I've heard him mention that, at least not directly."

"That's one of the benefits of staying as close to Jesus as Mary did. Listening to his every word with her heart, she learned the will and ways of God."

"Wow!" Mr. Pilgrim shook his head from side-to-side. "She wasn't wasting any time at all."

"Nope," Jesna said. "One minute of action by someone who has spent a day listening to God will accomplish more than a day of action by someone who has given only a minute to divine listening and loving.

"Amen," was Mr. Pilgrim's succinct commentary.

It wasn't long until our procession came to a halt about halfway up the Mount of Olives.

We were standing in the midst of a beautiful grove of gnarled trees. Their twisted shade provided welcome refreshment from the spring sun.

Jesus turned and faced his followers. Their faces were a patchwork of sun and shadows. Pointing to two of them he said, "Go to that village over there. As soon as you enter it you'll find a colt tied to a tree. It's never been ridden. Untie it and bring it back here."

"Are they just going to colt-nap it?" Pete asked.

Jesus answered Pete's question. "If anyone asks, 'What are you doing?' just say, 'My master needs him.'"

The two disciples left without question—as if they were well-trained soldiers. We waited together in the shade, conversing quietly as we sat in small groupings on rock piles. Jesna explained to us that the Mount of Olives was sort of like Jerusalem's park—a place for the people who wanted to escape the heat and crowds of the city.

Well, if this was a city park, Jesus had quickly become the fountain in its center, a wishing-well for the growing multitude. People began to discover that he was here.

About thirty minutes passed before the disciples returned with a very reluctant colt. With the help of a rope tied around the colt's neck, they brought their charge muzzle-to-face with Jesus. They were beaming. "It was just as you said, Master."

With that, they pulled off their cloaks and laid them across the back of the colt. The colt eyed them uneasily, but it remained motionless in apparent respect for its Maker. Jesus threw his leg over the colt's slender back.

The people who had gathered around Jesus erupted with shouts of praise. Half of them ran to gather olive branches, hastily blanketing the road in front of the Messiah-bearing colt. The other half became a roadside choir singing choruses of "Hosannahs" as they made their way toward the top of the mount.

They sang:

> "Blessed he who comes,
>   the king in God's name!
> All's well in heaven!
>   Glory in the high places![155]

Some startled, black-robed party-poopers began to rain on the procession. They shouted: "Hey! You had better get your disciples under control!"

But Jesus answered them above the shouting: "If I tell them to keep quiet, the stones and the trees will sing praises for them."

The detractors fell to the back of the cavalcade and began to inspect the ground, apparently waiting for the stones to do something.

The joyous procession continued on up the mountain until it reached its crest.

"Oh, look!" Mrs. Pilgrim exclaimed. "What a beautiful view of Jerusalem!" From the top of the Mount of Olives the Holy City had become a breathtaking poster. "What clear air! I think I can see every stone and water pot from here."

The view did more than take the breath from Jesus—it put tears in his eyes. To the background shouts of praises, Jesus' shoulders began to shake with sorrow.

"Lean in close," Jesna instructed. "I want you to hear this."

We heard Jesus' tear-streaked soliloquy:

"If you [Jerusalem] had only recognized this day, and everything that was good for you. But now it's too late. In the days ahead your enemies are going to bring up their heavy artillery and surround you, pressing in from every side. They'll smash you and your babies on the pavement. Not one stone will be left intact. All because you didn't recognize and welcome God's personal visit."[156]

In all of history there may have been no greater contrast: a joyous crowd singing exuberant praises for a sobbing King who wept over the future of his capital city.

FAMILY DISCUSSION

1. What would you have thought if you had seen Jesus crying over Jerusalem while a party was going on all around?
2. What can you do, right now, to recognize and welcome God's personal visit to your life?

SCENE 165
CLEAN TEMPLES AND DIRTY FARMHANDS: PART ONE[157]

As we made our way down from the Mount of Olives, through the Garden of Gethsemane and a large city gate, the crowd gathered in size, noise, and momentum.

Along the parade route, Jesna told us more about the Mount of Olives. She told us that in about forty years, the same spot where Jesus now wept would be covered by raucous legions of Roman soldiers. "They will call that crest of the Mount 'the Lookout,'" she said, "and under the direction of Titus, the son of the future emperor Vespasian, they will brutally capture Jerusalem and desecrate the Temple."

"Man!" Pete exclaimed after Jesna's description had helped him to better share Jesus' concern. "Being able to see into the future can be hard on the emotions." Mr. and Mrs. Pilgrim agreed. I'm just a dog, but I did whimper with sympathy for Jesus, seeing him in such grief.

The impassioned crowd had not even noticed their King's weeping. They had been too busy laying a layer of palm branches in front of Jesus. The new-road fabrication caused Pete to do some fabricating of his own—an off-key *Wizard of Oz* chorus of "follow the palm-branch road." The rest of us tried to quiet him, especially as we approached the Temple precincts.

In the center of the Temple courtyard, Jesus raised a hand and stopped the parade. The loud assembly quickly became reverently quiet.

Jesna whispered, "Half of the people in Jerusalem are probably waiting for Jesus to announce himself as the Messiah, the One whom everyone has been awaiting for centuries. One word from him, right now," she continued, "and all the soldiers in the city would be tossed over the walls."

But the Roman tyrants were not the villains Jesus had in mind for a good tossing. His voice thundered through the courtyard. "Holy Scripture says, 'My house is a house of prayer; you have turned it into a den of robbers.'"

Then, as the paraders stood frozen in disbelief, Jesus began to clean house. For the second time in three years, he sent donkeys galloping, doves flapping, coins raining, and red-faced entrepreneurs scurrying.

Pete was fired up. He changed his "yellow brick road" tune to a rhythmic chant of "Go Jesus! Go Jesus!" Somehow, no one else could share his enthusiasm.

Priscilla muttered the understatement of her life to everyone but her cheerleader brother: "I guess this isn't what they had in mind when they were wanting to make Jesus their king."

"No," Jesna said stolidly. "But it's what Jesus always has in mind, when he's asked to be king, either in the whole world or in one of our single hearts."

Then she went on, "there's something else I meant to tell you about the Mount of Olives. When the olives are ripe they are knocked down with poles and crushed to make oil. One of the chief uses for that oil is to supply fuel for the Temple lights."

She had our attention.

"Jesus' ministry is now like ripe olives," she continued. "Soon *he'll* be beaten and crushed. And his chief purpose will become fueling the light of the temple in his followers' hearts."

Then she looked directly into the eyes of each of the Pilgrims as she said, "Take care that you don't ever let that light go out. It's easy for a temple to become cold and dark."

FAMILY DISCUSSION

1. Jesus cleaned the Temple in Jerusalem both at the beginning and at the end of his ministry. What do you believe is significant about that?
2. What do you think the people in the "parade" were thinking when Jesus was turning over tables and chasing people around?

SCENE 166
CLEAN TEMPLES AND DIRTY FARMHANDS: PART TWO[158]

Once Jesus had his Father's house put back in order, he took a deep, slow breath. His surprising opening act had cost him a large slice of his audience. Scanning the astonished remainder, he proceeded to a stone bench to do some story-telling.

As usual, the ranks of his listeners included the committed, the curious—and the hostile. This kingdom-prophet's avid crowds were causing the religious leaders to plot new ways of holding onto their job security.

During the next few days before the beginning of Passover, Jesus taught with great urgency and passion. We all knew that he only had a few grains of sand left in the top half of the hourglass of his life.

As he looked out over his daily congregation, always a teeming mixture of eagerness, apathy, and back-row disdain, the sea of faces was like a harvest field—a fertile one—but with huge patches of weeds and rocks.

Eventually the "rocks" cried out. "Again we ask you, Jesus," someone in the black row sneered. "By whose authority are you saying these outlandish things?"

"A good question!" Jesus said. "And I'll answer it. But first let me ask *you* a question. Who do you say authorized the work that John the Baptist was doing? Heaven or humans?"

"Checkmate!" Priscilla triumphed.

"What do you mean, Prissy?" Pete asked.

"If they say 'heaven,' Jesus will ask them why they didn't believe him. If they say 'humans,' many in the crowd, whom I recognize from John's baptism lines, will turn against them."

"Good for you!" Jesna grinned.

The black-robed questioner, after consulting with his cohorts, admitted, "We don't know."

"Then neither will I answer your question," Jesus replied. "But I will tell you a story."

He began another farmhand story, a parable about a man who planted a vineyard and then, just before leaving on a trip, put it in the care of his farmhands. The man was gone for a very long time.

After the first harvest season he sent a servant to collect the profits from those who had been left in charge. But the farmhands beat the owner's servant within an inch of his

life, and sent him back bruised and empty-handed.

The owner sent another servant and then another. Each returned with bigger bruises and deeper cuts than the first.

At that point the owner said to himself, "I know what I'll do. I can't go myself, but I'll send my own son. They are bound to respect him as my flesh-and-blood representative."

But they did not. The greedy vineyard watchers said to themselves, "Here's our chance! Let's kill the heir! Then the vineyard will be ours alone." They murdered the owner's only son and tossed his body from the vineyard.

"So," Jesus said after letting a long silence rest on the audience, "What do you think the rightful owner will do next?

"Right. He'll come and clean house. Then he'll assign the care of the vineyard to others."[159]

Another long silence followed while God's Son looked out over the ripe grapes of his Father's vineyard. Black-robed "farmhands" began to huddle together in the back row as the stormclouds gathered. They *knew* the story was about them.

Eleven disciples and four Pilgrims waited for their new assignments. They were anxious to begin working in God's vineyard.

FAMILY DISCUSSION
1. What job do you think God will assign to you—in caring for his vineyard (the church)?
2. What can you do tomorrow to work for God?

SCENE 167
MORE TRICKS FROM
THE PHARISEES[160]

"Come on!" Pete said excitedly. "Let's go protect Jesus! Look how mad those mean men are, after *that* story!"

Jesna reached out and grabbed the little would-be storm trooper by the sleeve. "Hold on, Pete. They *would* like to snatch him up, they'd like to lynch him—but they won't. Jesus has the people on *his* side. So he's safe for now."

Pete dropped his assault. She dropped his sleeve.

"What will happen," Jesna said, "is that the religious leaders will try to win the people to their side. They'll be sending spies into the crowd to ask Jesus some trick questions. If they can cause even a slight shift in public opinion, they'll waste no time in seizing the moment—and Jesus."

Jesna was right. The next twenty-four hours brought in a ragtag assortment of malcontents who tried to challenge Jesus at every turn.

One of these Pharisee-hired-spies hissed, "Good Teacher, please answer this for me. We all know you are a righteous and wise man. So, tell us all, right out, is it proper to give Jewish money—taxes—to Caesar, or not?"

"He's got him now!" a scruffy character stage-whispered behind my left ear.

"Show me one of your coins," Jesus said to his inquisitor.

The well-dressed man reached inside his robe and pulled something out. It was a shiny, silver coin that flashed in the sunlight.

"Will this denarius do?" the man said in a proud voice.

"Look at that," Pete said. "It looks just like a dime. But who's that woman on it with the wavy 'do'?"

"That's not a woman," Jesna giggled. "That's Caesar

Augustus. And it's no dime. That coin is worth about a thousand dimes. It's equal to a day's wage for most of the ordinary folks here."

Jesus was studying the coin as the man held it out.

Jesna whispered, cocking her head toward Jesus, "He's about to set the hook."

Jesus reached out and gave the surface of the coin a light touch with a finger. The man looked nervous about this prized possession.

"This engraving here," Jesus mused, "who do you think it is?"

"Caesar, of course," the man snapped.

"Then," said Jesus, "I would recommend that you give Caesar what is created in his image, *and,* he continued, tapping lightly on the man's chest, I would urge you to give back to God what is created in *his* likeness."

"But you'd better hurry," Pete jumped in, as Jesus was giving the man's bosom a couple more taps, "from the sound of things, that heart of yours is getting pretty hard and brittle. Remember, it's worth a whole Temple-full of silver coins."

FAMILY DISCUSSION

1. What do you think Jesus meant by saying that the man should give what is in Caesar's image to Caesar and what is in God's image to God?
2. What do you have that has God's stamp on it?
3. How do you go about giving it back to him—each day?

SCENE 168
ANOTHER HARD QUESTION—
ABOUT THE RESURRECTION[161]

"Wait a cotton-pickin' minute!" Pete said, holding up his stubby hands. "Do you mean I don't have to give any of my money to the church; I can get by with only giving *myself?*"

Mr. and Mrs. Pilgrim seemed too stunned to respond.

"If that's true, Dad, then I want that dollar back. The one you made me put in the orphan's plate. I could've bought two giant Snickers bars with that dollar."

"Well, um," Mr. Pilgrim began. "I'm sure Jesus wasn't saying that you don't need to give money to the church, was he, Jesna?"

Jesna folded her arms across her small chest. "I think it's very important to remember that Jesus was dealing with a wealthy man, sent by the religious leaders, who was trying to trick him in front of the crowd. But don't forget Jesus' reply to them. He said that the kingdom of heaven is much higher, wider, better, than any of earth's kingdoms or concerns. Which plate you pitch your pennies into is all but insignificant. In reality it's a single human heart that is the most valuable commodity to God. More valuable than all the lifeless gold he sprinkled over the earth."

"So," Pete said while impatiently tapping his small foot. "Do I get my money back or not? I'm waiting.... "

"Pete," Jesna said while looking her student right in the eyes. "Which would make you happier? Eating Snickers bars, or seeing a little boy who had no food eat a delicious sandwich?"

"I guess, if you put it like that, watching him eat would."

"Then there's your answer," Jesna said. "When you give

your created-in-his-image heart back to God there'll be plenty of opportunities for things that are even more delicious than candy-eating."

"Wow!" Priscilla said to Jesna. "You're almost as good as Jesus at answering questions."

"Oh, I let him answer all the tough ones," Jesna said.

A movement behind them caught their attention. Apparently, another search-and-destroy squadron was arriving from the religious leaders' stronghold. Three well-fed gentlemen in embroidered linen robes elbowed their way to the front of the assemblage with artificial smiles, preceded by their perfume.

"Sadducees," Jesna whispered. "They're a well-to-do religious party of the Jewish aristocracy. They don't believe in life after death. The religious leaders must be getting pretty desperate," Jesna added, "if the Pharisees and Sadducees—sworn political enemies—are cooperating with each other to arrest Jesus."

"Teacher," a Sadducee asked through his nose, "Moses wrote that if a man dies and leaves his wife without a child, his brother must take the widow as his wife and give her a child."

Jesna huddled with the Pilgrims to interpret the scene which was unfolding. "He said, 'Moses wrote,' because the Sadducees only accept the written law. They don't welcome the added traditions of the Pharisees. So I guess that they're willing to help the Pharisees, but not without a knife-twist of their own."

"And, let's suppose," the insincere questioner continued, "that a tragic situation occurred, one in which there were seven brothers—each of whom were obligated to marry the same woman because each brother before had died before the woman conceived a child."

"Whoa!" Pete tittered. "Time to check your lunch for arsenic!"

"Now, Teacher," the Sadducee said in mock seriousness, continuing to set the mousetrap, "tell us, after the wife dies, whose mate will she be? All seven brothers married her."

Jesus had a ready answer:

"Marriage is a major preoccupation here, but not there. Those who are included in the resurrection of the dead will no longer be concerned with marriage nor, of course, with death. They will have better things to think about, if you can believe it. All ecstasies and intimacies then will be with God. Even Moses exclaimed [Jesus said, with a knowing nod to the Sadducees] about resurrection at the burning bush, saying, 'God: God of Abraham, God of Isaac, God of Jacob!' God isn't the God of dead men, but of the living. To him all are alive."[162]

Both the Pharisees and the Sadducees were staggered by the wisdom of Jesus' reply. "That's a great answer!" members of both political parties were heard to exclaim.

After that there were fewer trick questions from the religious leaders. I think they became afraid that if they kept getting close enough to Jesus to ask questions, the truth of his answers would begin to dissolve the lines that divided them.

FAMILY DISCUSSION

1. How do you think the people in the audience are feeling—when an ordinary-looking person like Jesus is able to answer all the toughest questions of the trained, religious leaders?

2. Reread the quote of Jesus above. If heaven is so much different from earth-life, what can you do to start preparing to live there?

SCENE 169
THE GREATEST COMMANDMENT[163]

"He's silenced the Sadducees!" rippled through the crowded courtyard.

"Jesus knows more about heaven than the Sadducees," a man next to me mused.

"I guess so," came a reply, "those rich, friends-of-Rome don't even believe in heaven."

"That's why they're so sad-you-see," Pete said as he gave the man an elbow through the knee.

"Hey," Pete continued. "Will you and Mom be married in heaven?"

"I hate to admit it but I was wondering the same thing," Priscilla said sheepishly.

"In heaven," Jesna began, "you will know each other as you are known in earth-life. It's just that the joy of being in God's presence will overshadow past relationships. Current relationships will become like the moon—real, present, beautiful, but primarily a reflection of a greater light."

"So I can still go out in the heaven-yard and play catch with Dad up there? And Priscilla can still plant flowers with Mom?"

"Yes," Jesna said with a smile. "But after a million years or so you'll probably want to come in for a cookie."

Pete seemed satisfied with the prospects of his after-life.

Someone—from his tone it was difficult to tell if he were asking for himself or the religious leaders who had just left red-faced—asked a question.

"Which commandment is the first of all, Jesus?"

"That man is a scribe, uh, a lawyer," Jesna enlightened them.

"Watch out, Jesus!" Pete shouted. "Don't answer! He's one of those evil scribe-lawyers! It's a trap!"

"Pete! Where do you get your opinions?" Mrs. Pilgrim asked, startled. Pete's dad opened his mouth and shut it again.

Jesus ignored Pete. He answered,

"'Love the Lord your God with all your passion and prayer and intelligence.' This is the most important, the first on any list. But there is a second to set alongside it: 'Love others as well as you love yourself.' These two commands are pegs; everything in God's Law and the Prophets hangs from them."[164]

"Isn't that interesting," Priscilla said. "Jesus told that man that the most important commandment is the same one he probably straps to his head in church—you know in that leather pouch, phylactery. You'd think he already knew that."

"It's a very long way from the head to the heart," Jesna said. "A very long way."

FAMILY DISCUSSION

1. What are some things you can do as a family to make sure that time is given each day to keeping the two great commandments?

2. Why not write out a "Family Rule of Life" to make sure that these commandments are kept each day. [e.g., "I will spend at least five minutes each day in silent listening before God." "We will spend at least one meal each day sitting down together as a family." "We will have a family devotion each night."]

SCENE 170
WOE TO THE SCRIBES AND PHARISEES[165]

With the Pharisees off regrouping, Jesus turned his attention to his disciples and faithful listeners. For a while he enjoyed the luxury of not having to teach in spite of trick questions.

As he lectured, I noticed that Priscilla had become absorbed in her wrist-computer, even more so than usual. For longer than it takes the Pilgrims to watch a TV sitcom, she was gazing at the tiny screen strapped to her wrist and punching buttons with the tip of a pen. Her parents noticed, too.

"Pssst! Priscilla. What are you doing?" Mrs. Pilgrim whispered. "You're missing what Jesus is saying."

"I'm just running a few calculations, Mom," Priscilla responded without looking up. "I really liked what Jesus said about the two most important commandments, and I'm calculating what effect it would have on the world if everybody followed them." Now she not only had my attention, but also Jesna's and that of her entire family.

"I warned you, Mom. I told you," Pete said. "It's happened. Too much learning has made her go nuts."

"No," Priscilla said, defending herself. "It's simple. I just punched in what our country's budget is for the last fiscal year and then subtracted all the spending that wouldn't be necessary if every person in the whole world *really* did love God with their whole heart, and their neighbors as much as they loved themselves."

"You did what?" the other Pilgrims said.

"Well, I just punched in how much money the federal,

state, and local governments spent last year, then I started subtracting the amounts that *wouldn't* have to be spent if everybody simply kept Jesus' two commandments."

"Hmm?"

"The first to go was the defense budget, over a trillion dollars. Then I sliced off the amounts needed to finance police departments, and prisons, and, well, I ended up taking off the costs for the entire judicial system."

"I read somewhere that over 80 percent of medical costs weren't due to disease but to sinful lifestyles and stress," Mrs. Pilgrim offered.

"Right, Mom. I took off the costs of addictions, and other lifestyle and stress-related medical costs. But it only came to 76.2 percent of the total medical expenses in the country.... ."

"She's making this up, Dad."

"No," Jesna said, "she's right on the button."

"I also subtracted the cost for much of the welfare and social security costs for the elderly—since churches and families would be providing most of the care. Anyway," she continued while punching at her wrist three last times, "it looks like we could easily save more than three-quarters of the costs contained in these budgets—trillions and trillions of dollars—if we would just obey those two laws.

"And all this would mean that people would have more time, too. Time is money too. For instance, if parents wanted to get more involved in the education of their own children, since they would have the time (because it would only take 12.4 hours of work each week to support your family—given all these savings and the fact that you no longer have to buy the *best* house and car on the block, since you love everyone and you're not competing with your neighbors anymore), you could subtract a lot from the education budget, too."

"Whew, Priscilla," Mrs. Pilgrim said, "your fingers must be sore."

"My brain is sore just listening to you," Pete exclaimed. "I need some mental floss to get all that stuff back out."

Priscilla was still glued to the screen. "The cost of breaking Jesus' two rules is staggering, and I don't think the cost is just financial!"

Mr. Pilgrim just wobbled his head. I'm never sure if he's responding to his daughter's intelligence or the dullness of his world.

But before his Priscilla could elaborate further, Jesus' words seized our attention.

"The religion scholars and Pharisees are good teachers of the Law. You should follow their teachings..."

"What!" Pete exclaimed. "See what you've done, Prissy. While we were listening to you, Jesus joined up with the Pharisees. I can't believe it."

"Keep listening," Jesna said.

"You won't go wrong following their teachings on Moses," Jesus continued. "You just shouldn't follow *them*. They're long on teaching and short on living. They don't take it into their hearts to let it change their attitudes, values, and behaviors. They're like polished and shiny toilet bowls.

"What God gives as simple, liberating rules of

life, they wrap with pounds and pounds of unnecessary doctrine, and then load you down like pack animals. They even seem to enjoy watching you strain under the burden. Meanwhile, they are busy clamoring for the choice seats at the head table and at church dinners, and basking in the rays of public praise, choice positions, and honorary degrees.

"But, I say,

"Don't let people do that to *you,* put you on a pedestal like that. You all have a single Teacher, and you are all classmates. Don't set people up as experts over your life, letting them tell you what to do. Save that authority for God; let *him* tell you what to do. No one else should carry the title of 'Father'; you have only one Father, and he's in heaven. And don't let people maneuver you into taking charge of them. There is only one Life-Leader for you and them—Christ.

"Do you want to stand out? Then step down. Be a servant. If you puff yourself up, you'll get the wind knocked out of you. But if you're content to simply be yourself, your life will count for plenty."[166]

"I don't get it," Priscilla said to Jesna. "Why is it so hard for the Pharisees to see the simple truth of what Jesus is saying? Or for modern-day folks to see the truth of these numbers I came up with?"

"Perhaps," Jesna began, "the difficulty isn't in seeing it; it's in *living* it, when living it requires the acceptance of two painful crosses. The one Jesus must bear, and our own.

FAMILY DISCUSSION

1. If tomorrow you decided to "be a servant," what would be different?

2. Jesus called the most respected religious leaders of the day, "polished toilet bowls." What does *that* mean?

SCENE 171
A WIDOW'S GIFT[167]

Jesus' last few teaching sessions had been in the Temple treasury. The sharp clinks of coins being dropped into the thirteen "trumpet" baskets had often sounded like misplaced punctuations to his statements about the religious leaders.

Jesus had just finished his latest rebuke: " ... and all the time they are exploiting the weak, who cannot help themselves. You can tell the worst of the religious leaders. They are the ones who pray the longest. But in the end it will be them who are weak and helpless. The oppressed will be exalted." At that moment he looked over his shoulder.

Everyone followed his gaze. Just inside the door was a long line of men clothed in bright, clean robes, followed by one woman in a plain dull garment. The men appeared to be standing in order—each being dressed more splendidly than the one he followed. Each one held out, for all observers to notice, a fistful of silver coins. In turn, each slowly poured his gift into the appropriate offering basket.

"What are those guys doing?" Pete asked. "Trying to see who can pour the longest?"

Behind the column of high rollers, you could hardly see the woman. She was stooped over at the waist, it was hard to tell if from age or sickness or humiliation.

"Look closely at this woman," Jesus said to his listeners. "*She* should be your role model."

"Look" was all that Pete ever needed to hear Jesus say. It was like him saying "sic 'em" to me. He bolted in for a closer view.

The woman's cracked lips were moving with quiet prayer. She stretched out a frail hand and let two dull coins slide quietly into the basket. I hoped she had not heard one of the rich men snort.

"No, lady," Pete said. "You should keep that money. You look like you don't have much left, and like its been a long time since your last biscuit. I'll get them back for you, and," (he was now talking with his head and both arms inside the basket and his feet off the ground) "I'll pick up some of this rich money for you too." Try as he might, his little hologram hands were not up to the task. He came up empty. The woman had already disappeared into the next room.

Jesus made his assessment of what we had seen.

"The plain truth is that this widow has given by far the largest offering today. All these others made offerings that they'll never miss; she gave extravagantly what she couldn't afford—she gave her all!"[168]

"You mean those two dinky little coins are the most money anyone gave? They must have been made of platiminium or something!" Pete exclaimed.

"That's not the case," Jesna began to elaborate. "The coins she gave, which will become known as the 'Widow's Mite,' are called 'leptons,' and they are usually made of some inferior grade of bronze or copper. They are worth so little that only the poor would bother to bend over and pick up a dropped one."

"What was the picture on it? It looked like the sun."

"One side of a lepton does show the sun, with eight rays representing the Sun of Righteousness; the other side ... "

"'Tails,' right, Jesna?"

" ... has a ship's anchor on it. That symbolizes the steadfast-ness of God's promises."

"My," said Priscilla. "I didn't know the Romans could be so religious."

"The Romans didn't mint that coin," Jesna explained. "A Jewish high priest, John Hyrcanus, was allowed to make leptons about eighty years ago."

"And Jesus liked those coins the best?" Pete said. "He must like the pictures better than those Caesar-headed coins the rich guys were making such a show of plunking down."

"It isn't the coin Jesus prefers, Pete," Jesna said very seriously. "It is the gift."

"Hum?"

"The woman had attached her *faith* to those coins. And attached to her faith was her*self.* She put her whole self into the Temple offering basket. The rich guys just gave metal."

FAMILY DISCUSSION

1. What would you have to give to offer God a "Widow's Mite" gift?
2. Why not discuss the "pros" and "cons" of making such a gift?

SCENE 172
SIGNS BEFORE THE END OF THE WORLD[169]

Right after the poor widow left the Temple, Jesus and his disciples left too. They were going to spend the night under the stars in Jerusalem's Mount of Olives park.

While we were still walking with them through the shadowy, narrow streets of Jerusalem, Pete piped up, "Oh, *now* I get it! That old lady's *coins* became known as the 'Widow's *Mite!*'"

"What did you think, little brother? That's as plain as the mouth on your face!"

"Well I always thought the preacher was saying we need to give because the 'widows might.' You know, like they might or they might not. So we had better give just in case...."

"Peter Pilgrim," Priscilla moaned. "It sure is a good thing you took this ride. I've seen salads that weren't as tossed-up as your Bible knowledge is."

Pete was winding up for his comeback when he was interrupted by one of the disciples.

"You know, Jesus, I understand you're not high on the religious leaders—and with real good reasons, of course—but Judas was just saying, and I have to agree, the architecture of that place is truly amazing, don't you think so?"

"He's right," Pete said, dropping his retort. "I mean I bet you couldn't squash more than four or five Temples (counting the courtyard) inside the walls of Jerusalem, even if you used a shoe horn and lots of Crisco. It's *huge*. And it's gorgeous. I bet it took a million years to build it."

The look on Jesus' face showed that he wasn't nearly as impressed. He said to the disciple, "Don't be so easily awed by size and craftsmanship. There's not one stone there in that Temple which will not end up in a pile of rubble."

The disciple dropped back. Pete dropped back to walk by Jesna.

"Jesus is more concerned about the craftsmanship of this temple *here*," Jesna quietly told Pete, giving him a couple of light thumps on the chest. "And," she continued, "don't forget what he sees in Jerusalem's future."

Later that evening, Jesus was sitting in the shadow of an ancient olive tree near the crest of the mountain. Jerusalem lay unfurled before him. Its stone walls appeared to be made of gold in the last rays of the day's sunlight.

He had just started a fire for the evening meal. The fire was still popping with new life when the same disciple who had admired the Temple approached him hesitantly, the others clustering close behind him. The disciple said, "Tell us then, when will these terrible things happen?"

Jesus didn't look up for a long time. Then, reluctantly, he began. "Many terrible things will happen before the end of time." He did not break his gaze away from the dancing flames. "There will be wars and rumors of wars, there will be false prophets claiming to be me, the true Messiah, and there will be great famines and earthquakes throughout the earth. But all of this will only be early labor pains for what will follow—more severe pain and then new birth.

"All of you here, and many disciples after you, will be hated, hunted, and killed because of your love for me. But you must remember:

> "Staying with it—that's what God requires. Stay with it to the end. You won't be sorry, and you'll be saved. All during this time the good news—the Message of the kingdom—will be preached all over the world, a witness staked out in every country. And then the end will come."[170]

"Whoa," said Pete. "It sounds like that will be the time to grab hold of God's love like my teddy bear."

FAMILY DISCUSSION

1. What would you be feeling if you were a disciple, standing by a fire and listening to Jesus tell you about the end of the world?

2. If talking about the end of the world is scary or uncomfortable, talk to your parents and then together you can talk to Jesus about your fears. He doesn't want you to be frightened of what the future holds. He'll be with you always.

SCENE 173
FALSE CHRISTS AND
FALSE PROPHETS[171]

Jesus continued talking to his friends about the end of the world as the firelight became brighter than that of the setting sun. He had the disciples' spellbound attention.

He had mine too! Even though there were a lot of sticks around that needed fetching.

"This is getting a little spooky," Pete announced. "It's kind of like ghost stories around a campfire. But with Jesus telling 'em, I know they're all true."

"Yes, Pete," Jesna said as she put a small hand on his shoulder. "You've become Jesus' special friend. He's not telling these things to frighten you, but to give you extra courage when difficult times come. You'll then be able to help others who may not have become his friends yet."

"But why do so many bad things have to happen at the end of time, Jesna?" Priscilla asked.

"Time doesn't ever end. It's the rule of the Prince of Darkness over the earth that will be ending."

"And snakes don't die pretty, huh, Jesna?"

"That's right, Pete. They sure don't." She continued, "You see, right now (the Bible-time 'now') and on up through your 'now' there are two kingdoms. There is God's kingdom of 'other-love' that Jesus is planting. And there's the kingdom of 'self-love' that Satan heads up.

"What you've seen Jesus doing, and especially what he's about to do, is the beginning of the end of the dark kingdom.

That kingdom will die a slow-but-sure death. And just before it breathes its last it will die a flailing and convulsing death. Jesus is warning his disciples, and you, that you might get 'bitten' by the darkness. So, while what Jesus is talking about can be a bit scary, it's also a time of great comfort and rejoicing."

"Like that time when a big snake was staring at me and Dad jumped in front of me and started chopping it with a hoe? I know I felt scared and relieved all at the same time."

"Turn the hoe into the sword of God's Spirit and your earthly father into your heavenly One, and yes, that's the picture exactly."

"Thanks, Jesna," Pete said. "That helps a lot."

Jesus was still talking. "If you are in Judea when you see the monster of desecration set up in the Temple sanctuary, run to the mountains. If anyone is on the roof of his house he should not even go down to collect his valuables. He should just flee. If someone is in the field he shouldn't even take the time to pick up his coat. He should just go!"

"I bet God will pick up that person's hoe and put it to work, huh, Jesna?"

"Shhh. Listen."

"This is going to be trouble on a scale beyond what the world has ever seen, or will see again. If these days of trouble were left to run their course, nobody would make it. But on account of God's chosen people, the trouble will be cut short."[172]

"Then at that time," Jesus continued, "many fake messiahs and lying preachers are going to start popping up everywhere. They will put on quite a show, and many people will be deceived by their tricks. But I have given you fair warning."

"Count me in, Jesus!" Pete erupted. "I'll help you chop those snakes up."

A smile pushed at Jesus' lips. It was the first smile I had seen on his face since we left the Temple.

FAMILY DISCUSSION

1. When you think about the world (as we know it) coming to an end, what are your feelings?
2. How does it make you feel, as a Christian, to know that your life in God's kingdom will never come to an end?

SCENE 174
"TAKE HEED, WATCH!"[173]

Jesus paused for a moment to let his end-time words settle into the hearts of his disciples. Only the occasional snapping of the fire broke the silence.

Then Priscilla asked a question. "Jesna, is Jesus talking about what's going to happen at the end of the world, or about what's going to happen in Jerusalem when the Temple will be destroyed by the Romans in about thirty years?"

"Your memory never ceases to amaze me, Priscilla. So you remember what I said about Romans camping right here on the Mount of Olives and the way they'll ... "

"Sack the city!" Pete interrupted. "*I* even 'member *that*."

"Well the answer is ... " Jesna continued, " ... both."

"Hum?" said Pete and Priscilla in rare harmony.

"The new age that Jesus is introducing now will continue throughout the centuries until the dark kingdom's rule of the earth comes to an end," Jesna began. "The desecration of the Temple in Jerusalem in about forty earth-years will be a very dark time. But it hardly compares to what will happen at the very end of Satan's reign as 'Prince of this world.'"

"I hear that phrase, 'new age,' mentioned a lot now. I mean the 'now' before we got on this ride," Mrs. Pilgrim said. "Is that the same 'new age' Jesus is talking about?"

"Oh, no!" Jesna said emphatically. "When the term 'new age' begins to be used in the latter part of the 1900s, that's Satan's way of trying to cause confusion. He's trying to make it seem that it is *humans*, and not God, who are responsible for the 'new age' Jesus announced and that is fulfilled in your day. But what those others mean by 'new age' is as different from Jesus' meaning as self-rule is from God-rule. Satan never tires of tricking people."

Just then, Jesus ended his silence and continued teaching.

"Then, the Arrival of the Son of Man! It will fill the skies— no one will miss it. Unready people all over the world, out-siders to the splendor and power, will raise a huge lament as they watch the Son of Man blazing out of heaven. At that same moment, he'll dispatch his angels with a trumpet-blast summons, pulling in God's chosen from the four winds, from pole to pole.

"Take a lesson from the fig tree. From the moment you notice its buds form, the merest hint of green, you know summer's just around the corner. So it is with you: When you see all these things, you'll know he's at the door. Don't take this lightly.

I'm not just saying this for some future generation, but for all of you. This age continues until all these things take place. Sky and earth will wear out; my words won't wear out."

"But the exact day and hour? No one knows that, not even heaven's angels, not even the Son. Only the Father knows."[174]

"Pete. Pete! Are you OK?" Jesna asked her little friend who was staring straight ahead. Much of the color had drained from his face.

"Oh, uh, yeah, I guess. I was just thinking of how bad it will be for people who forget to look at their fig trees."

Jesna gave him a tender hug. "I'm sorry for what you're feeling, but it's good for Jesus' special friends, like you, to have a little fear like that. Holy fear and holy love will keep you on alert to examine your heart, and to watch the times. Keep that up, Pete, and all of what Jesus is describing will simply mean—to you—is that God's wonderful kingdom is about to get more real than you can now imagine. That's the good part—the new baby that the earth's labor pains will precede."

"I think I understand, Jesna. But do you mind if I do something? I'd really like to pray right now."

"That would be wonderful," Jesna said.

Pete closed his eyes and bowed his head. The Pilgrims joined hands around him, and Jesus stopped his lessons and looked over at his littlest disciple. I'll never forget what Pete prayed. As he patted me on the head he whispered, "Lord God—and you, Jesus, of course—please make sure that I am always the kind of person that my dog, Wisdom, already thinks I am. Amen."

FAMILY DISCUSSION

1. What do you think Pete meant, that he would like to be the person his dog thinks he is?
2. What would you need to do to become that kind of person?

SCENE 175
THE PARABLE OF
THE TEN VIRGINS[175]

Jesus paused and listened to Pete's prayer; a pleased chuckle bounced up and down in Jesus' throat. But, speaking as a dog, I didn't see what was so funny.

Then Jesus continued, "The coming of my Father's kingdom is like a wedding night. The bride is spending her last night in her parents' home. With her ten bridesmaids, she awaits the arrival of her bridegroom. Each of her maidens has an oil lamp. When the groom approaches, they will run out and use their lamps to light the path to the bride's house."

"Kind of like human luminarias?"

"But," Jesus continued, "what if five of the ten were thoughtless and did not bring extra oil? And what if the groom did not show up when they expected him? They might fall asleep and awaken to discover that their lamps had burned up all the oil.

"The five silly bridesmaids might say to the other vigilant virgins, 'Let us borrow some of your oil. Our lamps have gone out.' But the response would come back, 'There will not be enough to go around; go buy your own.'

"Even if they ran to do so, the groom would have already arrived, and escorted his bride back to his house for the wedding feast. The feast would begin without them and they would find themselves on the wrong side of locked doors.

"Pound as they might, they would only hear the bridegroom say, 'Do I know you? I don't think we've met before.'

"So stay alert and expectant. For as I have said, no one knows when the bridegroom will arrive."

That was the end of Jesus' story. No one said a word. It was a long time before even nervy Pete became bold enough to break the silence.

"Let me make sure I got that one. Jesus is the bridegroom."

"Right," Jesna said.

"OK. Then what? I mean who's what?"

"The bride is the church—the whole collection of people who have decided to live by God's rules in his kingdom instead of living on their own terms."

"The wedding represents Jesus' coming back at the end of time to have a more intense and loving relationship with the church. And, it *is* a little confusing because the ten bridesmaids are also us—the church. They are the religious leaders and professors who light the path between Christ and his bride. They also represent 'anyone-else-in-the-pew' and their task of keeping the faith, keeping watch for Jesus' return."

"That's not so complicated, then," Pete interpreted. "Sounds like Jesus is just saying that there's going to be a big pig-out, piles of good food, when he comes back. If you want a place to sit, you'd better keep your lamps lit."

FAMILY DISCUSSION

1. What are some things you can do, both as a family and individually, to make sure you are faithfully watching for Jesus' return?

2. Why do you think Jesus talks about weddings so much? (Remember, his first miracle occurred at a wedding, and the church is often referred to as "the Bride of Christ.")

SCENE 176
SEPARATING SHEEP AND GOATS[176]

The fire blazed up. Jesus continued his prophecy about his second coming to earth.

"When I finally come again the skies will be ablaze with glory. All of the angels in heaven will be with me and I will sit on a glorious throne."

"That doesn't sound like the Jesus I know," Pete whispered.

"You've only seen Jesus, the man," Jesna responded. "You've yet to see Jesus, his Majesty, King of all creation, dressed in robes of light."

"Oh."

"The people of all the nations of the earth from all of time will be gathered before me. It will be my job to sort the people out, like a shepherd sorts out his sheep from his goats. I'll put the sheep on my right hand and the goats on my left.

"Then I will say, 'Enter, you who are blessed! Take what has been prepared for you in this kingdom. It has been ready for you to enjoy since the world was a blueprint and you were just sparkles in my Father's eyes'. And this is why you will be rewarded:

"I was hungry and you fed me,
I was thirsty and you gave me drink,
I was homeless and you gave me a room,
I was shivering and you gave me clothes,
I was sick and you stopped to visit,
I was in prison and you came to me."[177]

"And then all the blessed sheep will say with one voice, 'Father, what are you saying? When did we see you hungry and feed you? When were you thirsty and we gave you a drink? And when did we ever see you sick or in prison and come to you?'

"And I will say to them, 'Whenever you did one of these things for someone who was insignificant in the world's eyes, you did it for me.'

"Then I will turn to the ones on my left—the 'goats.' To these who have decided to follow their own wishes instead of the desires of the Shepherd of Souls, I will say, 'Get out, worthless goats! You are going to spend eternity with the father of self-centeredness and his hard-hearted demon helpers. It was to their songs, and not to mine, that you spent your lives dancing.'

"Your fate is sealed because when I was hungry, you went back for second helpings. When I was thirsty, you guzzled my share. When I was homeless, you sank into your warm sheets, you gave no thought to where *I* would sleep. I was shivering and cold and you kept your closet stuffed with coats. I was in prison, and you left me to rot.

"Then the goats will ask the same questions the sheep

asked. 'When did we ever see you hungry or thirsty or home-less or shivering or sick or in prison?' And my answer will also be the same. 'Whenever you failed to do one of these things for the most insignificant person, you failed to do it for me.'

"There are no insignificant people," Jesus continued. "That's because a part of *me* is in everyone. If you could truly see who it is that you are helping, or ignoring, you would be awestricken. *There are no mere mortals.*"

FAMILY DISCUSSION

1. What do you think it is that makes a "sheep" worthy of eternal reward and a "goat" due eternal punishment?
2. Which animal did you act most like today?
3. What are some "sheep" things you could do tomorrow?

SCENE 177
THE MINISTRY OF JESUS IN JERUSALEM[178]

"Jesna?"

"Yes, Priscilla."

"What did Jesus mean, 'there are no mere mortals'?"

"He was saying that every person has a little piece of God inside."

"You mean, after they become Christians, right?" Priscilla asked.

"No. When they become Christians, they have a *big* piece of God living inside."

"But ... "

"But," Jesna continued. "The 'little piece' is the Holy Spirit's voice that whispers to them to give their life to Jesus. Because of that 'holy spark' inside all of us, there are no *mere mor-*

tals, only immortal souls headed for life everlasting—in one kingdom or the other."

"I remember," Mrs. Pilgrim began, "that Leo Tolstoy wrote a story about what Jesus just said. It's called, *Where Love Is, There God Is Also,* I think."

"This is getting over my head," Pete blurted out.

"Hold on, son," Mrs. Pilgrim encouraged. "You'll get the story."

"Tell us the story, Mrs. Pilgrim."

"It's about a poor shoemaker, Martuin Avdyeitch."

"Mother!" Pete exclaimed as he was putting his hands over my doggie ears. "Don't talk like that in front of the dog."

Mrs. Pilgrim continued, ignoring him, "The shoemaker became a Christian late in his life after he had found a copy of a New Testament and gotten into the habit of reading it before falling asleep. One night he had a special dream. In it, Jesus appeared and told Avdyeitch that he would come by to visit him the next day.

"Well, as I remember, the shoemaker spent the day getting his shop cleaned up for Jesus' visit. But Jesus didn't show. The shoemaker's only visits were from an old, broken-down man, a poor mother who could not feed her child, and a little boy who had stolen an apple because he was hungry.

"Even though he was expecting a much more significant guest, the shoemaker invited each of these 'insignificant' people into his humble home and shared his few possessions with them.

"That night, he stayed up late to wait for Jesus. Finally, he gave up his vigil and began to read from the New Testament. Still hoping to be interrupted by Jesus, he began to chastise himself, saying, 'You must be crazy. Who do you think you are that Jesus Christ would stop by for a visit?'

"The next morning, as he was beginning a new work day, he was still grieving about his silliness. Then, all at once, he was surprised by the sounds of small voices. He turned and saw standing in his shoe shop the three people he had befriended the day before. But he was even more surprised when each one stepped forward and said, 'What's wrong, didn't you recognize me when you invited me in from the cold and gave me food and shelter? I was God's Son. I paid you not one, but *three* visits yesterday. Now I've come back to thank you for your kind hospitality.'

"Is that sort of what Jesus was saying?"

"Nope," Jesna said to Mrs. Pilgrim.

"*Nope?*"

"Not 'sort of'—that's it *exactly.*"

"So," Pete followed. "That shoemaker was a 'sheep' and not a 'goat.'"

"That's right, Pete. Sheep don't have their fingers crossed when they say, 'The Lord is my Shepherd.' They willingly give him control of their lives, and share with those in need. They often get to enjoy green pastures, still waters, and a life free from 'want.'

"Impatient, willful goats go racing off away from the Good Shepherd. They keep a tight control of their lives, living lives of never-ending 'want' and.... "

"They," Pete interrupted, "eat rusty tin cans and are always butting in and butting out."

"That's right, Pete. But they *get* it, in the *end.*"

"*Ooooh!* Good one, Jesna." Pete affirmed.

For the next couple of days we stayed close to Jesus as we camped on the Mount of Olives at night and listened to him teach in the Temple by day.

FAMILY DISCUSSION

1. The next time you see someone who is hungry, look closely. Do you see Jesus in their eyes? With your parents' permission, do whatever you would do if you saw Jesus hungry.
2. How did you act like a goat yesterday? How can you act like a sheep tomorrow?

SCENE 178
JESUS' DISCOURSE ABOUT HIS DEATH[179]

One bright morning, Jesus and the disciples awoke under an olive-green and sunlight-yellow canopy. There was something special in the air that morning. I could almost smell it.

The dawn had cracked open and let out all the anticipation of a Christmas morning, but without the lightheartedness. It's hard (especially for a dog) to explain, but I felt I had awakened to a day that would be crammed with all the emotions of a birthday and a funeral, all rolled into one.

"Do you know what day this is?" Jesna asked.

"No, *tell* me!" I wanted to bark.

"It's the morning of the day before Passover. Before we go to sleep again, Jesus and his disciples will celebrate the Passover meal together."

"You mean we'll get to see the real Lord's Supper today!" Priscilla shrilled. She sounded strangely like Pete.

"That's right, Priscilla. Tonight, Jesus and the disciples will be together in the 'Upper Room.'"

Only Pete didn't seem impressed. Jesna noticed and asked, "What's wrong, Petie?"

"Well, you know, I might have been born at night, but it

wasn't last night. I know what happens after
Passover," Pete mourned. "Jesus is going to
have to die. And I'm not sure I can stick
around and watch that without biting a
hunk out of somebody's leg." Pete ran to
his mother's side. "He's not really going to
die, is he, Mom?" Pete asked.

"Yes, Petie, I'm afraid he is," she said with
quivering voice and a squeeze.

"Well," Pete began, "I've been giving it a lot
of thought since Jesus first brought it up a few Bible-months
ago. I'm not sure I can stand to see that."

"But you know what that means!" Priscilla said. "You
remember what Jesna said. We'll all have to go back to Daffy
World, all because of *you*."

"Well, I'm soooo sorry, computer-heart! But some of us un-
evolved humans still have feelings," Pete said sarcastically.

"That will be enough!" Mr. Pilgrim said emphatically. "Jesna
is our guide, and we'll do whatever she says."

"Thank you, Mr. Pilgrim, for your confidence. But really it's
up to the four of you."

"Arrrf!"

"I mean the *five* of you. This is a very special ride and you
can only stay on it as long as there is no other place in the universe you'd rather be. Pete's concerns mean that he'd rather
be back home. Well, that's exactly where he'll be. And I can
imagine that if he's there, all of your hearts will follow him.
But, let's not talk about it right now. There's a big day ahead."

Before an hour had passed, we were all back inside the
stone walls of Jerusalem, by Jesus' side, in the middle of a circle of listeners.

By the time the sun had climbed directly overhead, two of

Jesus' disciples, Philip and Andrew, approached him and whispered in his ear. "Jesus, there are some Greeks in the audience. They've heard about you and want to talk with you."

"Mom says it's not nice to call people 'geeks.'"

"They said 'Greeks,' Pete."

"Oh. That's different. Do you think they can get us tickets to the Olympics?"

"Shhh!"

Jesus responded to Philip and Andrew, "My time is up. The day has come for the Son of Man to be glorified."

Then he turned to the crowd and spoke. "Whether you are Jew, or Greek, or Roman ... "

" ... or American!" Pete couldn't resist shouting.

" ... the way to real life is the same. Listen carefully:

"Unless a grain of wheat is buried in the ground, dead to the world, it is never any more than a grain of wheat. But if it is buried, it sprouts and reproduces itself many times over. In the same way, anyone who holds on to life just as it is destroys that life. But if you let it go, reckless in your love, you'll have it forever, real and eternal.

"If any of you wants to serve me, then follow me. Then you'll be where I am, ready to serve at a moment's notice. The Father will honor and reward anyone who serves me."[180]

Just at that moment a thunderous noise rolled across a clear blue sky. It sounded like a sonic boom.

"Thunder?" many in the crowd wondered aloud.

"No! It was an angel!" someone shouted.

"No," Jesus said. "That was my *Father,* speaking for your benefit. A new era is dawning. Satan, the ruler of this world, is about to be thrown out. And

"I, as I am lifted up from the earth, will attract everyone to me and gather them around me."[181]

"He's talking about how he's going to die, isn't he, Jesna?"

"That's right, Pete. He knows that he will be lifted up on a wooden cross."

Pete shuddered as if a freezing-cold wind had hit him in the face.

"Who is this 'Son of Man' you keep talking about?" a Pharisee asked.

Jesus answered.

"For a brief time still, the light is among you. Walk by the light you have so darkness doesn't destroy you. If you walk in darkness, you don't know where you are going. As you have the light, believe in the light. Then the light will be with you, and shining through your lives. You'll be children of light."[182]

At that several Pharisees whirled abruptly and walked away, their dark robes billowing. But the rest of the crowd, including the Greeks, leaned in toward Jesus to better absorb his words of life.

"Boy, those Pharisees are amazing," Pete gestured. "They can start a party just by walking away."

FAMILY DISCUSSION

1. What do you think Jesus meant by saying that you must "die" (to yourself) like a grain of wheat to find new life?

2. If you wanted new life tomorrow, what would be different about how you lived the day?

SCENE 179
THE UNBELIEF OF THE PEOPLE[183]

Jesus' listeners shifted position this way and that, trying to hear and see better. Sometimes we lost sight of Jesus for a while. Pete was the first to notice that Jesus had stopped talking and had slipped away. Jesna theorized that he just needed to be away for a little while, to hear some more encouragement from his Father.

"Hey, what you just said made me remember something Mother Teresa is supposed to have said about people going off to be alone like that."

"What's that, Mr. Pilgrim?" Jesna asked.

"I read it in a newspaper article about her. She said, 'In solitude we find prayer. In prayer we find faith. In faith we find love. In love we find service. And in service we find peace.'"

"Oh, that's real good," Jesna responded. "I bet I know where she got that one."

"From Jesus' Daddy?" Pete asked.

"Yes, and I think Jesus is asking his Father for some encouragement about making this last trip—from 'love' to 'service.' He's faced with laying his life down, like burying the grain of wheat he talked about. That sacrifice will bring the world immeasurable peace!"

"Jesna. I thought you weren't going to bring up the dying part again."

Jesna stared at the ground. "Sorry, Pete. Sometimes I forget how big that little heart of yours is."

"Yeah, well it's so big it's about to push its way out of my chest. I can already feel it in my throat."

Mr. and Mrs. Pilgrim each draped an arm around Pete.

An hour or two passed. We listened to people in the crowd

speak their minds. From all the comments, it appeared that almost all of the common people were with Jesus. But what was really surprising was that it seemed many of the *religious leaders* also believed Jesus was who he said he was.

When Priscilla asked Jesna if she were amazed that so many of the religious leaders had sympathy for Jesus, she said, "No. But their fear of losing favor with the Pharisees, of getting kicked out of their place of importance at the meeting places, is often greater than their faith. When push comes to shove, they care more about human approval than for God's glory."[184]

"Well, I can see how that could keep their grains of wheat from dying," Pete summarized. Then he said, "It sounds like they need to spend some more time doing what Jesus is doing—listening to God—if they ever are going to find enough love to die for."

FAMILY DISCUSSION

1. Do you think Mother Teresa is right about the source of peace?
2. If you were going to live your life to bring peace, what changes would you have to make in how you will spend your time tomorrow?

SCENE 180
JUDGMENT BY THE WORD[185]

When Jesus returned, the sun was at its three o'clock position. He walked through the middle of the crowd that was still debating his claims. Then he opened his mouth and spoke with the assurance of someone who had just come from the presence of God.

"Let me make this clear for all of you,

"Whoever believes in me, believes not just in me but in the One who sent me. Whoever looks at me is looking, in fact, at the One who sent me. I am the Light that has come into the world so that all who believe in me won't have to stay any longer in the dark.

"If anyone hears what I am saying and doesn't take it seriously, I don't reject him. I didn't come to reject the world; I came to save the world. But you need to know that whoever puts me off, refusing to take in what I'm saying, is willfully choosing rejection. The Word, the Word-made-flesh that I have spoken and that I am, *that* Word and no other is the last word. I'm not making any of this up on my own. The Father who sent me gave me orders, told me what to say and how to say it. And I know exactly what his command produces: real and eternal life. That's all I have to say. What the Father told me, I tell you."[186]

"Go, Jesus!" Pete shouted to his Friend. "That's telling 'em! It's time to fish or cut bait."

A long pause followed. It was Jesna who broke the silence.

"Well, speaking of 'go,' it's time to do just that."

All four Pilgrims were stunned. Then Pete complained,

"What do you mean 'go'? There's that famous supper that will happen tonight. I don't want to miss *that!*"

"I know, Pete. But things are about to heat up for Jesus—for all of his disciples. And we shouldn't be part of what is soon to follow, unless there is nowhere else in the universe we would rather be. So we're going back to Daffy World to let you breathe some familiar air before you each make a final decision about whether to come back or not. I'm not even sure that I will still be on duty to be your guide."

"No!" Pete and Priscilla gasped.

"You've become part of our family, Jesna," Mrs. Pilgrim said. "I don't want to think about your not being with us."

Jesna smiled a sad, knowing smile. Then she said. "Well, let's all get in the car. We'll soon see what the future holds."

It was a solemn march to the time-car. It would have been a silent one, too, except for Pete observing, "Boy, it's been so long since we've ridden anywhere I'd forgotten about the car being parked in the city." He and his family were all staring at their shoe-tops, but they did break their downward gaze long enough to give Jesus a goodby wave.

Pete couldn't leave it at that. He made a quick run to Jesus and gave him a bear hug. It was hard to tell if Jesus was patting Pete's arm to show compassion, or to plead for air.

"If I don't see you again in person," Pete sniffled, "I'll be seeing you in my Sunday school book."

Jesus just smiled a kind smile.

"Sunglasses on, everyone," Jesna said. Then she pushed a new pattern of buttons and the mid-afternoon sky of the Holy City became as bright as the noonday sun and our ears were bursting with the whistling sounds of twenty centuries blowing past in a second.

The car stopped. I opened my eyes. We were back in the

huge dome-shaped room where we had begun our ride—almost thirty-three Bible-years ago.

"I don't believe this," Priscilla said. "It's 1:30:59 P.M. Just like Jesna said it would be."

"Yeah," Pete followed, "but I bet they've torn the old park down. It's probably all high-rise office buildings out there."

Pete and Priscilla both jumped up from their seats with wide eyes and ran in the direction of the huge golden doors.

"Come on, Wisdom," Pete called. "Hurry, girl."

"Wait for us," Mr. and Mrs. Pilgrim cried.

Yes, wait for us, I thought, as I used my nose to nudge Jesna in the direction of the departing Pilgrims.

Through the golden doors, back through the maze of winding aisles, and through the huge, rusted metal doors at the entrance to the ride we hurtled. The doors opened automatically as we approached, and early afternoon light and the thousand smells of an overcrowded amusement park came pouring in like water through floodgates. The four of us who were bringing up the rear bolted through the large doors before they could swing shut.

Pete exclaimed "Wow!" as he drank in the view. Then he focused his gaze straight ahead.

"That big man there—the one with the plaid shorts and the hairy back—is the same one we were standing behind when we decided to get out of that line. He hasn't moved an inch. Nothing has changed."

"But *we* sure have moved, haven't we, son?" Mr. Pilgrim said affectionately.

"We sure have, Dad," Pete said.

Then, glancing around, casually at first, then frantically, he exclaimed, "Hey! where's Jesna?"

Scene	Note	
Preface..	1.	Please see page 134 of part two of *The Life and Times of Jesus the Messiah.*
91.......	2.	From Matthew 13:44-46.
	3.	Matthew 13:44-46.
92.......	4.	From Matthew 13:47-50.
	5.	Matthew 13:47-50.
93.......	6.	From Matthew 13:51-58. See also Mark 6:1-6a; Luke 4:16-30; John 7:15; 6:42; 4:44; 10:39.
	7.	Matthew 13:52.
	8.	Matthew 13:57.
94.......	9.	From John 5:10-18.
	10.	John 5:8.
95.......	11.	From John 5:19-47.
	12.	John 5:39-47.
96.......	13.	From Matthew 9:35; 10:1, 7-11, 14; Mark 6:6b-13; Luke 9:1-6.
	14.	Mark 6:8, 11.
97.......	15.	From Matthew 14:3-12; Mark 6:17-29; Luke 3:19:20a.
98.......	16.	From Matthew 14:3-12; Mark 6:17-29; Luke 3:19-20.
99.......	17.	From Matthew 14:12b-13a; Mark 6:30-31; Luke 9:10a.
100......	18.	From Matthew 14:22-23; Mark 6:45-52; John 6:16-21.
	19.	Matthew 14:33.
101......	20.	From Matthew 14:34-36; Mark 6:53-56; John 6:16-21.
102......	21.	From John 6:22-25.

	22.	John 6:26, 27, 29.
	23.	John 6:32-33, 35, 39-40.
	24.	John 6:47-51, 56.
103......	25.	From Matthew 15:1-20; Mark 7:1-23; Luke 11:37-41; 6:39.
	26.	Mark 7:6-7.
	27.	Mark 7:21-23.
104......	28.	From Matthew 15:21-28; Mark 7:24-30.
	29.	Mark 7:27.
	30.	Matthew 15:28.
105......	31.	From Matthew 15:29-31; Mark 7:24-30.
106......	32.	From Matthew 16:1-4; 12:38-39; Mark 8:11-26; Luke 11:16; 12:54-56; John 6:30.
107......	33.	From John 6:60-66.
	34.	John 6:61-65.
108......	35.	From Matthew 16:13-20; Mark 8:27-30; Luke 9:18-21; John 6:67-71.
	36.	Matthew 16:18-19.
109......	37.	From Matthew 16:21-23; Mark 8:31-33; Luke 9:22.
110......	38.	From Matthew 16:24-28; Mark 8:34-9:1; Luke 9:23-27; John 12:25; 8:51-52; 21:20-23.
	39.	Matthew 16:24-27, RSV.
	40.	Mark 9:1, RSV.
111......	41.	From Matthew 17:1-9; Mark 9:2-10; Luke 9:28-36; John 12:28-30.
	42.	Matthew 17:4, 5b, RSV.
112......	43.	From Matthew 17:14-21; Mark 9:14-29; Luke 9:37-43a; John 14:9.
113......	44.	From Matthew 17:22-23; Mark 9:14-29; Luke 9:43b-45; John 7:1.
	45.	Mark 9:31.

151......	129.	From Matthew 19:13-15; Mark 10:13-16; Luke 18:15-17; John 3:3-5.
	130.	Mark 10:14-15.
152......	131.	From Matthew 19:16-22; Mark 10:17-22; Luke 18:18-23.
	132.	Matthew 19:21.
153......	133.	From Matthew 19:23-30; Mark 10:23-31; Luke 18:24-30; 22:28-30.
	134.	Matthew 19:26.
154......	135.	From Matthew 20:1-16; Mark 10:31; Luke 13:30.
	136.	Matthew 20:14-16.
155......	137.	From John 10:22-39; Luke 4:29-30.
	138.	John 10:34-38.
156......	139.	From John 10:40-11:44.
	140.	John 11:41b-42.
157......	141.	From Matthew 26:1-5; Mark 14:1-2; 11:18; Luke 22:1-2; 19:47-48; John 11:45-53.
158......	142.	From John 11:54-57; Matt. 20:17-19; Mark 10:32-34; Luke 18:31-34.
159......	143.	From Matthew 20:17-28; Mark 10:2-45; Luke 18:31-34.
	144.	Mark 10:33, 34.
	145.	Mark 10:38-45.
160......	146.	From Matthew 20:29-34; Mark 10:46-52; Luke 18:35-43.
	147.	Luke 18:42.
161......	148.	From Matthew 18:11; Luke 19:1-10.
	149.	Luke 19:9, 10.
162......	150.	From Matthew 25:14-30; Mark 13:34; Luke 19:11-27.
	151.	Luke 19:12-27.

163...... 152. From Matthew 26:6-13; Mark 14:3-9;
Luke 7:36-50; John 12:1-8.

153. John 12:7-8.

164...... 154. From Matthew 21:1-9; Mark 11:1-10;
Luke 19:28-40; John 12:12-19.

155. Luke 19:38.

156. Luke 19:41-44.

165...... 157. From Matthew 21:10-46; Mark 11:1-12:2;
Luke 19:5-20:9.

166...... 158. See note 157.

159. Luke 20:16.

167...... 160. From Matthew 22:15-22; Mark 12:13-17;
Luke 20:20-26; John 3:2.

168...... 161. From Matthew 22:22-23; Mark 12:18-27;
Luke 20:27-40.

162. Luke 20:34-38.

169...... 163. From Matthew 22:34-40; Mark 12:28-34;
Luke 10:25-28.

164. Matthew 22:37-40.

170...... 165. From Matthew 23:1-36; Mark 12:37b-40;
Luke 20:45-47; John 13:4-5, 12-17.

166. Matthew 23:8-12.

171...... 167. From Mark 12:41-44; Luke 21:1-4.

168. Mark 12:43-44.

172...... 169. From Matthew 24:1-14; Mark 13:1-13;
Luke 21:5-19.

170. Matthew 24:13-14.

173...... 171. From Matthew 24:15-28; Mark 13:9-20;
Luke 21:12-24.

172. Matthew 24:21-23.

174...... 173. From Matthew 24:29-51; Mark 13:24-37;
Luke 21:25-36.